The New Republic
A VOICE OF
MODERN LIBERALISM

The New Republic
A Voice of Modern Liberalism

by
David Seideman

PRAEGER SPECIAL STUDIES • PRAEGER SCIENTIFIC

New York • Westport, Connecticut • London

Library of Congress Cataloging-in-Publication Data

Seideman, David.
  The New republic.

  Bibliography: p
  Includes index.
    1. New Republic (New York, N.Y.)   2. Liberalism—
United States—History—20th century.   I. Title.
PN4900.N328S4   1986   051   85-30776
ISBN 0-275-92015-1 (alk. paper)
ISBN 0-275-92016-X (pbk.: alk. paper)

Library of Congress Catalog Card Number: 85-30776
ISBN: 0-275-92015-1
ISBN: 0-275-92016-X(pbk)

First published in 1986

Praeger Publishers, 521 Fifth Avenue, New York, NY 10175
A division of Greenwood Press, Inc.

Printed in the United States of America

∞

The paper used in this book complies with the Permanent
Paper Standard issued by the National Information Standards
Organization (Z39.48-1984).

10 9 8 7 6 5 4 3 2 1

To Michael F. Foley

Foreword

ON WRITING A HISTORY OF THE FIRST TWENTY-FIVE YEARS of *The New Republic*, David Seideman has also written an important chapter in the history of American liberalism. It is not only, as Seideman shows, that *TNR* has an inordinate and unrivalled influence on both policy and public debate; the weekly journal of opinion also made its mark on the life of culture, when that movement called modernism in literature, art and music was beginning to emerge.

In retrospect, of course, a cohort of writers and intellectuals which included Herbert Croly and Walter Lippmann, Felix Frankfurter and John Dewey, Edmund Wilson and Randolph Bourne could not have failed to stir the minds and affect the decisions of those they saw as their readers. Still, it would be a mistake to see *The New Republic* as a magazine of establishment insiders, however liberal or even left-leaning. First of all, there was, in the early years and among some of the New Republicans, a certain clinging to the idiosyncratic politics of Theodore Roosevelt. Then came, from the midwest the insurgency of Robert La Follette which reverberated through the paper's pages. The twenties, from the failure of the League of Nations to the Great Crash, were a period at once of intellectual ferment and political alienation, even social and psychological churlishness. So it was at the beginning and at the end of the quarter century under discussion, with Woodrow Wilson's presidency and then with Franklin Roosevelt's, that the magazine was tested in the ambit of power.

If even from time to time it or one of its writers toadied to the mighty, its real function—historically demonstrable and with this book decisively demonstrated—was as relentless critic. The vocation of political criticism is harder now to understand than it was then, when a smaller but far more literate audience was what comprised the opinion elite. To such readers, an historical exegesis of some contemporary event, a philosophical meditation on some legislative option, a psychological excursion into character or even (dare I say it?) into the national character were as intrinsic a part of civilized life as the 7 o'clock news shows, with their breathless revelations, are to our more frantic lives.

Yet *The New Republic* certainly was not all sobriety and distance. One of its first editors, Walter Weyl, said he chose Socrates over Isaiah, reason over passion. But the magazine certainly was passionate and often quite certain, all too certain, and wrong as well. These enthusiasms put distance between the journal and political power. At times, however, the editors seemed persuaded that they were instead part of the fuel for the great engine of history, revolution. This was exhilarating, to be sure, and also morally and intellectually disastrous. Seideman's treatment of the magazine's off-and-on-again infatuation with Stalinism (sometimes, when the editors were in ideological confrontation, it was just one section of the magazine), is scrupulous, balanced, and yet vividly evocative.

There are also lessons, as in all good histories, for our own time. The author ends with the eve of the Second World War. In the twenty-five years preceding, the country's economy, politics, culture, values and expectations had been altogether transformed. *The New Republic*'s role in that transformation, at least to the historian of ideas, was there for all to see. David Seideman has made it comprehensible. It is surely to be wished that he will over the next years apply himself to a not less complicated relationship, that of this small but great magazine with the nation it has been presumptuous enough to want to instruct during the ensuing half-century of the career and ordeal of that nation as a global power.

Martin Peretz
Editor-in-Chief, *The New Republic*

. . . .

Preface

*T*HE NEW REPUBLIC (*TNR*) WAS CREATED "LESS TO INFORM OR entertain its readers than to start little insurrections in the realm of their convictions," Herbert Croly, the magazine's founder and first editor, wrote in 1922.[1] This was the *TNR* idea. Going against the grain of the day's conventional wisdom, the publication occupied a unique place in U.S. journalism from its founding in 1914. Its uncommon virtue lay in its editorial independence. Freed from the profit motive and the relentless hustle for advertising revenue, the magazine was never bound by the ordinary standards of the trade. Croly did not intend to reach the general reading public—only the thoughtful, the curious, and the uncommitted.

Although it was heralded at its founding as an organ of reform, the magazine never fit into tidy categories. The surprises found in the magazine each week attested to the wide latitude of opinions expressed in its pages. "We will be radical without being socialistic . . . and pragmatic rather than doctrinaire," Croly promised a friend while preparing the first issue.[2] Whether they labeled themselves "progressives" or "liberals," the editors rarely permitted the prevailing orthodoxy of the times to define their own high-minded purposes. From *TNR*'s inception at the peak of the latter stages of the progressive era and the outbreak of World War I and through the New Deal and World War II, the editors nimbly adjusted the instance to a constantly changing environment. But a single, bold theme underpinned philosophy: the establishment of a strong central government.

In the first half of the twentieth century, the forward momentum of U.S. history seemed stalled. The previous century's scattered and diffused economic and political institutions proved ill equipped to master the complexities of the modern industrial age. The traditional liberal principles of individual rights and natural freedom impeded national progress. During both active and dormant eras, *TNR* guided the United States away from self-reliance and laissez-faire and toward collective identity through the active intervention of the state.

The new liberalism propounded in *TNR* promised more than practical results. Suffused with the moral hues of social regeneration and good will, it always appealed to its audience's heart, as well as mind. *TNR* was not just a publication, Alfred Kazin has noted, but a "cause and the center of many causes."[3] No cause was ever as tirelessly and faithfully championed as social justice, a keystone for reform and civilized societies in the modern age. *TNR*'s editors believed a stronger central government was the means by which social justice could exist. Liberal editors at *TNR* devoutly believed that future generations would judge them by their humanity and care for the poor. Indeed, on various occasions, the editors proudly declared themselves the spokesmen of the oppressed minority. The broad class of exploited ranged from working men and women living in the Northeast's squalid urban slums to destitute farmers and sharecroppers in the South and West. Countless editorials and articles on their plight appealed to the public conscience and admonished public leaders who failed to act.

While the magazine's concern for the downtrodden remained constant, the tone it adopted usually mirrored the cultural ethos and general direction of liberalism. The Progressive Era's spiritual awakening evolved into righteous indignation during the conservative decade that followed and into full outrage at the height of the Great Depression. The inevitable political and economic cycles usually set the tone of the debate. *TNR* waged a two-front war of words. On one level, it analyzed and dissected U.S. institutions and on another offered its own individual programs to improve conditions. The severity of the problem at hand of course determined the solution.

This volume consists of a series of case studies of *TNR*'s philosophy for approximately 25 years. Each chapter seeks to examine and evaluate the editors' successes and failures on their own terms, as well as in the context of the times in which they lived.

For all its independence, throughout the struggles the magazine remained a victim of circumstances as much as a vehicle for change. It was forever at the mercy of persons and forces beyond its control. The historical intervals I have used provide a convenient, if somewhat subjective, means of charting a complex course. Rather than representing a vast continuum, the chapters deal with issues of particular significance to the period that raise fundamental questions about liberalism's general place in history. *TNR*, for its own part, recognized the value of honoring tradition and remembering the past to avoid repetition of mistakes in the future. When it moved too quickly, it usually fell out of step with the rest of the nation. Intermittent bouts of memory loss distorted priorities and seriously limited the magazine's efficacy. Even in the best of times, uncontrollable forces tended to dominate it. *TNR*'s successes and failures reflected upon the nature of the society it sought to reform.

In adherence to its stated objectives, *TNR* constantly struggled to resolve the dilemma between pragmatism and idealism. Whether it acted on its principles depended largely on the state of liberalism and a writer's personal convictions. "Liberalism is a tendency rather than a concise body of doctrines," wrote Lionel Trilling. The tendency of disinterested and independent opinion formed the binder of *TNR*'s eclectic philosophy.

For the purposes of this work, I have focused on a distinct and vital segment of the magazine—the work produced by the editors themselves. The views expressed in the editorials they hammered out together at weekly conferences constituted the magazine's "line." *TNR* thrived on internal debate and, sometimes, fostered it publicly through the editors' signed pieces. It also opened its pages to dissenting voices. But its reputation ultimately rested on the consistency and quality of the magazine's official policy.

This book by no means purports to offer a comprehensive history of either liberalism or *TNR*. The well surveyed terrain of twentieth century

U.S. reform has allowed me to do my own exploration. For their brilliant insights and exhaustive research, I am deeply indebted to many of the scholars cited in my text and bibliography. The sheer volume of the magazine, moreover, prohibits the thorough discussion of a number of issues involving *TNR* and liberalism. Instead, I have tried to dwell at length on the highlights. With extensive quotations and background, I have striven to do justice to the editors' creed, while giving the reader the feel and texture of *TNR*—much as a biography attempts to recreate a life. The glaring flaws and virtues in this "biography" reflect those of the editors' lofty mission to chronicle and make sense of U.S. affairs.

Today, liberals are searching for their souls. Recent trends and elections have not treated them kindly. Indeed, "liberalism" has become a term so stigmatized that few of its proponents dare use it. In the course of rethinking the philosophy for the future, liberals must, of course, remain mindful of their obligations to its past. History, to paraphrase Mark Twain, does not repeat itself; it rhymes. Many of the issues liberals are currently struggling with, such as the size and scope of government, have gnawed their forebears since the first wave of reform at the turn of this century. At the center of much of the debate and intellectual ferment has stood *TNR*, a major forum for liberalism's trials and tribulations.

. . . .

Acknowledgments

I AM INDEBTED TO SEVERAL INSTITUTIONS AND INDIVIDUALS for their help.

My first acknowledgements begin with a group of very gifted professors at Georgetown University where this book originated as an undergraduate thesis. John Glavin offered sound advice and wisdom. In the history department Dorothy Brown, an exceptional scholar, served as a mentor and invaluable resource, giving much of her time and knowledge. The late Michael Foley not only excelled as a professor, but was a figure students rarely encounter at a university who nurtured intellectual curiosity and inspired them to stand by their convictions. He is missed by the many he deeply touched.

Many thanks of course go to *The New Republic*, which continues to be, as it has been for the past seventy years, one of the finest magazines in America. Martin Peretz's intellectual spirit and generous impulse have sustained innumerable beneficiaries, including myself. At *The New Republic* I have been fortunate to keep some extremely good company over the years, and wish to express my gratitude for their encouragement to Dorothy Wickenden, Ann Hulbert, Marc Granetz, Leon Wieseltier, Jefferson Morley, Hendrik Hertzberg, Jack Beatty, Ronald Steel, Fred Barnes, and Morton Kondracke. In the course of finishing this work, it was my privilege and pleasure to work for a brilliant essayist, Charles Krauthammer. He is writing new chapters in *The New Republic*'s history and, what's more, is a good friend. I would also like to thank my editor at Praeger, Dotti Breitbart. Her inexhaustible patience helped keep the project alive.

And, finally, heartfelt appreciation goes to a good friend and my family. Amy Schwartz magnanimously set aside her own deadlines to review the manuscript at crucial stages. I also feel blessed to have such special parents, brother, and sister. They saw me through many a long day and even longer night. This book might never have been completed without their love and support.

. . . .

Contents

inculcated in their son an almost missionary zeal for social reform that he would carry with him all of his life.[1]

Herbert Croly undertook his enormous intellectual tasks with the utmost gravity. The thick, rimless glasses resting on his bulbous nose lent him a professorial air he was slow to dispel. Even his closest intimates felt uncomfortable in the presence of this painfully diffident man who swallowed his words and rarely spoke above a whisper. Editors at *TNR* compared him to a "stone crab in the middle of lively company" and were often taken aback by his "profound, often anguished seriousness." Much of his peculiar behavior stemmed from his own perception of himself. Croly's bold and daring philosophy concealed a private person who seriously doubted his talents and the efficacy of his ideas. The surefootedness and lucidity of his arguments did not always strike readers as immediately as the works of such contemporaries as Walter Lippmann or George Santayana. Almost every day, Croly buried himself in his study at home and at the office with foolscap and pen in hand and spun his elaborate theories in virtually illegible handwriting, which his secretary later deciphered and transcribed. It was time well spent. The endless hours the philosopher spent gazing at the nation's historical and political landscape yielded results. Croly was struggling to create a new, liberal philosophy to confront the problems of the twentieth century United States. At the peak of the progressive era, he founded *The New Republic* to serve as his vehicle.[2]

The birth of *TNR* occurred at a critical juncture in U.S. history. Walter Lippmann's apt phrase, "the end of innocence," conveys the uncertainty of an era in which the collision between the nineteenth century's faithful optimism collided with the next century's realism, ending in the utter despair of World War I. The fierce individualism and brutal social Darwinism of earlier eras contributed to the rise of robber barons and subsequent violent labor unrest. Businessmen, politicians, and public-spirited citizens agreed on the need for government to restore stability and ensure a modicum of economic and social justice. As president, Theodore Roosevelt fined Standard Oil for monopolistic practices, authorized the regulation of railroads, and banned the use of harmful drugs and chemicals and preservatives in food and medicine. After a brief retirement, the restless colonel reentered the world of politics in 1912 to lead his band of progressive insurgents against the laconic Republican standardbearer, William Taft, and Democrat Woodrow Wilson, the scholarly president of Princeton University and governor of New Jersey. At the crossroads of "Armageddon," Roosevelt's Bull Moose party advocated a "new nationalism" for the United States and presented a platform constructed of standard progressive planks, including direct primaries, initiative and referendum, control of business for the general welfare, workmen's compensation, a minimum wage for women, and the eight-hour work day. "We are engaged in one of the great battles of the age-long contest waged against the privileged on behalf of the common people," he declared to the delight of the convention crowd. Several future members of *TNR* listened in rapt attention.

Progressivism's human face had two sides. A strong conservative impulse for domestic tranquillity underlay its reforms. The prospect of social disorder frightened Roosevelt and shaped his view of the social climate of his day. He opposed the closed shop and distrusted unions in general. "I have never believed, and I do not now, that . . . a class war is upon us or ever need be upon us, nor do I believe that the interest of wage earners and employers cannot be harmonized, compromised, and adjusted," he once explained. Samuel Gompers represented the model labor leader. The head of the American Federation of Labor concentrated his efforts on the immediate short-term goals of the open shop (for plants prohibiting the hiring of union employees) or eight-hour work day and had no patience for the fantastic dreams of socialism. Drawn almost exclusively from society's middle echelons, the progressive movement honored moderation and looked askance at what Roosevelt contemptuously termed the "lunatic fringe." Considered too radical, Eugene Debs and his Socialist party and Bill Haywood of the Industrial Workers of the World were not welcome. Liberals were united by a belief in evolutionary, gradual change, as opposed to sudden or drastic upheaval. No matter how far they might wander from social conventions, they refused to abandon them.[3]

At the forefront of progressivism, Croly was well prepared to become founding editor of *TNR*. He served as an advisor to Roosevelt and wrote *The Promise of American Life*, arguably the movement's bible. When first publised in 1909, the book sold only about 7,500 copies, a small number even by those days' standards.[4] Its influence, however, was not measured at the bookstore rack nor by the number of people who actually read its dense contents. "It was a powerful book, powerfully hard to read," Alvin Johnson, a *TNR* editor once quipped.[5] Many readers were undoubtedly frightened away by Croly's ponderous writing style and the sheer abstruseness of his convoluted abstractions. Roosevelt claimed to have digested the work and effusively praised the soundness of its arguments, but his adherence to its philosophy may not have extended beyond his casual use of the phrase "new nationalism" for the theme of his campaign. The sudden prominence of an expression that only appeared once in the entire book stemmed more from "similarity and sequence" than emulation, explains Charles Forcey in his seminal study of the early *TNR*. For "Croly believed in democratic reform as strongly as he did in nationalism. . . . TR believed in himself."[6] On the other hand, David Levy, another astute student of the subject, insists Roosevelt devoured Croly's volume, assiduously underscoring and circling important passages.[7] The former president's seal of approval notwithstanding, *Promise* stood on its own merits as a landmark manifesto in the evolution of modern liberalism.

The novelty of Croly's vision for reform lay in its call for employing Hamiltonian means to achieve Jeffersonian ends. The republic had undergone dramatic changes since Jefferson argued that government was best that governed the least. Traditional Jeffersonian and Jacksonian liberalism favored rugged individualism for fear of centralized power in the hands of a tyranny. They could not foresee how a small minority would exploit this freedom to their own advantage by oppressing the majority. In defiance of these concepts, Croly hailed Hamilton's contrasting vision of a unified, national government. Hamilton was

> the sound thinker, the constructive statesman, the candid and honorable, if erring gentleman, while Jefferson was the amiable enthusiast, who understood his fellow countrymen better and trusted them more than his rival, but who was incapable either of uniting with his fine phrases . . .a habit of candid and honorable private dealing or of embodying those phrases in a set of institutions. The conservative designed the public machinery with which to promote the liberal's value of social, political, and economic liberty for all citizens.

The United States must find a medium between Hamilton's aristocratic sympathies and Jefferson's spirit of democracy as "self-reliant, undisciplined, suspicious of authority, equalitarian and individualist." Fusing the influences of Comte's positivistic "religion of science and humanity" taught to him by his father with the philosopher Santayana's theory of "government by men of merit," Croly urged U.S. citizens to produce a leader in the mold of Abraham Lincoln to embody democratic ideals and fulfill the national promise. The Civil War proved pivotal in the formation of the young union. The significance of this national tragedy to the author centered on the emergence of Lincoln as the "most human statesman who ever guided a nation through a great crisis." Roosevelt filled the bill in no small way. The Colonel demonstrated Lincolnesque qualities necessary to realize the United States' vast potential for "social regeneration."[8] Croly had found the man to lead his national revival.

The agenda in *Promise* consisted of the customary progressive measures for the moderate redistribution of political and economic resources. The first task was to curb the "excessive money power" of a "few irresponsible men" by the gradual expropriation of huge fortunes through income and inheritance taxes on unearned corporate wealth and family fortunes. The progressive antitrust orthodoxy did not fit into this national plan. Croly belonged to the sect in the movement to which monopolies signified an advanced stage of capitalism above the primitive and inefficient competition of the early Industrial Revolution. In certain cases, he also recommended the nationalization of the railroads, telegraph system, and other monopolies to convert them into "express economic agents of the whole community." *Promise*'s blueprint for industrial peace contained designs for only selected unions. The author discriminated between good, law-abiding unions and those other "bad unions." By implication, the American Federation of Labor's goals of a minimum wage and maximum hours furthered the common good. Conversely, the International Workers of the World (IWW), "persistent, unscrupulous" agitation promoted its "class interest" at the expense of the entire community's safety. To protect the public, therefore, unions would be legalized and encouraged only on the condition that they be placed under government auspices where they could be carefully monitored and disciplined. The double-edged sword Croly brandished from the left in the name of "socialized democracy" against private concentrations of wealth and from the right against the freedom of unions appealed to the middle-class centrist—"the common citizen" Croly hoped would become "something of a saint and something of a hero."[9]

The political philosopher had serious misgivings about his own programs after the disappointing results of the 1912 election. In the largely forgotten *Progressive Democracy*, Croly reevaluated his convictions a month before starting to publish *TNR*. Through much of the book, he haphazardly juggled his democratic instincts with his dream of a virile, national state. To establish his democratic credentials, he reiterated his support for the direct primary, initiative and referendum, and an amending clause to facilitate the revision of the Constitution to reflect majority views. A third alternative to the insulated Democratic and Republican parties, such as the Bull Moose party, offered a quick route to "pure democracy." Croly also exhibited increasing empathy for workers in whose "impatient spirit there seems to be no way of imposing such a radical change of attitude upon economic society save by the use of organized violence." Croly laid the groundwork for "industrial democracy" through worker self-management, a bold move to break the hold of autocratic capitalists. Hence it fell on government to impress upon "responsible businessmen" that benefits can accrue from the improved morale of an efficient workforce.[10]

Yet, programs in *Progressive Democracy* for the rationalization of national plans dwarfed the reformer's democratic ideals. His "torch of truth" that shone to light the way for "popular control" flickered before his proposal for a "fourth branch of government" directed by a class of "social experts." The "successful performance" of such elite specialists "modifying social behavior," he wrote, "depends upon a condition of indifference to political opinion. . . . He has received his orders from the state, and until the orders are changed he must be preoccupied by the task of carrying them out with the utmost efficiency." The scope of the power Croly granted this officialdom remained a mystery. The impenetrable thicket of his snarled syntax and winding sentences offers few clues:

> A certain part of the social program would be embodied in achieved legislation, upon the desirability of which opinion was, for the time being, sufficiently agreed, and which was actually accomplishing or was failing to accomplish the desired results.

Croly's flair for suffocating his points with extraneous verbiage became most obvious when he wanted to disregard the undemocratic drifts of his arguments. Having repudiated "dogmatic socialism or individualism," the totalitarian intimations of his scheme raised the possibility of a mightier form of government than he could have ever imagined.[11]

As a cofounding editor, Walter Weyl added excitement to the *TNR* staff. Croly's arguments frequently sank under the weight of his plodding prose. Weyl's additions to the annals of progressive literature, by contrast, were lucid and sparkled with sardonic wit. An economist by training but journalist in practice, Weyl earned his reputation from the publication of *New Democracy* in 1911. An ingenious metaphor that described U.S. history as one big democratic gamble, with a few plutocrats the winners and everyone else a loser—"the public be damned"—set the book's theme. For their own pecuniary gain, the plutocrats invoked an archaic constitution and a perverted form of Jeffersonian individualism. This group functioned not so much as a Junker class (the ultrareactionary landed aristocracy in Prussia,) or U.S. oligarchy, but as a "group of wealthy men loosely united . . . by bonds of wealth and prestige" and the "economic influence" they exercised over "industry, politics, and public opinion." Moreover, while the gap between the haves and have-nots widened, the country squandered its most precious resources—people:

> Below the economic level of democratic striving, men are for the most part too ill-fed, ill-clad, ill-conditioned, too depressed by want or sickness, too harassed by debt or insecurity, too brutalized by child-labor or overworked to maintain the morale required for the attainment of democracy.

According to this version of the stake-in-society theory, the sense of utter desperation and deprivation planted the seeds of an imminent class conflict. "However spirited a structure civilization is," Weyl explained, "it is nevertheless built upon wheat, pork, steel, money, and wealth." Weyl's direct involvement and first-hand observation of violent industrial strikes left him leery of absolute socialism or Marxism, dogmas at odds with the "common interests," and "national ideals" of all classes. Man lived by bread, not chimerical utopian visions.[12]

For Weyl, the United States still represented the land of opportunity. He took care to demand the "equalization, not of men but of opportunities." The nation created a vast, unprecedented wealth only to see it appropriated by the industrial oligarchy. A product of the whole society, this abundance could guarantee all people "meat, potatoes, school books, public parks, and surcease from excessive toil." This optimistic doctrine of progress through prosperity turned the Marxist concept of a permanently impoverished proletariat on its head. Once the dispossesed rose above the poverty line and reached levels of democratic striving," they would act as the engines of revolt. A new class could then invoke their formidable "consumer power," as full-fledged participants in the economy, to ensure a peaceful redistribution of the nation's abundance. "Step by step, as the chance presents itself," Weyl argued, the people would demand government ownership of railroads, coal mines, and other industries. Progressive property, income, or inheritance taxes could further diffuse wealth, allowing it to be channeled into socially useful purposes.

The battleground for the attack on plutocracy was the voting booth. With the aid of democratically controlled parties and nominations and the initiative and referendum, citizens could press for the extension of worker health and safety reforms, legislation prohibiting child labor, socialization of health care, and enlargement of educational programs. How Weyl intended to piece together all the fragments of his strategy and translate "consumer power" and similar alluring slogans into tangible political results, he left vague. Whereas Croly deferred to his band of technocrats, the thrust of Weyl's "social democracy" emerged from the people themselves. Both shared, in principle and in their patchwork reforms, a preference for a highly homogenized form of socialism. Both also believed the U.S. system could heal itself.[13]

Walter Lippmann completed the triumvirate of *TNR* editors. The ambitious 24-year-old prodigy served as a cub reporter for muckraker Lincoln Steffens and a socialist mayor in Schenectady, New York, until he grew despondent over the impossibility of applying socialist theory to practical politics. The sobering experience led him to sever his ties to the socialism of his college days and develop the central themes of *Preface to Politics*, a major work that enormously impressed Croly, Roosevelt, and other progressives in 1912. Politics, Lippmann declared, must satisfy basic human desires instead of hypothetical rights and concepts. Goo-goo reformers cursed the wrong evils. Though it may have been corrupt, Tammany Hall succeeded because it recognized the value of "solid warm facts of kindliness, clothes, food, and fun." The young philosopher's enthusiasm for the prospects of humanity branched off in different directions. He hoped to tap into an age "rich with varied and generous passions." Touching only slightly the specifics of a liberal agenda, Lippmann embraced Henri Bergson's idea of the living over the inert. Borrowing from Santayana's lectures at Harvard, he also expounded on naturalism to link the creations of living people to human desires. A critique of the human proclivity toward "irrational politics" bore the mark of another figure at Lippmann's alma mater, the English philosopher Graham Wallas.

Among the potpourri of William James, H. G. Wells, Nietzsche, and others in *Preface* ran a single, dominant influence. Lippmann relied heavily on Sigmund Freud's taboo theory to demonstrate how politics was governed by a method as "naive as barbarism, as ancient as human failure." All too often, he argued, politics repressed human instinct rather than attempting to "sublimate" and direct society's evils toward desirable ends. Of course, the knottier problem lay in the precise definition of evil. Lippmann, for example, may not have found it so easy taming the malevolence of the average trust by diverting it to social uses. In a world only beginning to take notice of Freud, *Preface* seemed daring. But, within the context of U.S. reform, it broke little ground for constructive progressive policies.[14]

Lippmann's stature as a political thinker rose to loftier heights after the publication of *Drift and Mastery* in 1914. "We have lost authority. We are 'emancipated' from an ordered world. We drift," he complained. Lippmann singled out various villains for being out of tune with the times. Jeffersonian liberals worshiped the chaos of freedom to the exclusion of all else. The Socialist party occupied the fringe of irrelevance in U.S. politics. The IWW, the syndicalist union, forged solidarity among workers and satisfied some of their urge to revolt but "was quite ready to destroy the union for the sake of militancy." Lippmann sympathized with their pentup anger; no one, after all, could "expect civic virtue from a disenfranchised class." In short, constant fear of unemployment and wretched living conditions of workers undermined the general welfare. "You can't build a modern nation of Georgian crackers, poverty-stricken negroes, the homeless and helpless of the great cities," he concluded. Lippmann echoed Weyl's stern warnings against the dangerous course on which the United States was headed.[15]

Unfortunately, Lippmann proved stronger on the problem than the solution. *Drift* took a few pages from Weyl's book on consumer control and readily affirmed Weyl's confidence in a "social surplus" to pay the price of genuine democracy. Above all, mastering the nation's destiny involved the "substitution of conscious intention and unconscious striving" for scientific management and science itself. Management's eventual acceptance of unions as a fact of industrial life would eliminate much of the strife that wracked the nation. The business world had already begun to produce a "new kind of businessman"—a professional manager freed from the profit motive and an inveterate opposition to unions. Lippmann predicted the "nationalization" of business, not by the government, but through dispersed ownership.

It took little knowledge of economics or the nature of gargantuan trusts at the time to understand that his assessment did not square with reality. Trusts were neither "sucking the life out of private property" nor allowing private property to "melt away." The ease with which Lippmann dismissed socialism and replaced the irrational in *Preface* with a rational strategem for the reorganization of society signaled a sharp turn, if not a certain caprice, in the evolution of his political convictions. Lippmann had clearly purged himself of his college leftism to become firmly entrenched in the camp of middle-class liberalism.[16]

That these three very gifted, contemplative men should search for an outlet to express their views on a regular basis was no surprise. Prior to the advent of television and radio, people turned to print journalism to be entertained and to keep abreast of current events. Just how popular and prosperous magazines were was evident from the hefty stipends, from 400 to 500 dollars per article, which Weyl earned from his contributions to *Harpers* and the *Saturday Evening Post* in 1913.[17] Lippmann also had worked for a muckraking magazine and dabbled in freelancing. Croly served as editor of the prestigious publication, *Architectural Record*. None of these, however, fully quenched their thirst for politics and the arts. The new periodical they envisaged would occupy a niche unique among all others of the era. They never wished to imitate Randolph Bourne's *The Masses* and its close relative in the arts, Van Wyck Brooks' *Seven Arts*, in their paeans to the IWW's radicalism or the general cause of anarchy. *TNR* would take the lead in a national renewal in education, literature, and government. While its sister journal, *The Nation*, devoted most of its attention to Einsteinian and Freudian theories and uninspiring cultural matters, *TNR* ushered in a new age of progressive thought and bid farewell to the liberal philosophy of yesteryear.

Of course, an enterprise as grandiose as the three men contemplated required capital—a lot of it. The generosity of the project's backers, Dorothy and Willard Straight, appears to have had no limits. Dorothy's father, the extremely wealthy William C. Whitney, made his fortune in municipal streetcar lines and investments in Standard Oil and served in Grover Cleveland's cabinet. Her position as an heiress to the estate and member of the famed Whitney family of New York endowed her with plenty of time and resources to fight for her favorite humanitarian causes, ranging from the Settlement House movement (which sheltered, educated, and fed immigrants) to campaigns against sweatshops and for fair wages and women's suffrage.[18] Before joining the J. P. Morgan firm, Willard Straight served a close, personal apprenticeship with Theodore Roosevelt. At the J. P. Morgan firm, he led a U.S. banking group in China in negotiating the "Open Door" policy, in close contact with the U.S. Department of State. The life of a businessman did not suit his eclectic talents and interests, including politics, music, art, education, reading, writing, and especially journalism. He had long considered shopping around for a newspaper or magazine to purchase. He longed for a daily to be read by hundreds of thousands. In 1913, he briefly entertained the thought of buying the *New York Evening Post.* Never did he foresee, in his wildest dreams, the beginning of a new progressive journal of opinion.

Perhaps, the idea of *TNR* could have only germinated in the collective minds of these extraordinary individuals. Mrs. Straight acted out of a sense of noblesse oblige and dedication to the public good. Beatrice Webb, her closest British equivalent, probably would have referred to the society to which she belonged as the "world of three b's, bureaucracy, bourgeois, and benevolence." One afternoon, the Straights invited Croly to their country home on Long Island to discuss Croly's work and sundry matters.[19] In the course of criticizing the recent revision of *Harpers Weekly*, Dorothy interjected to ask him why he did not "get out" a weekly himself. Even if he had a bit of extra money, he responded, "it would take at least $100,000 and five years to make it self-supporting." "It may take longer, much longer. But let's go ahead . . . I will find the money," she assured him.

While his wife supplied the idealism and encouragement, not to mention the greenbacks, Willard operated on another set of assumptions. He sought out the author of *Promise* because its messages conformed to the robust visions of nationalism and imperialism he had learned under his mentor, Roosevelt. Croly was already in the process of writing a report for Straight on the feasibility of founding a National University in Washington to train students to serve in the government and diplomatic corps.[20] The concept for the publication they tossed about would not reach the large audience of a daily newspaper, but Straight could settle for the tens of thousands a "little" magazine might reach.[21] After the death of his employer, Croly reflected how little Straight cared about "speculative or critical thinking whose relationship to practical affairs was not immediate and direct."[22] Though too young to know his father before his premature death during World War I, Straight's youngest son and future *TNR* editor Michael later recalled—on the basis of posthumously read letters and talks with his mother—that his father "described himself as a 'conservative.' "[23] At times, in fact, Mrs. Straight took it upon herself to remind her husband of the magazine's primary function as an instrument of progressive reform.

Croly's initial enthusiasm for the Straights' attractive offer was tempered by professional and personal observations. His dilemma reflected Charles Beard's perceptive dictum: "Reform leaders in the

United States . . . [had] better have money, or next best marry it."[24] Croly warned his patrons that it might cost as much as 150,000 dollars over a five-year span until the magazine became self-supporting.[25] Digging further into their wallet (or pocketbook), Croly delicately broached the subject of his personal deficit between 5,000 or 6,000 dollars. (A healthy sum, if one remembers the dollar back then was then worth approximately ten of today's.)[26] A late legacy and tardy payment for a series of lectures he had recently delivered forced him to post debt at the Harvard Club, procure a loan from friend Judge Learned Hand, and gently request from Straight remuneration for the report he had written on "social education."[27] Furthermore, "it would not be fair to Mrs. Croly," Mr. Croly informed Straight, "to cut down on our standard of living"—which called for 8,000 dollars per year—by having to move from her modest surroundings in New Hampshire to the costlier lifestyle of New York.[28] Mrs. Croly might also have been distressed to see her spouse forego his epicurian tastes for fine wine, giving dinners and dining out, lawn tennis and golf.[29] Croly doubted whether he was even qualified for the job. Though he promised to visit the office "regularly," he did not feel "strong enough" to act as anything more than a "steady contributor." He could be counted on to "always [attend] editorial councils," but wished to be "relieved, if possible, of editorial detail . . . for his own good and that of the publication,"[30] A troubled Croly informed a close friend, Harvard Law Professor Felix Frankfurter, of his nagging anxieties about involvement in the vaguely defined project.[31] The broad scope of his observations, he warned, permitted him to examine "much more clear at a distance than at close quarters."[32] Croly appraised, for the benefit of Straight, his "disinterested and somewhat detached thinking" as the richest "gift" he could give the magazine.[33] Far from thanking the editor for his "gift," Straight often prodded him to stop trifling with his beloved abstractions and get to the point. Their different philosophies of the magazine were to collide head on in coming years. Fully aware of his own liabilities and assets, Croly was caught in a quandary. His own retiring personality and antipathy toward the daily details of running a magazine prevented him from ever assuming a forceful position at the helm of *TNR*. The liberty he granted his editors would precipitate many a fierce editorial squabble during his reign.

Straight's powers of persuasion and purse ultimately rescued the embryonic operation from premature extinction. Dorothy was "very insistent" that Croly receive an annual salary as high as 10,000 dollars.[34] Her prospective employee demurred. He appreciated her generosity but worried that it might "gravely compromise the success of this enterprise."[35] He had no intention of becoming wealthy from the magazine; he wanted only making enough to live comfortably. He was yearning, he reminded himself and friends, for intellectual rather than material enrichment. Straight's offer to forward payment for the investigation he conducted about the feasibility of a national university and to purchase real estate Croly owned for the magazine's offices eased his burdens considerably. Now the two parties could turn their attention to practical matters such as finding a name for the publication.

The ensuing debate over the title did not revolve around a merely cosmetic issue. It was a vivid example of the two men's different conceptions of the magazine and the direction they wished to see it take. Straight bubbled with excitement over his suggestion: "FACT: For, Against, Consultation, Truth."[36] When Straight "sprung it upon" his friend, Felix Frankfurter, Frankfurter objected at first, then "scratched his head and thought there was a great deal in it." Straight sincerely believed that his name was "much more striking, and really much more representative of" Croly and his "aim than any other." "New Democracy, Progressive Ideas, the Republic, Nationalism, Federalism, and all the rest" were only "sound if based on *FACT*":

> *FACT* is what people will want. *FACT* is what they have been unable to get in the old publications and *FACT* is what we are setting out to supply. If we make a fight for any one thing we expect to base our faith on *FACT*. If we criticize any person our arrows will be barbed with *FACT*, not prejudice. We want to tell *FACTS*, not stories. In *FACT*, it is in telling *FACTS* that *FACT* will differ from de FACTo publications.

Straight revealed more than an obvious affinity for a particular word; he was showing faint respect for progressivism. In blending the diverse elements of federalism, "progressive ideas," and "all the rest" into a meaningless whole, he thoroughly misjudged its spirit. As a reform movement, progressivism's inspiration for people lay in an optimistic hope for a better future. The objective, scientific formulas Straight so valued actually figured little in the cause. The businessman appeared to place "clear and impartial judgment" above political idealism. Approaching the enterprise with a publisher's sense of what sells and a reporter's eye for data, he, was, in effect, still nurturing his ambition to own a newspaper instead of a magazine of opinion.

Croly struggled to dissuade his employer from adopting his pet logo. The bashful editor reiterated their goal of starting "a critical and constructive review" whose

> primary purpose will not be to record facts but to give certain ideals and opinions a higher value in American public opinion. If these ideas and opinions were accepted as facts it would be unnecessary to start the paper. The whole point is that we are trying to impose views on blind or reluctant people.

Hence, the "paper," as Croly dubbed it," ought to imply a political purpose and a national outlook" and provide "information which people cannot get elsewhere." He preferred "One Nation" or the "New Nation" but, perhaps owing to their close resemblance to the extant *Nation*, finally opted for the "Republic" as a fair substitute. Croly tried to placate Straight. Of course, he reassured him, he recognized the importance of buttressing judgments with facts and admitted it would "be fatal . . . to specialize as much in social reform as the Webbs do. The publication, however, he warned Straight, would "give a good deal of space to it." The culture-bound Webbs had little use for literature and arts. Croly viewed these as integral elements of the U.S. tapestry. Yet, like the Webbs, he was not about to shy away from social reform either.[37]

After further deliberation, Straight relented. Only one obstacle stood in the way: the name "Republic" had already been taken. A paper by the same name belonged to John Fitzgerald, a popular Boston politician and grandfather of John F. Kennedy. Straight traveled up to New England to haggle with "Mr. Honey Fitz," but to no avail. The Boston politico informed him that this publication had already been "entered as second class matter," to which Straight had to restrain himself from rudely retorting that perhaps "that was rating it too high."[38]

Straight consoled a "greatly disappointed Croly." "Regardless of the man's character, or his paper," he conceded, he was "just as much entitled to it as though he were an angel of light." "The appellation 'Plato . . .' always seemed particularly fitting" for their use, so Straight broke the news gently to his partner in a seriocomic fashion:

> It's too bad, but I think that it is the only thing for us to do. I think it would be very unfortunate for a group of young men like ourselves, standing like houses of light and

towers of strength and moral purpose in this proverbial fog and murk of materialism and corruption, to enter upon our career with a lawsuit for endeavoring to appropriate the title of a paper published by the notorious Ex-Mayor of Boston.

"The New Republic" was not a poor consolation prize. After all, the 1912 election had pitted Roosevelt-cum-Croly's "new nationalism" against Wilson's "new freedom" and newness, as always, was still in vogue. Coincidentally, a few years earlier, H. G. Wells, a Fabian socialist, had called for replacing the old order with a "new republic" led by an "intellectual samurai"—a group of superior men and women who would manage society for the public good.[39] At times, the new *The New Republic*, albeit not in the antidemocratic overtones of Wells, preached a similar message to its readers.

The task of assembling a staff proved less difficult for Croly than deciding on a name. While Straight and he agreed to keep salaries down as far as possible, they could not skimp if they wanted to "get the best . . . men in order that the [New] Republic may astound the world."[40] Walter Weyl welcomed the idea of the paper and was invited to become an editor. Journalist Philip Littell was an old friend of Croly's at Harvard and a business associate. Croly selected him as "one man in ten thousand" to take charge of the letters department and a book column.[41] Charlotte Rudyard, a graduate of Vassar, had done stints at Harper and Row and *Harpers Weekly* and copyedited *Promise*, surely an onerous task that would have eliminated all but the hardiest from the profession. Francis Hackett, an erudite Irishman, had arrived in the United States 13 years earlier and edited the highly acclaimed literary supplement of the *Chicago Evening Post*. He was appointed to the books and arts section. Robert Hallowell combined a practical business sense with political idealism and an interest in the arts.[42] Also a Harvard alumnus and member of the Greenwich Village crowd, he was stationed at the post of business manager and unofficial art editor.

Walter Lippmann, whose *Preface* deeply impressed Croly, became the paper's final acquisition. During a dinner in early 1914, Straight silently watched Hackett and Lippmann become embroiled in a heated exchange with Ogden Mills, a leading progressive Republican and affiliate of a major railroad and several large corporations. A couple of days later, an agitated Straight dashed off a note to Croly:

> [Mills] remarked to me today that Lippman [sic] was an
> avowed socialist with leanings toward the IWW, and said
> that if Lippman was going to be on your paper and got
> that sort of stuff off his chest you wouldn't be doing what
> I said you would. I told him that you believed you would
> be able successfully to muzzle some of Lippman's wilder
> notions, and that while you recognized his point of view
> you felt him to be sufficiently sane always to yield to
> reason; in fact, I painted quite a rosy picture of what a
> value Lippman would be to the Republic in the guise of a
> reformed socialist.[43]

Straight left the content of his side of the discussion open to
speculation. Lippmann was no socialist, and the thought of "muzzl-
ing" anyone violated the very idea of *TNR*. Straight may well have
been simply humoring his friend, Mills. (Straight's companion, it
turned out, would have a peculiar history. He supported various
liberal measures in the New York State Senate before World War I,
and became assistant Secretary of Treasury to the ultraconser-
vative Andrew Mellon during the Coolidge administration,
whereupon he succeeded Mellon under Hoover and later became a
scathing critic of the New Deal.)[44] Lippmann might not have found
his employer's behavior so amusing. In the course of supplying a
"thousand . . . things" as "grist" for the editorial "mill," Croly was
advised to keep certain labor issues "out of Walter Lippmann's
sight." "Go slow," Straight cautioned him, and do not tip over the
"apple cart."[45] The owner always insisted his "connection" with the
paper "was not a very close one" and Croly had "entire charge of the
personnel."[46] The staff was skeptical and wanted to establish some
ground rules before the magazine came out.

Several members of the staff demanded firm guarantees of
editorial independence. From the outset, Hackett, Weyl, and Littell
expressed concern over the dangers of receiving subsidies from a
banker with unsavory friends. An agreement was worked out
limiting editorial meetings to the staff to keep out the likes of
Mills.[47] At Croly's insistence, a compromise was reached ensuring
the Straights would be consulted about all important questions of
policy and management but would not play a role in editorial decisions. "I would have felt better," Straight once modestly told Croly,
"if you'd said I don't like and won't use you[r] brilliant but indigesti-
ble suggestions."[48] Of course, the Straights implicitly exercised
another form of power. If they ever radically objected to the
magazine's policy, they could simply stop the subsidies and let it go

out of business. From every indication, in all their years as financial angels, Dorothy and Willard never did cut off the flow of money, nor even threaten to.

Straight and Croly decided to throw a gala dinner to celebrate their new venture and spared no expense in doing so in November 1913. All the elements were provided but one: the festivities were marked by the conspicuous absence of female guests. The guest list the two hosts carefully drew up included Ida Tarbell, the famous muckraker, and a few other distinguished women. After giving it some thought, however, Straight decided the event "would be much more successful if held out at some club as a dinner."[49] Croly concurred, adding that it was "just as well . . . to cut the women out of this larger meeting . . . [because they] might feel lonely in such preponderantly masculine company."[50] For fear that they could not entertain those other ladies in the style to which they . . . [were] accustomed," Straight bemoaned, invitations went out only to the wives of Croly and Judge Learned Hand. In April of the following year, a "Dinner of Introduction and Anticipation" was given at the fashionable Players Club in New York to honor "Counselors, Contributors, and Friends"—qualifications, it seemed, few women could meet.

Had the women attended, they would have been wise to skip the appetizer, which consisted of a bland Croly speech on "human emancipation and fulfillment," and proceed to the sumptuous main course of Smith Island oysters and spring lamb.[51] Straight, the magazine staff, and Felix Frankfurter enjoyed the fare. So did another individual. "You can decide better than I whether his presence is worthwhile," Straight told Croly before extending a welcome to Mills.[52] Eventually, even the persona non grata himself came to wine and dine. In this "pre-liberated" age, human behavior was clearly dictated by a different code of social mores. Croly and Straight's patently sexist behavior explains why, for many years, no woman held a high-level editorial position at *TNR* and Dorothy Straight abstained from direct contact with the magazine, preferring to act through her husband.

The men at *TNR* wanted their product stamped with a prominent seal of approval. Croly hoped to stay on friendly terms with Roosevelt and preserve "some close cooperation without close association" with the Progressive party. Weyl and Lippmann prepared a labor policy for the colonel in the summer of 1914 in which the latter advised him to endorse unions and all their "crudities."[53] Weyl, for his part, counseled the former president on the "best way of evolving a . . . permanent, constructive, dynamic labor policy for the Progressive Party" and averting violent strikes such as that occurring in Colorado. The two editors' efforts were met with staunch resistance. A "little surprised and rather a little shocked," Weyl looked on as Roosevelt exploded over the "murders and outrages of the strikers."[54] This exchange marked the first in a long series of squabbles between Roosevelt and *TNR*, eventually culminating in the relationship's break-up. A few days before the publication of the first issue, the editors called on their hero at his home at Oyster Bay, Long Island. They all talked, according to Lippmann, for hours, while their host was "as fresh as a daisy at two in the morning . . . Weyl as alert as ever, and Croly [was] dozing in his chair."[55]

During the months preceding *TNR*'s debut the dramatis personae put final touches on the magazine and rejoiced over the inspired mission they planned to lead. The staff had spent months busily seeking out contributors and testing various type designs and formats. In a moment of rare elation, the normally stoic Croly confessed to Straight that he dreamed about the paper "every night." "If anybody ever had a vision about anything," he wrote, "I have one about this editorial weekly. The only difficulty is that it will take a company of intellectual and moral Sir Galahads to make it come right."[56] Not missing a beat, the poetic Straight rose to the occasion with a stirring tribute to their endeavor: "a large splash is a great thing," he exclaimed, "for the little ripples keep on circling even after the noise of the splash has passed into history. Of course our aims must be to make the pond, if not pot, boil."[57] However high the temperature of this body rose, it was a pond, nonetheless, in which *TNR* intended to cause the splashes and ripples of liberalism rather than the oceanic tidal waves of radicalism.

The Business
of Living

. . . .
1914–16
. . . .

DOROTHY STRAIGHT HAD TRULY DESCENDED FROM THE heavens to bless the *TNR* enterprise. In all her years as the paper's financial angel, her grace and beneficence never ceased to awe the staff. She enjoyed many of the trappings of high society with few of the pretenses. As W. S. Swanberg, noted historian of the Whitney family, describes her class:

> Scions of the most affluent families, with townhouses in New York and country houses elsewhere (Dorothy could choose among four country houses), they took for granted servants, opera boxes, private railroad cars, yachts, horseflesh, and exclusive clubs.

The genteel tradition, which Santayana so ridiculed, was indeed thriving at the turn of the century. Dorothy treated herself to these luxuries and partook of a nonstop regiment of balls and proms. Unlike many of her peers, however, she managed to escape from this tinselland to take advantage of the opportunities her privilege afforded. She was well educated in the classics and modern philosophy, an uncommon achievement for females in her day. While traveling in Europe, Dorothy paid Edith Wharton a call and toured Paris art galleries with Henry Adams. Her involvement in the suffrage movement and other social causes reflected as much a commitment to public good as an insatiable urge to edify herself. *TNR* suited her tastes perfectly. "The power of the paper is really extraordinary," she once wrote her husband. "I believe it is going to

19

do more for the education of this country than any other force I know of . . . [and] is the best thing that you and I ever put over."[1]

Willard Straight occupied the outer fringes of the upper class. Orphaned at ten, he had to work his way through Cornell and graduated with little money. As luck and determination would have it, he earned the confidence of Roosevelt, and of an influential railroad magnate with connections to important financial firms. While traversing China, he also had the good fortune to meet Dorothy who was enjoying a sightseeing trip. After a long courtship, they decided to marry only to confront a tall wall erected by her family. Swanberg describes the situation:

> A formidable opposition had developed. Even the fact that he worked for J. P. Morgan—normally a high recommen-dation in society—could not save him. His college background was scorned by those who saw prestige only at Princeton, Yale, and Harvard and regarded Cornell as a small rural place devoted mostly to instructing farmers.

This bitter experience and Willard's difficult childhood drew him even closer to Dorothy on whom he relied for constant encourage-ment and moral uplifting. Straight never let his occasional bouts of depression drag on for long; he had too much zest for life. His fascination for and proficiency in politics, diplomacy, music, art, reading, education, and sports cast him in center stage at any social gathering; a position which, by dint of his infinite charisma and charm, he wanted gracefully held for the evening's duration. "Play the game!" he roared in the robust, virile spirit of Kipling, his favorite writer. The adventurer approached *TNR* with the same fer-vor. While in his lighter moments he treated it as if it were a toy, he was well aware of its importance as an instrument of power. No matter how far he stayed in the background, the magazine bore the imprint of his dynamic personality.[2]

"*TNR* is frankly an experiment, it is an attempt to find a na-tional audience for a journal of opinion," the editors announced in their inaugural issue in November 1914.[3] A few weeks later, the magazine further defined itself as a "representation of the layman who meets the expert, acknowledges him, and endeavors to relate his work to the larger issue and the general business of living."[4] The "larger issues and general business of living" were indeed flourishing in its pages. Novel for the times, the magazine's ar-resting graphics spawned a host of imitators. *TNR* opened with a series of short editorial paragraphs, called "leaders," and proceeded to longer editorial "light middles" and signed articles by the staff and outside contributors. In the years before the United States entered World War I, *TNR* was especially distinguished by the regular appearances of John Reed, John Dewey, Santayana, the historians Charles Beard and James Harvey Robinson, and other cultural luminaries. The work of H. G. Wells, philosopher Graham Wallas, George Bernard Shaw, James Bryce, and the Webbs lent it a particularly British flavor. The glow of Anglophilia burned even more brightly with the outbreak of World War I. The "back of the book" displayed the formidable literary talents of critics Van Wyck Brooks and Randolph Bourne and poets Amy Lowell, Conrad Aiken, and Robert Frost, whose "Death of a Hired Hand" was first published in the magazine. At the heart of this rich, eclectic assortment of writing stood the editors' prodigious body of work. Their weekly output, in private and public form, shaped the destiny of the magazine and, to a larger extent than could possibly be imagined, a U.S. liberal philosophy.

While other magazines existed to earn their backers money, *TNR* knew it was futile to compete for hundreds of thousands of subscriptions or the customary revenue derived from advertising. The day before the second issue, publisher Hallowell discharged the advertising manager, one Mr. Tobey, because "he didn't seem to wake up to the news and opportunities of the paper or his job" and his "drowsiness . . . caused much trouble."[5] Tobey's legacy survived him, however. As future editor Malcolm Cowley once put it, advertisements were merely "tolerated."[6] As did the *Nation* and similar high-brow publications, *TNR* catered to the book-buying public with pitches, for example, for a 1,200-page, two-volume set of *Shakespeare's England*, which no educated reader could do without.[7] Social appeals frequently tugged at the audience's heartstrings. Help "Tenement Tommy," the "New York Association for Improving the Poor" entreated, with a small donation so that he and other "victims of poverty" might enjoy a few days in the country away from the slum.[8] Periodic promotions were cooked up to discount subscriptions—4 dollars per year and 10 cents a copy—with the purchase of one of the editor's books or trial combinations with either *Harpers* or the *Atlantic Monthly*, two established magazines that benefited from a long-standing and devoted corps of readers.[9]

TNR celebrated its first anniversary with a grand announcement. Although circulation was "not yet large enough to make it self-supporting," it was "larger than anyone thought it would be at the end of the first year,"[10] From an initial base of 875, circulation had grown to 3,000, a figure that would increase at least tenfold within the next five years. An exclusive audience of some 30,000 was not about to put *Colliers, Hearst's,* or *McClures,* averaging sales of .5 million each, out of business. Nevertheless, *TNR* was writing a unique chapter in the history of U.S. magazines. One reason for this success was an unlikely source of subscribers: word of mouth. By mid-1915, as much as 15 percent of the circulation came from the names subscribers sent in, a remarkably high rate for any magazine. (Croly was embarrassed to learn that Dorothy paid for hers.)[11] A direct mailer was privately issued to subscribers in the hope that "every reader would secure one new subscriber." Only then, the mailer asserted, could *TNR* reach the "breaking-even point," a "necessity" if it were to stay alive.[12] This clever advertising ploy stretched the truth a bit. Far from being a "necessity," an abundance of subscribers merely reduced the editors' dependence on the Straights. In its entire history, *TNR* rarely reached the elusive goal of self-sufficiency.

Behind the scenes, *TNR* functioned quite harmoniously. The magazine was located in two adjoining old brick houses in New York's fashionably run-down Chelsea district across the street from the General Theological Seminary and a few doors away from a home for wayward girls (as if by "some coincidence of symbolism," historian Eric Goldman suggested).[13] The offices were smartly furnished with handsome antiques and other articles of impeccable taste.[14] Lucie and Etienne, a resident caretaking couple, prepared elaborate meals for meetings and special luncheons and dinners in honor of dignitaries. Each Monday or Tuesday, the staff convened around an ornate table to lay out the week's issue. After lengthy discussions, the editorial board assigned a writer to a particular topic. The editors, according to Croly, determined the paper's policy, participated in its management, and operated "in all important matters by practically unanimous consent."[15] Alvin Johnson—an economist recruited from Cornell to write unsigned editorials, and later invited to become a permanent member of the staff—related how the editors were in "constant consultation." Whenever disagreements did arise, they were allowed to "iron themselves out in the staff discussions" to everyone's satisfaction.[16] In terms of actual pencil editing, it seems, for the most part, that writers were left to their own devices. "The organization of *TNR* was based on the theory," Lippmann recalled, "that none of its editors wished to do much editing, that none of them would remain at a desk very long, and that there would be a place on board for men who were not wholly organizable."[17] Because the editors shared similar assumptions on most issues, they could entrust one another to the task of carrying out the "official" word of *TNR* in signed and anonymous articles.

In the midst of his hectic schedule, the magazine's benefactor did his best to keep abreast of the latest happenings at the office. Each week, Hallowell sent Straight cumulative statements on subscriptions, disbursements, and receipts, as well as acknowledgement of his regular 5,000 dollar checks to cover salaries, supplies, and other expenses.[18] Straight dutifully gave his authorization without comment, but his interests really lay on the editorial side.

Straight's peculiar relationship with the enterprise was, at its calmest, cordial, and, at its stormiest, somewhat tense. He canvassed his own ideas "about ten thousand . . . things" for articles with Croly and Lippmann.[19] When turned down, which occurred more often than not, he thanked his principal editor for being so "very kind." "I would have felt better," he modestly told Croly, "if you'd said Willard Go to the Blazes."[20] How sincere was his humility and deference to his editor? As historian Swanberg astutely points out: "Croly was nobody's yes-man and would always stand up for his beliefs, but he also knew that Straight was well informed, clear-minded, and a far more interesting writer than Croly himself."[21] The editor-in-chief was thus forced to placate the owner without conceding to him on crucial matters. The "disinterested loyalty" Croly claimed he maintained occasionally became strained:

> Willard never participated with sufficient intimacy in the writing and editing of *TNR* to feel that it was to any great extent an outlet for his own personality. It was at times irksome for him to be so closely associated with a publication and so responsible for its existence without himself contributing more positively to its policy and contents and frequently without altogether approving of what those contents were.[22]

No sooner had the magazine been out for a week than it occurred to Straight that it "should have paragraphs" on the Federal Reserve banks and foreign trade.[23] Croly might submit an article on the Steel Trust case for his perusal and Straight, in turn, would offer a piece he had written on Japan, consigning it to his "tender care—prayerfully."[24] Once in a while, the owner invited his employee "up to the country to get a chance to chin-wag."[25] In Croly's absence, Straight was not averse to sending Lippmann a message recommending a "subject which . . . [he], with his trenchant pen, . . . [was] preeminently qualified to deal with."[26] Throughout the war, Dorothy was bombarded with a steady barrage of "let H. C. know" and "tell Herbert" letters from her husband overseas.[27] In short, Straight behaved much like a coach on the sidelines, rooting his players on and letting the manager make the vital decisions.

In at least one case, Straight's involvement with *TNR* may have violated the code of ethics set up between the editors and him. At the peak of the magazine's crusade for the appointment of Louis Brandeis, a respected lawyer in Boston and friend of Woodrow Wilson, to the Supreme Court in 1916, Croly beseeched his employer to see him as soon as possible to discuss an urgent matter. An editorial entitled "The Motive of Class Consciousness" had already been set in galley form. Croly and Lippmann wished to publish it with an accompanying chart linking Brandeis' opposition to 35 prominent Bostonians who had sent a petition to the president. All these men, the piece contended, worked together, married into each other's families, had the same stocks and investments, went to the same board meetings, and belonged to the same clubs. The social pattern of "these gentlemen" amounted to nothing less than a "class psychology." Indeed, the "proud line" whence they came epitomized the "class consciousness of their section, the Backbay." Croly, in a feeble attempt to appeal to his boss's conservative instincts, cited these items as a "good contemporary example" of the tendency of such groups as labor and socialists to become insulated and "imperious to wholesome outside influences." Of course, the crux of the indictment centered on the close social and business connections of the petitioners. Croly wanted Straight to "understand right away" that this spicy fare would not be served without his "consent." If he took exception to it, the editor hoped he would at least give the rest of the staff the "precise weight" and "ground of difference" and listen to the "full bearing" of their arguments in favor of the article.[28]

Brandeis successfully repelled his foes' attacks to gain the nomination, but without the aid or firepower of his friends at *TNR*. Neither the chart nor article was ever published. Perhaps, on aesthetic grounds, one can understand the decision to withhold the unsightly chart; the tangled webs of interconnecting lines were an eyesore. And yet, the content scored telling points against Brandeis' detractors. Unfortunately, "The Motive of Class Consciousness" appeared only in a highly pasteurized version. Though scores of pro-Brandeis articles were published, in the unsigned and untitled one that most closely resembled the original and ran the week following the encounter between Croly and Straight, Lippmann exorcised the Marxist jargon; instead of being dominated by "class psychology," the men were victims of their own "group psychology."[29] All personal references were deleted. No names were named until two months later when a lone Boston newspaperman was accused of representing the "forces of evil and ignorance."[30] These two items retained all the vitriol of the untampered text, sans the class-conflict analysis. The editors apparently had backed up against the limits of Straight's political tolerance. The owner had no intention of seeing the image of his publication tarnished with an ideologically tainted condemnation of men with whom he probably associated.

Straight was not the only individual trying to check *TNR*'s leftward drift. R. M. Easley served as chairman of the National Civic Federation (NCF), an organization of capitalists and labor representatives established to promote the peaceful settlement of labor disputes. His mildly progressive attempts to secure industrial justice through collective bargaining and other methods of conciliation were matched by an almost neurotic compulsion to ferret out socialists in high places. Pressed by an angry friend in the federation about a subversive journal lurking in their midsts, Easley responded that, to the best of his knowledge, J. P. Morgan "had nothing to do with . . . another radical sheet which under the guise of high intellectuality and great responsibility, is insidiously preaching the doctrines of the revolutionaries, feminists and other cubists,"[31] The fault lay with the naive Straight, he wrote, a "very estimable, high class young man . . . [who] unfortunately . . . got mixed up with Herbert Croly, a progressive-populist, Walter Lippmann . . . more of a syndicalist, plus a modicum of Progressives." Easley could not have agreed with his friend more, "If the time ever came when J. P. ever advocated government ownership of Socialism," he replied, he too would "throw up" [his] "hands in disgust and quit it all." The agitated Easley quickly fired off a note to another official at the federation and close partner of Straight at J. P. Morgan:

> Mr. Gompers and the other big labor men expect to stand shoulder to shoulder with them to fight socialism in all its aspects at every stage of the game and I should feel a traitor to their cause if I "let down" on this for a moment. Is it not strange that it should be the labor men who are fighting the battle of capitalists.[32]

Gompers and other labor leaders certainly joined the NCF to enhance their respectability and oppose socialism. But there was by no means a consensus about its tactics or purpose, which some union organizers blamed for "chloroforming the labor movement into a more submissive mood."[33] Croly harbored enormous doubts about the organization's nonpartisan status. At the end of 1915, the socialist slayer struck again in a report, (Croly told Straight, with a "pretty lively attack on *TNR* as a purveyor of pernicious Socialist doctrines."[34] The assault amused the editor and intensified his urge to see Easley expelled from the association. Croly also realized that it marked the boundaries of the magazine's reformism. No matter how far he took his magazine in a liberal direction, the likes of Easley would be gunning for him.

Disparagement of *TNR* extended beyond a few socialist-baiting zealots. Roosevelt was not a man to brook personal reproach. An editorial critical of his belligerence toward Wilson's policy in Mexico prompted a stinging rebuke of the "three circumcised Jews and three anemic Christians" at the paper.[35] (Actually, there were two Jews at *TNR*, of whom only one had undergone the religious ceremony.) Lippmann had written the item in Croly's absence and without his consent. Croly, in an effort to mend fences, responded to the colonel's charges by reaffirming his magazine's principles: "*TNR*," he carefully explained to his most famous reader, "has never pretended to be a party organ, and its whole function depends on the impression which it makes upon readers of being able to think disinterestedly and independently."[36] More was at stake for the magazine than Roosevelt's vanity.

Overall, reviews were mixed. From the left, one important socialist intellectual denounced the "venality of Walter Weyl" for joining the venture, while another labeled the editors "kept idealists" for their association with Straight.[37] The *Catholic World* was bored by its "inspired vagueness" and "intellectual dilation." Echoing a wag's barb at the paper's "Crolier than thou air," Straight patiently admitted to his editor that the magazine suffered from "a little too much opinion and perhaps not quite enough knowledge." At times, Straight worried that it had become "too high-brow" for the audience to enjoy. "Lighten up the tone of the paper and give it a sugar-coating to get it across even with the semi-intelligent reader," he implored Croly.[38] In fact, the magazine's stiffness and unflagging solemnity bespoke a seriousness in keeping with its editor's high-minded purpose of molding public opinion. Even if no one exactly stormed his local newsstand to read Croly's latest expatiation, the rising circulation and awesome list of contributors in the arts and politics sections attested to the magazine's growing influence.

In the first few months, *TNR* rapidly moved to establish its identity as a vehicle for social justice. The editors constantly harped on the "inordinate amount of misery made in the U.S.A."[39] The "paradox and human" factor was that the very "modern industry" that provided food, shelter, clothing, the basis of life, health and education "also destroyed them; forever condemning men and women struggling under the burden of impossibly low wages" to their horrible jobs and "wretched shanties" and tenements, stripping them of any hope for the "wealth" of life.[40] Women were forced to work, if they could find it, out of "dire necessity" to keep their families fed. "The girl living alone, the country girl in the city, the immigrant girl, and the orphan" were inexorably dragged along the road to "prostitution, pauperism, and degradation."[41] In attempting to prick the "private consciences" of "disquieted" New Yorkers, the editors explained the causes of violence among the jobless:

> For there is no torture so refined as that of the man who is willing—even anxious—to work and yet slowly starves because, for reasons he cannot understand, he is not permitted to work. . . . What has become of the thousands of men and women who were . . . homeless, who slept in cheap lodging-houses, immigrant homes, employment agencies, missions, in the rear rooms of saloons, or lay shelterless on public streets, bridges and docks, or in the parks in midwinter? Some are dead; some are in prisons and in brothels; some are on the wide road, begging, stealing, occasionally working, freed from all manner of restraints and ancient inhibitions.[42]

How could men not act unlawfully as long as society's "chronic evil" continued to trap them? United States civilization was regressing to the days of Tudor England when "sturdy rogues . . . were trapped along the highroads and did some stealing . . . were hanged by the neck until they were dead." Charity drives across the country for the "one hundred neediest cases" failed to reach the thousands in need and were all too reminiscent of the Elizabethan method of "licensed beggary." "For God's sake, let's do something," *TNR* exclaimed in the midst of a steadily worsening depression in 1915.[43] The plaintive cry sounded none of progressivism's usual optimism. Hollow appeals to charity for the poor were relics of the nineteenth century. These twentieth-century liberals were developing new standards by which to judge society's performance in this crucial area.

Walter Lippmann ventured out in the field to gather material to mobilize public opinion. As a young student at Harvard, he had volunteered to aid the victims of a massive fire in Boston's slums. The upper-class Lippmann's first exposure to poverty so overwhelmed him that he joined the college socialist club, declaring to his girlfriend "I long to reach a small portion of the 'masses' so that in the position not of a teacher but of a friend, I may lay open real happiness to them."[44] The young journalist had lost little of this concern by the time he arrived at *TNR*. In an article entitled "Life is Cheap," he noted that one man was killed for every floor added to a skyscraper. The tragedy of the statistic was lost on the general public because the value of life increased only if it emerged from a "mass" and became "individualized."[45] The same collective indifference could not appreciate the number of "so dull, so degrading, or so useless" tasks such as those of bellhops, chauffeurs, ladies' maids, and caretakers for empty houses. Human beings degraded themselves with these jobs in order to survive. The "appalling insensitiveness" to the high death rate of infants and widespread use of women as "drudges" convinced the angry young man that "the notion that every person is sacred, that no one is a mean to someone else's end, this sentiment which is the meat of democracy . . . has taken only slight hold upon the modern world."

This was Lippmann at his best—sensible and incisive. In a lengthy supplement, he called for a "campaign against sweating."[46] According to the reporter's extensive research, countless females in paperbox, shirt, and candy industries would have died of "slow starvation" without the assistance of family, friends, and—as a last resort—charity. A woman who toiled away all day long deserved a minimum or "living" wage large enough to "sustain her health, buy decent food, clothes and lodging, and secure a little recreation," Lippmann argued in a rerun of *Drift and Mastery*'s message. A country could only be ruined by "stupidity, waste, and greed," he warned, and it need not so recklessly follow this course if it obeyed his and *TNR*'s dicta.

Liberals of *TNR*'s stripe found themselves in an awkward position. As affluent and well bred representatives of the middle and upper class, they were certainly cognizant of the social gulf between them and the masses they so earnestly wished to help. Almost 75 years before, Frederic Law Olmstead had commented on the tendency of "men of literary tastes" and "superior rank" to "overlook the working classes, . . . the dumb masses so lost in the shadow of egotism."[47] The fact was, Alvin Johnson argued, that the proletariat had a "small place" in U.S. fiction.[48] Outside the middle-class view lay the life of the "vast majority" and the "rawness of American existence." The "social-sentiment workers" or "bright reporters" noblest intentions could not bridge the wide gap.

Weyl also sensed this distance. Although he observed and wrote about strikes before joining *TNR*, he never participated in any. To keep from "jumping to false conclusions about the temper of the working class," in his spare time, Weyl liked to mingle with the common folks on movie lines.[49] In the event of any commotion on the street, he struck up a conversation by asking for a match: "I put myself under his slight obligation and the man feels kindliness toward me and is willing to talk," Weyl said. In another attempt to probe the proletariat's psyche, a group of prominent social reformers once cordially invited a few unemployed men from breadlines and lodging houses to lunch in the parlor of an exclusive residence. Weyl confidently began the meal with the "stubborn conviction that after all they were human beings and citizens." Much to his dismay, the festivities ended in utter frustration with the "vagabounds'" inability to "reason a thing out; they were too obsessed by the sordid trifles that had become their life":

> We tried desperately to be equal. It was the least we could
> do. Were we not all men and brothers? We used the title
> "brothers" as men do when in the absence of all social
> bonds that appeal to the last shred of common humanity
> . . . but could not use . . . that term of equality
> ["gentlemen"] to one who came from slow starvation.

The contrasts in appearance and behavior were too stark even to allow Weyl to bridge the social gap with this gesture of elementary courtesy. Economic and political inequality sapped the underprivileged of intellectual vitality, thereby reinforcing their disenfranchisement and prolonging their subjugation. Lippmann propounded a similar theory. Yet, the tone of Weyl's story was laced with bittersweet condescension. The editors' contempt for egalitarianism liberated them from tailoring their ideas to popular taste and limited them to a small minority, as opposed to the vast majority. If the only hope for the masses' salvation lay with Weyl and his fellow middle-class reformers in the ruling class, the road to equality was longer and rockier than he could have imagined.[50]

Weyl did not have to travel uptown to meet the poor. A 15-minute walk from the *TNR* offices would have placed him in the center of New York's lower east side slums and revealed the cruelty of the local garment industry. The scattered unions representing the mass of Jewish and Italian immigrants in this trade went on strike in 1910. The ensuing unrest continued unabated until, through the efforts of Brandeis, a "Protocol of

Peace" was reached, abolishing home work and enacting the six-day work week, weekly pay in cash, and regulation of overtime work.

Six years later, cloak manufacturers retaliated by invoking the lockout against 60,000 unorganized "green immigrant laborers." The manufacturers' refusal to uphold the principles of mediation or arbitration was, Weyl argued, a "return to the wild" of labor strife.[51] The editors saluted the wage earners as representatives of "industrial and progressive democracy" locked in a bitter struggle against manufacturers representing "despotism tempered by anarchy."[52] Due to the seasonal unemployment in the industry, the strikers' meager savings had already vanished. As the strike dragged on for months, a shortage of meat for adults and milk for babies and eviction from housing aggravated their plight. *TNR* not only asked the public for donations but, more importantly, for its sympathy for the workers' cause of joint control of the industry. In July, a settlement collapsed and employers resorted to their most effective weapon in 1910: the yellow-dog contract under which workers agreed not to join a union during their term of employment. Pronouncing the cause lost, the editors surrendered their claims, praising the "splendid solidarity" of the workers and their peaceful behavior. Their "grim determination" in the face of insurmountable odds was unsurpassed in "the history of American unionism." *TNR* reserved few kind words, however, for the AFL or Gompers' aloofness from events and disinclination to array his forces behind the garment workers. This criticism marked neither the first nor last time *TNR* positioned itself far ahead of the conservative labor leader.

In Colorado, a bloodier confrontation between coal miners and their employers confirmed the magazine's worst suspicions about the inequities of industrial relations. In the small towns, workers possessed nothing they could call their own; companies owned stores, houses and, roads, and even censored movies, books, and magazines. When miners attempted to organize in 1914 and 1915, management resorted to the usual union-busting tactics of summary discharge, the blacklist, and armed guards and spies. A local sheriff deputized several hundred employees, armed them with guns and ammunition, and ordered a specially built armored car, "The Death Special," to intimidate picketers and strikers.[53] Once the militia began attacking, looting, and firing at tents (in which the strikers lived after management evicted them from the company-owned houses) and killing women and children, the National Guard (a traditional ally of management) was sent in to quell the clashes. *TNR* placed the blame squarely on the mine owner's obstinate refusal to compromise and meet union representatives. "By provoking harassed and embittered men who . . . [needed] no provocation," it said, the owner precipitated and fueled the unrest:

> The torture of guilt rests indelibly upon the mining companies, their agents, and the politicians they control. They left open no remedy but rebellion; they offered the men the alternative of a strike or absolute submission. . . . [u]nder conditions where self-respect allowed them no other choice . . . [but to] . . . take up arms. . . . If in pursuit of a few human rights they themselves committed crime, the only answer is that tyranny breeds tyranny, that stupid injustice is not broken by planned violence.

Of course, the editors were not endorsing violence as an instrument for social justice. It was, however, a natural outcome of the industrialists' irrational suppression of unions. The resulting savagery could have been avoided had they only confronted the twentieth century reality of dealing with organized labor, the hallmark of a new civilization.[54]

Lippmann examined the incident as a test case in the securement of industrial peace. The industrial autocracy's "prejudice and mental rigidity" had caused the mayhem, he concluded.[55] As director of the conglomeration in control of the mines, John D. Rockefeller, Jr., was summoned before the federal government's Industrial Relations Commission to justify his role in the affair. Feigning ignorance, he absolved himself of all complicity in abetting the strike breakers and assigned responsibility to his subordinates. In an unsigned note, Lippmann could only marvel at the man's "intellectual helplessness," his embodiment of the "supreme negation of all equality, and unquestionably . . . the most menacing fact in the life of the republic."[56]

Several months after posing his lame defense, Rockefeller authorized an "Industrial Representation Plan" to give workers the opportunity to settle their grievances, arrange wages and working conditions, and establish a joint committee on health, housing, and recreation. The editors cut through the facade. The selection of delegates from the ranks of company employees deprived workers of genuine representation, an essential component of collective bargaining. The employees evidently agreed, and, through protracted negotiation, finally gained the right to collective bargaining. Industry initially resisted the employees' overtures. Finally, after the loss of numerous lives, it gave in to their demand—the way *TNR* believed that disputes should be settled. In the heat of the battle, the editors took direct aim at Rockefeller, the epitome of ruling-class intransigence, to urge him toward the sensible center.

The averted railway strike of 1916 challenged the convictions of *TNR* in a different context. In fighting with the railways over the eight-hour day and overtime pay, engineers, conductors, and trainmen risked pitting the public interest against the private needs and aspirations of workers. The disruption of the United States' lifeline threatened to wreck havoc on the nation. "The image, which is flashed through our minds," the editors fretted, is "of cities wihtout milk or food or coal, with unemployed men rioting, and thousands literally dying of starvation." It was difficult to shed tears for the "aristocracy of labor," which consisted of skilled workers "without much consideration for the interests of the unskilled and lower-paid workers in their industry." *TNR* was willing to acquiesce to the workers' demands to forestall the strike's devastating effects on the public. While welcoming President Wilson's intervention in the conflict and the Adamson Act, which promised an eight-hour work day, the magazine objected to provisions for compulsory investigation before future strikes or lockouts, a tool that industries could use to neutralize the striking power of employees by buying time to rally public opinion against the workers.[57]

Lippmann choreographed most of the magazine's editorial stances in this contest. As an informal advisor during the presidential campaign, he urged the president to oppose compulsory arbitration, and sent a note dismissing Republican Charles Evans Hughes' talk of "legislating first investigating afterwards" as "pure bunkum."[58] The president's "statesmanlike action" expressed "the temper of the country," Lippmann announced in the pages of *TNR*. As a "matter of social policy," he argued, the basic work day and Adamson bill were a "small price to pay for the prevention of a terrible national calamity." It was a "pity that the nation . . . [had] not yet developed the enterprise and public spirit seriously to face the labor question except when labor shakes its fist." The act "opened a new era of intervention by the government," presenting it with the opportunity to fix wages and hours and renew "the confidence of organized labor" in its capacity to perform a truly national task for all the people.[59]

Over the years, few strikes occurred in which *TNR* failed to champion the cause of labor. From a streetcar dispute in Chicago to mining communities in Arizona, the magazine sometimes read like a union newsletter. It was all part of the crusade to sell the idea of unions to the nation. Workers banded together collectively, the editors reasoned, because of their individual inabilities to bargain with employers. In essence, unionism offered a "means to gain control over the terms" of the wage earner's employment and, therefore, the "very substance of citizenship in an economic community."[60] Attempts to thwart unionism invariably reduced citizens to the "status of a commodity" and risked igniting a "warfare between unionism and anti-unionism" that endangered public safety. A population "too docile to protest, too dull to wish for better things" was a ticking time bomb. In a revealing moment, *TNR* asked those who disliked social "agitators" what exactly they proposed to substitute for them:

> Just how for example, do they intend to arouse interest in obscure injustice? Do they suppose men will think who have not first been made to feel? Do they suppose that they will feel until they have had the brutal facts forced upon them? Surely it is idle to suppose that the "public" is a sensitive, wise, interested, courageous, active body of responsible people. We are all members of the "public," and we might as well confess that these adjectives do not describe ourselves. . . . On the whole we do not move unless we are prodded, and we are the gadfly every bit as much today as when Socrates recommended it.[61]

Socrates defined his gadfly not only as an individual who acted as a provocative stimulus—the labor leader—but also as one habitually engaged in provocative criticism of existing institutions—the writer at *TNR*. The editors rarely held back their scorn for the popular press. Subsidized by the same corporate power structure hell-bent on sabotaging unions, mainstream newspapers and magazines "poisoned the public mind" and fomented "class suspicion and hatred."[62] This unreliability of daily news sources only enhanced *TNR*'s stature as a gadfly, giving it the additional role of the fourth estate's conscience.

Unfortunately, the largest impediment to labor's progress was labor itself. Gompers's conservative political instincts were based, a noted labor historian explains, on "the eighteenth century concept of liberty and the nineteenth century belief in individualism."[63] A faith in voluntary institutions and hostility toward government formed the bedrock of opposition to the minimum wage, maximum workday, and state insurance for the unemployed. *TNR* admitted "middle-class" reformers could "adapt the law, prepare public opinion, and shape programs which translate into results."[64] But it was up to the working class to actually generate "enduring, meaningful reforms." Such advances were delayed by the American Federation of Labor (AFL) a "strongly entrenched" craft union "based on skill, exclusiveness, race discrimination, high fees" and led by a man who avoided "dangerous issues" and bolstered the "conservatism of age and power with a kind of whig liberalism dating from England in 1850." Gompers's extreme caution came to the fore after passage of the Clayton Act in 1914. Hailing the law as labor's "Magna Charta," he rejoiced over the fulfillment of the AFL's long-sought goal of immunity from antitrust prosecution. *TNR* remained unconvinced. The act, the editors cautioned, was designed to protect property instead of personal rights. The sadly "defrauded" officials at the AFL were misleading the rank-and-file. In fact, not even J. P. Morgan himself could have framed "sections more favorable to capitalists and more hostile to labor."[65] In the glow of labor's ostensible crowning achievement, *TNR* still cast a pall on workers' lowly status as citizens.

Swimming against the AFL's strong currents, *TNR* presented its own legislative agenda for the construction of an industrial democracy. Its policies emerged from the toughest progressive tradition. To the editors, the employment of nearly 2 million children under the age of 16 symbolized the "evil . . . of callousness and apathy and greed."[66] The passage of the Keating-Owen Bill in 1916 outlawing child labor was heartily endorsed. As long as "general weakness, anemia, or premature old age" plagued the worker during the typical 12-hour work day and 60-hour week, "agitation and strikes and threats of strikes" would continue to fester.[67] People were entitled to the 8-hour day and a minimum wage to guarantee "health and decency." Brandeis' "overwhelming indictment of the chaos and cruelty and the stupidity by which women's wages were fixed" (in his famous defense of the Oregon minimum wage law before the Supreme Court in 1908) proved that on "human grounds . . . the burden of proof" rested on the opponents of such laws.[68] The extra burden imposed on the private sector did not bother Lippmann: "Industries which can't support themselves are uneconomic and should not be subsidized out of the health and sanity of their employees."[69] Nor did *TNR* have much patience for the Supreme Court's reflexive rejection of prolabor laws. To overhaul the court's historical "veto . . . upon social legislation" it recommended an overhaul of the Constitution through measures as drastic as amendments and curtailment of the power of judges.[70] In their books or magazine work, the editors rarely allowed the sentimentality of tradition to interfere with their visions of the future.

The implementation of the rest of *TNR*'s social program meant broadening the scope of government. "What Uncle Sam . . . [did] not do for women in industry" was protect their welfare and security. A "Women's Division" in the Bureau of Labor Statistics might be spearheaded by a "flying squad of expert investigators" to publicize the results of their research and stir "wholesome publicity" for future legislation.[71] An "industrial commission" might also be set up in each state and on the national level to work "with all bureaus or divisions that deal with all conditions of labor, including safety, and sanitation and child labor."[72] The commission-happy editors' programs often seemed innocuous and vague. The government only recognized the problem and did little else.

In a rarer instance, the magazine sketched concrete plans, including maternity insurance patterned after European models. "The most womanly woman and the most radical burden of risk . . . from hazard," had to be transferred "from the shoulders of unfortunate individuals to those of society."[73] To alleviate "inadequate diets, housing conditions, and infant mortality," the editors demanded a "government plan for health insurance" in the place of the paltry plans private companies operated.[74] Out of the 50 cents per week allotted to each individual, the employer would agree to contribute 25, the employee 20, and the "public" 5 cents. Unfortunately, the typical employee was already struggling to eke out an existence on meager wages. Forcing him to hand over a chunk of his paycheck to insurance companies left even less to pay for life's essentials. The noticeably low priority of the "public" participation indicated the limits of *TNR*'s acceptance of big government in these pre-New Deal Days. It was only a beginning.

Once in a great while, *TNR* envisioned a much larger role for the federal government. To reemploy "hundreds of thousands" in 1915, public work initiatives, which bore a slight resemblance to the WPA projects of the 1930s, were bandied about.[75] Toward that end, the federal government might issue loans or provide credit to the jobless —as long as the "short-sighted reluctance" of the government to increase the national debt in peace was overcome. This was rather strong medicine in the days before Keynesian deficit spending. Even stronger was the demand for the transfer of wealth from "private to public possessions." The resulting "fund for social welfare" was to fund workman's compensation, disability, or old-age insurance.[76] Contrary to the editors' optimistic forecasts, it was unlikely that the proceeds of a federal inheritance tax could possibly have covered the project's astronomical costs. There were clearly degrees to which the rich could be soaked. Despite its crudity, the program at least signaled the great leap forward the magazine was taking. On these small foundations, progressives mobilized their forces to build the modern state.

In the rush to advance their proposals, liberals occasionally left democracy behind. Their multifaceted tenets did not always mesh. Early on, the magazine became embroiled in a controversy over vocational education.[77] In deference to the theories of John Dewey (a frequent contributor and probable author of the editorial in question), "the younger generation" with "industrial callings" was advised to pursue practical training to the exclusion of the leisure class' "bookish education"—surely a device that would reinforce class stratification. In addition, certain articles on scientific management, a dominant issue in Lippmann's and Croly's books, might have given serious liberals pause. It represented a "force," the editors were wont to concede, "promising great good, and possibly threatening serious evils."[78] They were "compelled to defer... [their] blessing" on Henry Ford's benevolent strategy toward workers until he actually "committed the supreme insanity of sharing not only profits, but his power."[79] Rigidly applied, scientific management risked reducing labor to "abject dependence upon the whim of the employers." Specialization and the interchangeability of the work undermined unions and cost jobs. After all, optimal plant productivity and human satisfaction, the editors maintained, should never be mutually exclusive goals. Or so it seemed—for, on another occasion, *TNR* claimed that organized labor's "lack of scientific knowledge" sacrificed U.S. prosperity. Indeed, the unions' intransigence posed a "serious menace" to the sacrosanct "public interest." This uncharacteristic indictment revealed a certain capriciousness toward organized labor. While Croly expressed his concern about the more radical elements within its ranks in *Promise*, Lippmann focused on its "crudities" in his report to Roosevelt in 1914. A latent fear of social upheaval and unruly unions tempered their enthusiasm. They were willing to support them only so far as their demands coincided with progressivism's goal of orderly and incremental change.

Science, in the wrong hands, risked becoming a dangerous tool. The editors' excesses were especially evident in "Salvaging the Unemployable," a piece so barbaric it deserves to be reviewed in its entirety.[80] The "rational program for disposing of the problem" of unemployment consisted of collecting "from the city and country the hordes of tramps and loafers, to restore as many of them as possible to independence, and force the rest to draw their own weight." These "unemployables" could then be assigned hundreds of "simple" [tasks] "at the point where private industrial employers would gladly take them off the hands of the state at living wages." Since the "work-shy" in general cared very little for money and often suffered from "neurasthenia, originating, perhaps in obscure physical lesions," they surely would be satisfied with less remuneration. As for the "irredeemables," it was essential that they be "interned" and restrained from contributing their quota of defective offspring, to the relief of the society of the future." A tramp—"who, by the way, is probably at least nine-tenth of an ordinary man"—could finally cease and desist "sponging off the rest of society" and "pay for his food." "All this, you say, is Utopian?" the editors asked:

> [O]ur social energies and charitable impulses will no longer be frustrated as now by the helpless confusion of need and worthlessness, of genuine misery and pretend hard luck. Not even the most dogmatic exponent of the doctrines of laissez faire and the survival of the fittest would have the heart to propose social reforms in the interest of an unadultered class of the deserving poor.

How can a piece such as this be classified as anything but parody on the highest stage? The writer must have derived a Swiftian pleasure in firing at conservative bogies—social Darwinism, charity for only the demonstrably neediest cases, and laissez-faire. And yet, the piece lacked a vital ingredient of satire: wild exaggeration to tip off the unsuspecting reader. Furthermore, amusing farces were not the sober *TNR*'s strong suit. Not until the free-wheeling 1920s did the magazine deign to play with the comic side of life. None of the editors, particularly the dour Croly and Lippmann, was ever renowned for a sharp sense of humor, and science, by their accounts, was no laughing matter.[81] With it, they seriously set out to build a new world.

TNR set out to "salvage" other groups besides the "unemployable." The fierce U.S. nativism that harassed Germans and Irish in the nineteenth century returned during the progressive era to the detriment of the great influx of European immigrants from southern and eastern Europe. Their low standards of living, foreign norms, and high illiteracy rate inspired a new school of racists. Edward Ross' paeans to the supremacy of the Puritan stock were required texts. Protestant progressives sought to defend immigrant restrictions on rational grounds. The abundant, cheap supply of immigrant labor in slow economic periods undercut the unions' control and allowed business to squeeze out a larger profit, as the magazine portrayed them, of "restless millions of former wage-earners."[82] The editors were not overly eager to lend a helping hand to immigrants.

In vague appeals to improve the newcomers' lot, the editors admitted that "immigration is a problem which begins, not ends, at Ellis Island." The "ignorance, congestion . . . and political corruption" plagued the "swelling populations" they conceded. Something had to be done, the editors warned, "to protect ourselves and the immigrant" from the "lawlessness of the economic struggle." Once again, the "highly trained . . . government expert" was called into service. Under this plan, he would serve in a "federal system of supervision of the alien" to personally screen out "aspirant immigrants" in their homeland before they could emigrate to the United States. Only then could the selected candidate enjoy the privilege "in every stage of his career" of learning to become a U.S. citizen. As part of the effort to prevent "extortion and exploitation" and "diminish that unequal distribution of aliens" (a recurring term in the magazine's discussions of the question), "interstate employment bureaus" could be established to monitor their locations and "industrial and social conditions."[83] The totalitarian cast of this scheme betrayed ulterior motives to exclude immigrants from the United States, rather than facilitate the painful process of assimilation.

The debate over immigration was not confined to pages of journals and books. It was a serious bone of personal contention among the editors at *TNR*. Weyl and Lippmann were born to the first generation of Jewish immigrants who fled to the United States in the mid-1800s. Neither practiced Judaism. As children, they enjoyed the amenities of comfortable, middle-class lives. The newly arrived immigrants from Eastern Europe mired in the lower east side slums were as foreign to the editors as Germany itself, yet both suffered from nagging anxieties because of their heritages. Weyl once attempted a novel on Jewish life but abandoned it after the first draft for fear he lacked a sufficient knowledge of the subject.[84]

Perhaps it was better left unwritten. In an article on the cloak industry strike, Weyl attempted to explain why Jews were drawn toward this line of work: "No people has a more elastic standard of living; none is more willing to live on little or anxious to make much. The nervous, febrile energy of the Jew attracts him to this industry."[85] Such stereotypical and distorted depictions did little to extinguish the flames of nativism in the United States. Lippmann's biographer, Ronald Steel, has brilliantly documented the impact of his encounters with antisemitism at Harvard and at New York's posh clubs, which catered only to "restricted clientele" (such as the Straights). The victim placed the blame squarely on the Jews themselves, whose failure to assimilate stemmed from, in his words, their own "blatant vulgarity" and conspicuousness.[86] On the major issues of the day for Jews, Lippmann maintained a discreet silence. His analysis of the Brandeis controversy indirectly hinted at the possible anti-semitic aims of the cabal in Boston but, in the end, settled on a predictable progressive versus conservative dialectic. He opposed Zionism because it raised the profile of Jews. In *TNR*'s letter column, an indignant editor vented his rage at an editorial on Zionism that raised the "alien" issue and accusations of dual allegiance.[87] He had fled Europe in the first place, he admonished the editors, precisely to escape from that sort of rubbish in the German, Rumanian, Russian, and Austrian papers. If the item offended Weyl or Lippmann, they kept their feelings to themselves. To succeed in the predominantly Protestant world of U.S. letters meant submerging one's own native identity. As social climbers, Weyl and Lippmann could ill afford to muscle their "alien" religion around such a devout Presbyterian as Croly without creating trouble. It was an odd variation of Richard Hofstadter's theory of "status revolution," whereby, since the republic's founding, the monolithic Protestant ruling elite surrendered control to a rising, heterogeneous middle class.[88] Lippmann and Weyl, in essence, were protecting their own status as cosmopolitans who preferred to keep their Judaism under wraps.

The angriest editorial dispute in the magazine's early history erupted over Francis Hackett's own ethnic passions. He was, Alvin Johnson wrote, "born in Kilkenny on soil so provocative that even the cats have an eternal place in the folklore."[89] Early in the century, Hackett worked closely with Jane Addams in the Hull House movement. It, he later recalled, "had no leadership, had no doctrine, no dogma, and tried, more than anything else, to create a faith in life and to link bewildered or benumbed immigrants to the American community.[90] Upon joining *TNR*, his identification with his nationality and the plight of immigrants intensified. He wrote regularly on events in Ireland and, at the height of the Easter rebellion in 1916, the tone of his work rose to a fevered pitch. The Anglophile Lippmann could not bear to see his colleague behave so foolishly while he was preparing the magazine for eventual U.S. intervention in World War I on the allies' side. The two men quickly fell out of each other's graces. Lippmann deliberately stayed away from the office for long stretches to avoid confrontation with his adversary.[91] Despite his Irish father, Croly clung to his mother's English Protestantism throughout his entire life and barely touched on the issue of immigration and ethnicity. He was primarily worried about the effect of the quarrel on company morale. By 1920, the bickering broke out in the open, prompting British writer Harold Laski (a close associate of the magazine) to comment to his friend Justice Oliver Wendell Holmes "Hackett is simply Sinn Fein with which Walter doesn't sympathize."[92] Two years later, Hackett requested a ten-month leave of absence from *TNR* to write a history of Ireland. Croly, in effect, gave his literary editor as much time as he wanted by informing him that his services were no longer needed at the magazine.[93] As a microcosm of the larger U.S. society, the dismissal and the magazine's peculiar attitude toward immigration corroborate sociological studies that debunk the myth of the melting pot. Truer to life, the United States was a tossed salad.

The intellectuals at the magazine were never completely satisfied with the mere presentation of their proposals each week. What they wanted most of all was to set their ideas in motion, and, every four years, election time afforded an ideal opportunity. In 1916, the editors frantically scouted around for a candidate in whose fertile mind they could plant their policies. Eugene Debs and the Socialist party were quickly ruled out. Although Debs polled an impressive 891,000 votes in 1912 (5.9 percent of the total), the magazine patronized him as though he were an obstreperous child in need of parental guidance. The charismatic socialist electrified many an audience in his day, but, except for a fervid defense on his behalf when he was incarcerated at the height of the war hysteria, the magazine largely ignored him. The party itself fared worse. "Its errors are less of the heart than of the head," the editors observed, and "its enthusiasm, its self-sacrifice, and its occasional spurts of courage more than compensate for its obstinacy, misrepresentation, and for a certain mendacity born of fanaticism."[94] By directing its appeal to middle-class farmers and small capitalists, the party had become "revolutionary in tone, less dogmatic in utterance, more apologetic, more matter of fact," the editors felt. Indeed, if any administration ever decided to act on the socialists' "sham issues and sham battles" and implement their "unwholesome" programs, the country would "land . . . in disaster."[95]

The editors refused to elaborate on any of the "issues" and "programs" they so scathingly denounced, as if an implicit understanding between *TNR* and the readers existed that the movement's irrelevance rendered a thoughtful discourse worthless. Instead, the editors rehashed the stale, conservative explanations for the failure of a genuine socialist movement to take hold in the United States.[96] In order to "clean house thoroughly," the socialists were advised to desist from foisting their European notions on an incongruous, unique U.S. situation. Unlike Germany, where the masses did not enjoy universal suffrage and were suppressed by a hereditary aristocracy, the United States functioned through a two-party system that "blurred the lines of class interest" and appropriated other groups' demands for its own purposes, the magazine opined. This was the ordinary argument used to deflate socialists, but not the extraordinary one expected of incisive analysts. Eight years later, in another election, Croly would eat his own words.

Considering their own irreverence for the two-party system, the editors' assaults against the socialists rang especially insincere. None of the editors was a stranger to third-party movements—all volunteered their services to the Progressive party in 1912, and Croly traveled the third-party route in two of the three subsequent presidential elections. Summing up the inadequacies of Democrats and Republicans in 1916, Croly concluded that "something had to be done to alleviate the grievances and win the confidence of the less favored groups of our hallowed citizens."[97] The editors offered to locate a "permanent political shelter" for "homeless radicals" to promote the interests of independent labor and farmers—so long as it was not the socialists, a movement too unwieldy for the centrist liberals at *TNR* to control.[98] Their benign neglect of socialists rankled the party's leaders to no end. W. J. Ghent, a prominent official in California, marshaled evidence to refute the magazine's "deproletarianization" theory.[99] Another socialist chief captured the essence of *TNR*'s hypocrisy. "If Socialists were only good that might make life quite as miserable for your periodical . . . they might ask with a persistent and undesirable utterance how it happened that a public so benevolent and richly endowed as yours could have taken to itself the task of damning the Socialist party because it was not sufficiently proletarian and revolutionary." Although John Reed also believed his beloved party had lost much of its revolutionary zeal, he could not stomach the magazine's insipid talk of "industrial democracy."[100] It was true that Debs' doctrine of universal brotherhood, as contemporaries put it, had "plenty of kindlin' power but very little stayin' power." But it still remained a force to be reckoned with. No other group on the left addressed social causes as innovatively and passionately, and struck as an illuminating contrast to *TNR*'s moderate liberalism. The editors' judgments pronounced on the bankruptcy of their leftist brethren revealed a serious shortage of intellectual candor and fortitude.

The other choices in 1916 left *TNR* cold. The Democratic president and his party stubbornly embraced their "new freedom" of classic laissez-faire economics and illiberal social policies. In his first term, Wilson opposed child labor laws, rejected farmers' urgent requests for long-term credits, and incurred the wrath of W. E. DuBois and Oswald Garrison Villard by shelving their recommendation for a National Race Commission to study the problem of race relations. Only the vociferous complaints from liberal northern Democrats finally forced the administration to reverse the pernicious segregation in the government. The Clayton Act not only deprived labor of antitrust immunity; with Wilson's tacit approval, the Chamber of Commerce ran its campaign for "self-regulation" roughshod through the conservative Senate. Wilson also invited delegations of businessmen to advise him on cures for the 1914–15 depression and appointed bankers to the Federal Reserve. (The Senate rejected one of these nominees under federal and state indictment for illegal restraint of trade.) When Wilson hailed these measures in 1915 as the consummation of his "new freedom," an irate *TNR* labeled him a "dangerous and unsound thinker upon contemporary political and social problems."[101]

Wilson's belated conversion to progressivism hardly endeared him to *TNR*. Ten months before the election, the editors reflected on the "oblivion . . . [that] descended on the New Freedom, and the Democrats . . . traveling by the light of a pale and fluttering candle which Mr. Wilson . . . hurriedly contrived out of Republican and Progressive materials."[102] Wilson's distinguished biographer, Arthur Link, has confirmed progressives' worst suspicions about "the dearth in administration circles of any impelling passion for social justice."[103] Ever the practical politician, Wilson recognized the exigency of bidding for independent liberals to secure his reelection. With the aid of a Democratic Congressional majority, he swiftly pushed through programs ranging from workman's compensation laws to the Keating-Owen child labor law. By the fall of 1916, the entire progressive platform of 1912 was enacted. "Wilson's concessions to the progressive concept had been made under duress," Link contends, "and were not the result of any genuine convictions of his own." *TNR* assessed these acts separately, while reserving comment on the total progressive picture. Options were limited. The Republicans' nomination of New York Supreme Court Justice Charles Evans Hughes, gave progressives little reason to cheer. The crumbling Progressive party retaliated by giving their beloved Roosevelt his final encore. He quietly bowed out and asked his disciples to join him in the Republican camp. Few followed him. Though Croly believed Wilson was "looking backward," he saw in the "huge increase of government power" the faint intimations of a program of "national reconstruction."[104]

The president began to employ a powerful tool to garner the support of the leading liberal magazine. Like any adroit White House tenant, Wilson exploited his office's majesty. In March 1916, he dispatched his confidant and alter ego Colonel House to lunch with Croly and Straight. The host graciously flattered his guests by proving, through a number of references to articles, that he was a regular reader of the magazine.[105] Croly found him "extremely reticent about all matters of domestic and foreign policy" but was satisfied to have established a "means of communication with . . . [House] so that in the future . . . [Croly could] get at the President through him, or get information from him when [the editors] critically" needed it.[106] On a trip overseas the following week, Lippmann arranged to interview the president privately for over an hour and a half for background information. Unfortunately, not "much knowledge" was gained on this occasion either. Croly was pleased to hear from Wilson that "when [the editors] had anything to say to him, or wished to have any better understanding of what he was getting at than . . . [the magazine] could obtain through the newspaper, he would always be glad to see some member of the editorial staff of the paper."[107] During the summer, Lippmann wrote speeches for Wilson and delivered campaign talks in upstate New York from the back of a trailer truck.[108] Earlier, he had praised the president for his heroic part in the railroad controversy. Now he informed a close associate of the president how "eagerly" he awaited a "decisive" acceptance speech at the Democratic convention.[109] Norman Hapgood, a magazine editor and friend of Wilson, singled out the young journalist as the "ablest of the New Republic editors and the one who is working to swing the paper openly to you." The *TNR* men were returning to the balmy Roosevelt days all over again. A savvy politician courted influential writers, who, lured by his power and prestige, were gratified to have such visible homage paid to their work.

Not everyone fell under Wilson's spell. In the international arena, his efforts to preserve U.S. neutrality and campaign slogan— "Keep us out of war"—deeply disturbed Willard Straight. As an ardent advocate of universal military training and an open alliance with Great Britain, Straight had become impatient with the president's "gum-shoe or soft-pedal" foreign policy and suspected for a long time that the president's "whole aim" was "to sit upon the lid and suppress information as regards our relations with belligerents."[110] Wilson's domestic reforms perturbed him, as well; he wanted a changing of the guard to protect U.S. international interests. In the spring, he still entertained hopes of drafting his good friend Roosevelt as a candidate. During Croly's brief absence in April, Lippmann took it upon himself to dissuade his employer from using the magazine to further the colonel's ambitions.[111] Roosevelt, he reminded the owner, was only one of many candidates and by no means the perfect choice. Had the magazine continued to remain silent about the former president's increasingly bellicose views on foreign policy and turned the other cheek to his barbs toward the editors, it would have been pretending that he had no flaws and automatically deserved the nomination. "You know that the *New Republic* was not created to play that kind of game," he admonished his employer. The magazine could not cozy up to Roosevelt without failing the "most crucial test . . . of independence." As soon as Roosevelt exited the scene, Straight set his sights on the Republican candidate. He had no qualms, according to Croly, about putting "up the stiffest kind of fight for his own side."[112]

Straight so adamantly opposed Wilson that he demanded a forum to air his views in the magazine and go on record in support of Hughes. Croly balked. By separating himself from the established editorial policy, he warned, Straight was handing over a harmful and "juicy piece of political gossip" to the Democrats. "The value which you attach," the editor argued, "to intellectual independence on the part of the people with whom you are generally in sympathy, but with all of whose opinions you do not agree . . . [is] the strength of the paper in the eyes of all disinterested readers."[113] After further deliberation, Croly agreed to give Straight space to dissent from the editors.[114] A preface to accompany the Hughes endorsement was carefully drafted and edited to both parties' satisfaction. A reference to Straight's "misunderstood . . . attitude" was deleted. Perhaps, sensing the irony of the situation, the editors removed the phrase "in any respect" from the sentence "Mr. Straight is not responsible for the editorial policy of *TNR*." The incident obviously embarrassed the editors. In the note's final version, they recapped the story of the financier's connection to the magazine, taking care to reassure readers, and themselves, that "Mr. Straight has been consulted on all important questions, but the ultimate decision has rested with the editors." Straight reiterated the editors' independence by insisting that neither he nor the editors "wished to be charged with carrying water on both [their] shoulders." But, the magazine was, in fact, carrying the buckets of both candidates and heavily on Straight's large shoulders. The disagreement between the editors and him over the value he attached to big-stick diplomacy presaged a wider and deeper flare-up of antagonism in the country once the United States entered the war.

TNR entered a new phase of its existence at wartime with an uneven record. Croly expected his creation to be "radical without being socialistic." It met half this criterion. The magazine harbored no socialist tendencies, but barely any radical ones either. Organized labor lagged far behind the liberals racing toward the government for assistance. To attain minimum wage laws and legal acceptance of unions required savage dogfights against entrenched obstacles. *TNR*, in step with other liberals of the same ilk, led the propaganda drive against J. P. Morgan and his fellow leaders of the plutocracy. The sensitive issue of poverty among women and children was treated with delicacy and intelligence. No political party owned this group of liberals. Disobedient Democrats were viewed with an equal portion of contempt as were Republicans. No candidate was worthy of *TNR* approbation who could not fit the designs of the proper progressive.

Yet, the independence the editors so highly prized crumbled under intense pressure. The problem stemmed, in part, from the oppressive ownership. If not the "kept idealists" of Mencken's gibe, they were not the freewheeling thinkers who stretched imaginations at *The New Masses*. From week to week, Straight hesitated to interfere directly in the operation. He did not have to. His periodic greeting cards during the Brandeis affair and the election kept his potentially mutinous crew in check. Based on their books and signed pieces, none of the top three editors differed greatly from their employer on fundamentals, and only in the rare instance did they differ on particulars. Even without Straight looking over their shoulders, the editors refrained from taking socialism very seriously. They preferred to work within the system close to the corridors of power. Perhaps too closely. As the 1916 election approached, the magazine came closer to sacrificing its editorial honesty in the close presence of the men from whom they should have remained detached. The burning urge to attain influence in the correct circles afforded Lippmann and Croly wide access to Roosevelt and Wilson. From this vantage point, *TNR* stature as the insider's source soared—but at a cost for which the editors did not bargain.

· · · ·

A Battalion
of Death

· · · · · · · ·

1917–19

· · · · · · · ·

BLESSED WITH AN ABUNDANCE OF TALENT AND UN-
flagging ambition, Walter Lippmann's life traveled smoothly down
the path to success. He attended the proper prep school and sailed
through Harvard with personal commendations from philosophers
William James and Graham Wallas, who were extremely impressed
by their student's brilliance. After graduating, he joined the Greenwich Village crowd and helped fashion the intellectual elites'
unusual brand of socialism and artistic freedom. The "Buddha-like
curves" of Lippmann's face, in the words of the village's maître d'
Mabel Dodge, accentuated his stern appearance and serious demeanor. Lippmann made his mark on journalism early on as an
assistant to the famous muckraker Lincoln Steffens, with whom he
collaborated in 1910 on an exposé of big business and Wall Street. In
his profession he had few peers in turning out lucid, incisive prose
quickly and consistently. Even though a skeptical Willard Straight
thought the young journalist too clever for his own good and "carried away somewhat by the music of his own words," he had to admit they were "very well used indeed." But as Lippmann honed his
razor-sharp mind, with maturity he also lost some of his youthful
excitement. He knew he could not preserve his key relationships
with Colonel House and Wilson and take the same risks he had during his socialist and muckraking days, or in his earlier career. As his
professional stature grew and his contacts with the powerful blos-
somed, his prior leftism and enthusiasm for *TNR* gradually
diminished. Foreign crises were brewing daily. Now that he was serving as House's shadow adviser and the president's point man at the
magazine, Lippmann's priorities were rapidly changing.[1]

The magazine's other Walter did not have as many friends in high places. Ever since his days as a student at the University of Pennslyvania's Wharton School of Commerce and Finance, Walter Weyl had researched and reported his articles with uncompromising care and vigor. His pen was almost as lively as Lippmann's. But he preferred detached, analytical objectivity to the exclusive stories and esteem acquired from hobnobbing with dignitaries. Ironically enough, the amiable Weyl's outgoing personality was probably better suited to earning the confidence of notables. Whether at the ballpark or on the street, people instantly took a liking to him. His moustache and dark goatee led Alvin Johnson to comment "he looked like a saint and fundamentally was one." This Walter's politics, by contrast, also veered further toward the left with age. Weyl was the first *TNR* editor to desert the liberal camp in search of a radical substitute.[2]

The two Walters and Croly thought World War I would be a war that would "make the world safe for democracy" and be the "war to end all wars." The editors shared these dreams in the company of virtually all intellectuals as the United States' ended its historical isolationism to enter the Great War overseas. The magazine developed a decidedly British hue from the steady contributions of Norman Angell, H. G. Wells, and a cast of English luminaries. *TNR* also had more than a passing interest in Wilsonian diplomacy. "I need hardly tell you that I suppose that *The New Republic* and all of us are entirely at your disposal," Lippmann wrote the president in a letter recommending military conscription.[3] The editors stayed in close touch with House through regularly scheduled meetings. Wilson's famous phrase in a keynote address to the Senate, "peace without victory," first appeared as a headline in *TNR*.[4] Rumors spread that the magazine was Wilson's personal organ, which he used to float trial balloons. On Wall Street, investors believed they could gamble successfully in the stock market by forecasting administration policy in the latest issues. Copies were gobbled up at newsstands, and attempts were made to bribe printers for advance proofs.[5] The publicity was welcome in the business office, as circulation soared from 16,000 in 1917 to 43,000 in 1919.[6] To be in the know, many believed, meant reading *TNR*.

The pace of events swept away the men at the magazine. While Lippmann left the magazine in 1917 to serve as a high-ranking aide to the secretary of war, Straight retired from J. P. Morgan to enlist as an officer. From Europe, he wrote ardent letters, imploring Dorothy to "tell Herbert that *NR* must demonstrate . . . our ability to fight-fight-fight, that's what is going to win—not talk-talk-talk."[7]

Back on the home front, Croly rhapsodically introduced his employer to the glorious prospects that lay ahead:

> But what a rare opportunity is now opening up, my dear Willard! During the next few years, under the stimulus of the war and its consequences there will be a chance to focus the thought and will of the country on high and fruitful purposes, such as occurs only once in every hundred years. We must try all humbly and indefatigably and resolutely to make good use of it.[8]

Before Croly ever had a chance to look back, those fruitful purposes rotted on the vine. The national resolve to unite in a common struggle dissolved in the crucible of a war-torn United States.

The conflict held out the promise of enacting the editors' treasured domestic agenda. "If the new world that is to follow in the wake of the war is to be a democratic world it is inevitable that the labor movement should be at its very heart and driving center," they asserted.[9] A National War Labor Board was established to set up machinery for adjusting labor disputes. To prevent strikes and lockouts during the war, the government officially granted workers the right to organize into trade unions and bargain collectively. The board also applied pressure to employers not to discharge workers for engaging in union activities. The eight-hour day and the principle of a "living wage" finally became national standards. In return, workers agreed to accept a "no-strike policy" and refrain from using "coercive measures of any kind to induce persons to join their organizations."[10] Although these laws included no penalties to compel acceptance, their authority was usually accepted in the clauses of contracts. Numerous labor leaders served on government boards or commissions, and the ranks of union membership during the war swelled from 3,014,000 to 4,168,000—the highest level in the labor movement's history.[11] Labor had, indeed, gained unprecedented power during the war.

Optimistic liberals viewed these hopeful signs as the answer to their prayers for social democracy. They claimed the Supreme Court earned their enmity for poisoning the atmosphere with injunctions against the United Mine Workers. This was no time to stir "the suspicion of workingmen that the war, with the appeal to patriotic sacrifice, would be used as opportunity for strengthening capital and undermining labor," *TNR* argued"[12] Nor did the Court have any business in overturning child labor laws: "If our resources become so fully engaged that we must enlist the toil of children in order to win the war, we shall hesitate to make the sacrifice."[13] The editors also demanded that munitions, ships, and other heavy industries obey the spirit of the eight-hour standard and provide decent living conditions and housing. Failures to do so, they said, were eroding the fragile base of the young "industrial democracy" the United States was finally on the verge of building.

TNR carefully laid the foundation for "industrial constitutionalism." The installation of collective bargaining signaled the first stage.[14] The various adjustment boards on which Gompers and his fellow labor leaders sat proved once and for all that "in the conflict between capital and labor, government . . . [could] no longer be considered neutral." "More has been accomplished for labor," the editors declared, "than during the preceding fifty years."[15] The effects of government's powerful mobilization of industry and regulation of the marketplace were not lost on labor leaders. The alliance they were forging with their traditional enemy created unimaginable opportunities for the movement.

TNR even managed to pay the dreaded socialist a rare compliment. The longer the war lasted, it explained, the "nearer" U.S. citizens would be to being "forced to approximate" socialist positions.[16] The war "opened many minds to the desirability of a larger measure of economic democracy than the world knew before." And yet Republicans would have "none of it," and Democrats viewed it "askance." The editors thus pondered for the first time the possibility of the Socialist party playing a "significant part . . . [in] American history." The model *TNR* chose to emulate was thriving on the other side of the Atlantic in the form of the British Labour party's mild, inoffensive brand of "socialism." Labor's significant, and lengthy, manifesto, "Report on Reconstruction," was republished in its entirety, occupying a full 12 pages in the magazine.[17] The term "socialistic" actually did not apply, the editors comforted readers, to the sweet-sounding proposals for a "Universal Enforcement of the National Minimum" and "Surplus Wealth for the Common Good." The British Labour party's rising fortunes during the war raised the hopes of Croly for a similar campaign in the United States in the near future. For the time being, however, he focused his attention on other concerns.

Women were unlikely beneficiaries of the war. A shortage of manpower as a result of the draft and the stepped-up activity of war-related industries created a void that they quickly filled in massive numbers. *TNR* had long championed the cause of women's suffrage. Now it aimed to supplement the political franchise with the "industrial franchise."[18] The appointment of a woman to the National

War Labor Policies Board helped blaze the trail for "full industrial citizenship of wage-working women . . . with rights and responsibilities coequal with the responsibilities and rights of men."[19] The AFL was rebuked for its "tepid interest" in enlarging the National Women's Trade Union League to expand the protection of working women.[20] The AFL's Neanderthal mentality did not surprise the editors. The organization was, they noted after all, directed by "men, average men, who although they think far enough to recognize the independence of labor, are still traditional males when it comes to the independence of women." Organized labor effectively removed itself from the women's revolution.

TNR's hopes of exploiting the war for democratic purposes were soon dashed. The editors might have heeded their own dire warnings. In a 1914 editorial, they sounded an alert:

> People with an aroused social conscience object to war not merely because it brings with it so much agony and brutality but because it diverts to essentially wasteful purpose the product of so much good human labor. . . . the economic and social consequences of such a step are nothing less than terrifying.[21]

The ethical blinders the editors donned to fight their crusade abroad impaired their vision on the home front. In 1918, Randolph Bourne published a contemporary critique, "War and the Intellectuals," in *Seven Arts*, dramatizing the conflict between practical moralism and practical politics. As a pacifist, he laid much of the blame for "opening the sluice of a sewage of a new spirit" on the interventionists at *TNR*. Oblivious to the war's sinister forces, the editors clamored for the "allies to subordinate military strategy to political ends, technique to democratic values," while forgetting that war, as they had said, "always undermines values." Their grandiose rationales for engaging in the conflict amounted to self-delusion. The low level of working-class patriotism and the violent IWW protests were symptoms rather than the causes of the nation's "social neurosis." In the rush to march off toward war, *TNR* completely misjudged the temper of the nation and ignored a fundamental rule of history: war subverts democracy as often as it fosters it and often stirs the darkest passions.[22]

Bourne's sweeping indictment barely grazed *TNR*. Contrary to all of his assertions, the editors battling for the minds of the United States nevertheless retained profound qualms about the war's impact. The severe strain the war put on U.S. institutions surprised Croly.[23] "I'm becoming a filthy conservative, I am afraid of these days," Straight wrote his wife from his post in Europe.[24] Before dying the in 1918 in the influenza epidemic that cost some 20 million lives, he became gripped by the sheer senselessness of it all: "this war appeals to me less and less . . . it's terribly unintelligent and unreasonable—the whole thing. I hate unfairness and greed and stupidity—and war is all that—and is not redeemed by the fact that it brings out heroic qualities in individuals and not peoples. It must in the end brutalize."[25]

To make matters worse, in the editors' view, the war failed to accomplish its stated objectives. As members of the "Inquiry" peace planning group, Weyl wrote a massive report for Colonel House, and Lippmann helped draft the 14 points for a postwar settlement before returning to the magazine. Both, however, took great pains to distance themselves from the treaty's final version. The "Carthaginian" peace terms—which included harsh indemnities, reparations, annexations, and German war guilt—betrayed the liberals' most democratic ideals. After a long, heated debate, the editors decided to oppose the treaty, thus forfeiting the highest expectations that they carried with them into the war—the hope of securing a liberal peace. Lippmann led the fight at the magazine against the treaty. In a fit of personal pique, Lippmann wondered whether the debacle might reflect poorly on him. He "found it easier to blame Wilson," his biographer argues, "than to accept his own complicity in believing that imperialist wars could be transformed into democratic crusades."[26] Although other *TNR* staff members battled against the treaty with the same ferocity as did Lippmann (who fed its opponents in the Senate information from secret treaties he had acquired while working for Inquiry), they all shared a similar guilt about the nature of war. "If I had to do it all over again I would take the other side; we supplied the Battalion of Death with too much ammunition," Lippmann later confessed.[27]

On the home front, the war unleashed forces so destructive that U.S. democracy seemed in mortal danger. The first victim of the war hysteria was the IWW. Spurning political action, the syndicalist organization frequently resorted to coercion and occasional violence. This strategy limited its appeal to a small segment of unskilled foreign workers and migratory U.S. citizens. Never a favorite among moderate unions nor conservatives, the IWW's brazen defiance of the president's no-strike ultimatum during the war won it even fewer converts. In 1917, a disastrous fire resulting in the death of 164 citizens in Butte, Montana, brought the Wobblies, as members of the radical union were commonly called, to the scene. The townspeople took matters into their own hands. Six armed men kidnapped the IWW's local chairman, beat and tied him to the rear of their auto with a rope, and drove him out of town where they finally hung him on a railroad trestle. In Bisbee, Arizona, armed deputies arrested 1,200 IWW strikers, packed them into cattle cars, and dumped them in the desert without food or water.[28]

The persecution of the IWW represented a difficult case for *TNR*. Though the editors thought even less of the outlaw union than of socialists, they tolerated it as an unfortunate consequence of volatile labor conditions. "Its guerrilla methods are alien to the spirit of the American wage workers," the magazine scolded.[29] "Conspiracies to harass the government by the reckless and disloyal fomenting of strikes [had] to be put down with a strong hand." On the other hand, the unskilled and underpaid workers the IWW had mobilized were so "harshly exploited that they . . . [were] on the point of spontaneous revolt and . . . [needed] only the touch of a match to set them off." The denial of workers' right to collective bargaining and barbaric acts of cruelty against them, *TNR* argued, only created breeding grounds for further violence. In an effort to broaden *TNR*'s coverage, Croly dispatched Charles Merz, the magazine's newly appointed Washington editor, to report on the strike.[30] His first-hand observations corroborated what the editors had suspected from afar: "To sensationalize about the IWW . . . is to obscure a very real social evil, and to misrepresent a courageous attempt to put control of an industry on a more democratic basis."[31] Yet, the editors were still plagued by self-doubt about their position toward the outlaw union.

Their endurance was tested once again in the Pacific Northwest in the lumber industry. In their struggle to obtain a minimum wage and eight-hour day, unorganized workers temporarily halted the nation's shipbuilding programs during the war. Instead of damning the "baffling and insidious strikes," *TNR* advised the public to find out their causes.[32] An editorial described the lumberjacks' wretched living conditions in Washington:

> Forty loggers occupied a bunkhouse that should not have been an accommodation, sleeping two in a bunk. A stove at either end sent the steam rising from lines of wet clothes strung at the length of the room; beds made in some cases by dumping hay into a wooden bunk; food that was unsavory; the crudest sort of provisions for cleanliness and sanitation.[33]

These men joined the IWW precisely because it stood as "their one hope for improvement," Merz concluded. He fiercely attacked the Associated Press' (AP) sensationalist reporting for spreading "malicious" propaganda about the IWW. An assistant general manager of the news service fired off a letter to his editors to dispute charges of dishonest reporting and collusion between the press and the management. A "publicity agent" for the strikers responded by sending a letter of his own accusing AP of deliberately concealing the workers' suffering. "For men do not go on strike and face hunger and prison for no cause whatsoever," he insisted.[34] *TNR* echoed such sentiments exactly. It differed only on the IWW's violent means of organizing, not its goals.

It was almost inevitable that *TNR*'s commiseration with the IWW would collide with the demand of the war in which the editors had so heavily invested their emotion. In Chicago, 100 prominent IWW leaders, including Bill Haywood, were indicted for un-patriotically conspiring to hinder the execution of the war in 1918. An editorial bearing the inimitable Croly mark condemned the IWW for carrying on "class conflict during the war at the expense of American national success." The editors were in no mood to tolerate loud dissent:

> Let revolutionary agitators take note, the temper of public opinion has undergone a radical change since America's entrance into the war. It will not brook opposition to the constituted social order in the country, and which advocates the use of violence to overthrow that order. Every American who loves his country and believes in it must rejoice at its pulling the country together . . . [and has] every reason to support the government in suppressing and punishing any agitation against the war and the authority of the U.S.[35]

No matter how noble its goals, the editorial concluded the IWW was guilty of treasonous acts. This view did not sit well with a jailed Wobbly in Chicago who wrote to take issue with "superficial intellectuals."[36] Opposition to the war, he claimed, extended beyond the small group of syndicalists who had become scapegoats. Other intellectuals agreed. John Dewey, Thorstein Veblen, and—interestingly enough—Walter Weyl (who had temporarily left the magazine to write a book on foreign policy) sponsored an advertisement in the magazine entitled "Never Mind What You Think About the IWW." The "American liberals" to whom the appeal was addressed evidently excluded Croly and Lippmann who, unlike Weyl, in their books had expressed distrust of "radical" unions. In *Promise*, Croly had hoped to curb their excesses by incorporating them into government. By contrast, Weyl's sympathies reached farther than the "respectable" unions of the AFL variety. He was becoming increasingly convinced that the IWW was the natural outgrowth of a hostile labor climate and, perhaps, the only effective means for labor to advance its goals.

Croly's resistance to leftism was steadily weakened by the government's vicious assault on civil liberties. For his role in leading protests against the war, Eugene Debs was incarcerated in late 1918. "According to the letter of the Espionage Act, Debs was no doubt justly convicted and sentenced," *TNR* noted, but his moral objections to the war did not stem from "malignance toward his country, or desire for its defeat." The authorities would have also exhibited "better discretion" had they not invoked the full force of the Espionage Act and misinterpreted "the uses to which a free people intended to put an instrument so easily capable of injuring the state instead of advancing its interests."[37] As progressives, the editors had spent close to two decades preaching the gospel of a powerful government. Now, under the strains of a war, *TNR* had to brace itself for the impact of an authoritarian state unlike any they could have foreseen.

The next casualty of the war was the first amendment. The Espionage Act authorized the federal government to ban from the mails any material advocating treason, insurrection, or forcible resistance to any law in the United States which would violate the act. The suppression of the socialist periodical *Masses* infuriated *TNR*. It only suceeded in alienating the "body of American opinion" in favor of the war. The *Masses*' outspoken pacifism clearly separated it from liberal interventionists. The editors at *TNR* admitted that they befriended the paper because they fraternized with the editor, Max Eastman, and they counted themselves among its "numerous and not unintelligent middle class audience." "Whenever the editors of the *Masses* became bored," *TNR* quipped, "with the daily routine of demolishing such institutions as property, the family, law, church, and the state, they could always fall back on an exposure of *NR* as purveyor of fictitious ideology and furtive militarism."[38] The two journals were merely playing their favorite sport of intellectual shadowboxing.

When the government censored *The Nation*, *TNR* lost its sense of humor. In 1918, the government suspended that magazine's mailing privileges for no apparent reason other than a piece it had run criticizing Gompers, who supported the war. The feeble justification for the action, *TNR* argued, proved, beyond a doubt, that this was "an extreme case in the exercise of arbitrary administrative discretion."[39] In Britain, where the press routinely leveled criticism against the war, the authorities had a "much better understanding of the art of free government."[40] Or, as Norman Thomas put it, the postmaster general "didn't know socialism from rheumatism."[41] If the government could so mindlessly harass *TNR*'s sister journal, the editors reasoned, they too might find themselves a victim of the government's clampdown.

Indeed, *TNR* did have trouble escaping the smear of disloyalty. In a letter to Willard Straight, a jingoistic Roosevelt accused the magazine of promoting "principles . . . destructive of our national honor and decency" and tantamount to "moral treason."[42] Although he and his wife did not direct editorial policy, the owner informed the colonel, they were "in hearty accord with most of the magazine's contents."[43] R. M. Easley's saber rattled as frantically as ever at *TNR* and other "mischief-making publications."[44] He "never agreed with the socialistic, anarchistic, syndicalistic, and populist leanings of the *New Republic*, but all that . . . [was] nothing in comparison with its poisonous emanations since . . . [the United States'] entrance into the War." Of course, a "patriotic citizen" like himself, Easley lectured Straight, "would not for one moment permit the use of his name as the financial backer of the paper." Straight politely thanked his well-wisher for the "friendly spirit" of his letter.[45] "One does not have to see red in order to fight," he wisely counseled his color-blind pen-pal, "at least those who assume to lead public opinion should not." As a conservative, Straight was troubled by the explosive potential of an overly aroused population. In this condition, he cautioned Easley, the country would fail to make the "calm consideration" of adjusting to peacetime. Easley appears to have had friends in high places. Before the director of Wilson's Committee on Public Information identified *TNR* as a friend of the administration, *TNR* came under surveillance by government agents.[46] "Instead of meeting argument with argument . . . on a fair field," the editors complained, the government was "erecting the Chinese Wall of repression."[47]

By war's end, U.S. economic and social institutions seemed on the verge of collapse. The cessation of war-related industries and return of thousands of soldiers threw an already unstable labor market into chaos. In 1919, 4 million workers, or one in five, were on strike. From a general strike in Seattle to a police walkout in Boston, labor unrest swept the country. The employment of women for the war effort had been limited and brief: one half of them who worked in heavy industry could not find jobs in peace time.[48] The foundation on which the war had established industrial equality fell apart. *TNR* noted the development with a tinge of sarcasm: "While the men were at war it was possible for women to run elevators, work drills, carry messages, or collect fares on street cars. When Johnny comes marching home again, however, woman's work is done and her proper place is the home."[49]

The abrogation of civil liberties continued with increasing fierceness. The Bolshevik revolution in Russia sent shock waves through the world's democracies. In the United States, the demagogic Attorney General, Mitchell Palmer, exploited the nation's paranoia by arresting thousands of "alien" communists and assorted anarchists and deporting hundreds to the Soviet Union. Palmer's carefree use of the Alien and Sedition Law convinced *TNR* that he was "bent on wiping out the last vestige of freedom of speech and press."[50] The "hair-raising Bolshevik melodramas" staged by the government quashed the magazine's dreams of directing the war effort's collective fortitude toward the domestic battle for social justice.[51]

In the wake of the war, Croly and Lippmann hastily revamped their prewar conceptions of the U.S. system. Croly found the process especially painful. Only a few months after the U.S. entry in 1917, he personally sent Wilson a note in which he warned of the fallout from recklessly "dividing the body of public opinion into two irreconciliable classes. It is extremely difficult," he explained to the president, to "occupy an intermediate position as NR does" and be "constantly . . . crowded between two extremes."[52] In the magazine, Croly blamed the "mob in high places" for intensifying the blind and unruly popular sentiment and its "passion for persecution." By undercutting the ground out from under "orderly constitutional agitation," the government was presenting "socialist agitators," he warned, with a pretext for violence.[53] The consequences would be disastrous. If, "for the first time in modern history," U.S. citizens were forced to "choose ultimately between a capitalist or proletarian dictatorship," and the latter prevailed, reactionaries would have to be held accountable for the "inevitable extermination and ruin of democracy." Progressivism had reached a standstill. The violent unrest Croly most feared clouded its original adherents' bright optimism.

Reflecting on the "Red Scare" a decade later, Lippmann regarded his defense of civil rights as his most "exhilarating experience" at the magazine and recounted how difficult it was to "remember the idiotic intolerance which descended upon the country

in those days."[54]   Hardly a model of sanity in "those days," Lippmann actually appeared to be cracking under the pressure. In a rare
mood piece, he attempted to explore the conditions for industrial
distress. The "American ideal of being above European class conflict" was expiring, he decided. But there was still time to restore it
by reviving the idea of a "Public" as a "short way of expressing the
great faith that a group of men and women will always disentangle
themselves from their prejudices." Lippmann's inexplicable lapse in
and out of "Public" and the lower case "public" seemed to suggest
his own uncertainty about the directions his views were taking.[55]
The unprejudiced "Public" he had in mind, it turned out, consisted
of a body of government experts empowered to protect people from
their own frailties. Lippmann would flesh out the details of his
theory in the early 1920s in *The Phantom Public*, a book that ir-
revocably severed his ties to the progressive tradition.

Alvin Johnson and Walter Weyl took a dimmer view of U.S.
resiliency. Johnson truly believed revolution was possible; so much
so, in fact, that he devised a domino theory of strikes whereby "one
long strike" would spread from "industry to industry . . . on a narrow belt of Southern New England, N.Y., N.J., Pa., W. Va., Ohio, Indiana, Mich., Min. . . . subsiding only to rage anew, until the tissue
by which economic life coheres is eaten away." Johnson hesitated,
he said, to "indulge in alarmism." The fierce strikes in the steel and
coal industries, however, convinced him of the urgency of giving
workers their fair share of control and industries "decent conditions of labor, adequate wages, housing and necessities of life."[56]
Weyl sounded similar notes of despondency. For seven years, he had
sporadically worked on a book about class conflict in the United
States. He entitled the final draft of his unpublished essay, "The Only
Truly Revolutionary Class." "The waste of childrens' lives, the
destruction of women, the killing and maiming of men through accident, industrial disease, overwork, insecurity and starvation wages,
and the robbing of workers' dignity," it noted, demonstrated how
"the sword of class consciousness" was being "whetted, and its
sharp edges . . . cut clear through the body social, sundering us into
two mutually antagonistic classes." The "proletarian" (a term he
and Croly had previously eschewed in describing the working-class
person) was a "giant awakening from the sleep of millenia." The
progressive pendulum had swung far from the utopian aspirations
of liberals at U.S. intervention in the war to the apostasy that followed. Weyl's U.S. landscape resembled Armageddon. "Fear vanishes
and if we wish to taste the ecology of the dead, we must join some
suicide club." The faith in human progress that Weyl had evinced in

New Democracy disappeared. It was a steep descent from the proverbial progressive "city on a hill" to the depths of his despair.[57]

Liberalism's meteoric fall caught *TNR* by surprise. The editors'
ambitious designs for a modern state signaled a radical departure
from the U.S. tradition. Croly's sharp break with the laissez-faire
model of liberalism vaguely sketched the contours of a new polity.
Forged under the white-hot pressure of a war, that scaffolding
became brittle. Though Croly believed that old-time liberal religion
of natural rights and individualism had outlived its usefulness, he
never quite reconciled the conflict between the individual's rights
and those of the state. Draped in the flag of patriotism in wartime,
the spirit of Croly's benevolent nationalism was thoroughly
disfigured. The "mob in high places" was leading the mob in low
places to destruction, and middle-class liberal reformers, such as
the editors, feared for their own stable positions in society.

. . . .

The Lost and Found Generation

. . . .

1920–24

. . . .

IN THE 1920s, NO SINGLE FIGURE DOMINATED *TNR*. THE stately institution appeared to have a personality all its own. The magazine's tradition of editorial luncheons, begun at its inception, was already legendary. The editors invited statesmen, foreign dignitaries, artists, literati, and just about every luminary of U.S. culture and politics to discuss pressing issues of the time. The fine Italian and French cooking and wines earned it the distinction of "the best club in New York." From his perch at the head of the table, Croly cast a stern gaze over the proceedings. Formality was rarely relaxed. The poet Amy Lowell, a habitual smoker, caused a terrible scene when the butler passed out cigars only to the men at the table. To break the mood of seriousness verging on pomposity, a mischievous staffer once filled a plate of eclairs with cotton and watched in gleeful amazement as the guest, a British diplomat, swallowed his whole. (She was summarily discharged.)[1]

Even the bookish Edmund Wilson found these occasions oppressive. (T. S. Matthews, a *TNR* literary editor for a brief period in the mid-1920s, quipped that Wilson's parents had once bought him a baseball uniform, which he put on—and then resumed reading.)[2] Wilson told a friend that *TNR* was "a chilly and unfriendly home for anybody but a respectable liberal of at least middle age."[3] Still, the food was good, and the conversation, even if overly solemn, was intelligent.

At times, the magazine itself floated adrift. Several of its most dynamic figures had left the scene. Walter Lippmann departed to become an editor at *New York World*. Major Willard Straight died in the massive influenza epidemic that swept across Europe in 1918. A year later, Walter Weyl fell victim to cancer. Croly still remained at the helm but did not captain the ship as forcefully as in the past. The editorial board operated as though it were a soviet, with decisions reached in conference presumed to be unanimous. When serious disagreements arose, Croly was "primus inter pares" and his views triumphed. Managing editor Bruce Bliven, recently recruited from *New York Globe*, compared his job to "conducting an orchestra with members who do not want to play, perform special compositions of their own, or make discordant noises that are the equivalent of Bronx cheers."[4]

If *TNR* did not prosper, it at least continued to survive. Willard Straight had asked his wife to provide financial support during his lifetime and ten years after.[5] The price was raised to 15 cents per issue and 5 dollars for a year's subscription, the paperstock changed to a mechanical wood pulp, and the size reduced to 26 pages.[6] Circulation slipped from a wartime high of 35,000 to the teens.[7] The ghost of Mr. Tobey still drifted through the sparsely advertised pages. Robert M. Lovett shared literary duties with Robert Littell and wrote on foreign affairs. British writers H. G. Wells, Rebecca West, Virginia Woolf, and Bertrand Russell and such U.S. cititzens as Lewis Mumford, Waldo Frank, and Edmund Wilson appeared regularly to deal with cultural topics.

A hostile climate afforded liberals plenty of time to explore apolitical matters. By the 1920s, the United States had managed to right itself socially and the revolutionary fervor vanished as quickly as it had appeared. The workers' fortunes had not markedly improved but so long as they kept quiet, the issue seemed irrelevant. The United States was preoccupied with the business of business. Basking in what Charles Beard labeled the "golden glow of prosperity," the middle class, which had spearheaded the progressive movement, now concentrated on pecuniary pursuits. A growing professional business and managerial class spent its working days perfecting the techniques of mass production, consumption, and advertising. It its leisure time, it found ways to strike it rich in the stock market and escape from cities to flourishing suburbs. Historian Arthur Link describes the deleterious effects on liberalism of the Versailles debacle and the suppression of civil liberties. The "spark plug [was] removed from the engine of reform," he wrote, inducing a "substantial paralysis of the progressive minds."[8] Van Wyck Brooks, John Dos Passos, and fellow artists and intellectuals of the so-called lost generation waged their aesthetic rebellion against a materialistic, shallow culture. Malcolm

Cowley later described how assorted Wobblies and socialists were being shunted aside by literary circles as "former people."[9] The goal of these literary rebels was to convey the "pathos and absurdity" of a standardized U.S. life, not to pass moral judgments on the political principles of others. The unfashionable topic of reform was left to a dwindling minority of liberals, who were shouting in the wilderness.

The respective political polarities of Lippmann and Weyl illuminated liberalism's disarray. The former's intellectual odyssey veered further toward the right. In 1920, he contemplated the possibility of "abandoning the strike as a tactic."[10] Gompers' "strategic minorities," he argued, disturbed the nation's "routine again and again and again," presenting the "salaried [middle] classes" with the "prospect of endless cycles of demands, strikes, settlements, and recriminations." To rid the nation of this annoyance, Lippmann proposed an elaborate "legal process . . . to safeguard the interests of a working man sufficiently to justify the prohibition of strikes." Thus, with one stroke of his pen, Lippmann dismissed labor's vital tool for defending itself and gaining leverage over employers.

After leaving *TNR*, Lippmann wrote *The Public Opinion* in 1922 in order to debunk "the intolerable and unworkable fiction that each of us must acquire a competent opinion about public affairs." His revision of "the original dogma of democracy" accounted for the average person's supposed obsession with his own microscopic world. Lippmann authorized "intelligence bureaus" to examine information outside the domain of unreliable press reporting to form uncluttered opinions about public decisions. John Dewey condemned *The Public Opinion* as "perhaps the most effective indictment of democracy as currently conceived ever penned."[11] Lippmann's theory foundered, Dewey pointed out, on the rock of liberal ambivalence toward the masses. If not government by the people, was it at least for the people? Lippmann, in opposition to *TNR*, would answer the question in the 1924 election.

The erstwhile editor's contempt for the multitude moved Weyl to write a devastating burlesque, "Tired Radicals."[12] Before his death in 1919, Weyl concluded that radicalism was a "young man's job." Such immature men "grow into clever reactionaries, or after shedding all ideas, become absorbed in business, practical politics, or pleasure; retaining only an ironical, half-regrettable pity for their callow days of radicalism." Some aging radicals concerned themselves with "butcher's bills and baker's bills, and the wife's dress and what the children's shoes cost," while others disparaged "all dogmas" in the choice of a philosophy "to suit their nerves, as one chooses a wall-paper." Weyl did not care if these jaded leftists married "pleasant wives, begot interesting children, and built . . . homes in the country"—so long as they ceased pretending to be "radical" and went away. Their acceptance of "all . . . sedative aphorisms that end in quietistic philosophy," he angrily declared, "turn you into pillars of salt." What seemed to irk Weyl the most was the sight of a conservative wolf in a liberal sheep's clothes. The obvious parallels between the object of Weyl's derision and Lippmann's own political evolution did not go unnoticed. Lippmann kept his colleague's essay out of *TNR* because he thought it was directed at him.[13] It appeared a few years later in a posthumously published collection of essays.

Progressivism had all but become extinct. With the deaths of Roosevelt and Wilson, liberals were deprived of a national leader for the first time in 20 years. *TNR* searched for a successor to marshall the forces of liberalism in the 1920 election. As the Belgian Relief Committee and Food Administration's effective and diligent director during the war, Herbert Hoover earned high marks for his humanitarianism. Though both Republicans and Democrats (including a young Franklin D. Roosevelt) vied with each other for the privilege of helping him secure his nomination, no one knew exactly where he stood on any issue. Hoover's invisible profile did not deter *TNR*'s efforts to launch one of the first major balloons on his behalf. The magazine touted the former engineer's "technical knowledge in modern economics" and record of achievements to prove that "the springs of his character . . . [were] generous, and his power of visualizing sympathetically the plight of ordinary people over wide areas and under all kinds of circumstances . . . [amounted] to genius."[14] He thus met all the qualifications of Croly's prototypical administrator and expert. (The fact that he was the only person ever to express interest in purchasing *TNR* stock—10,000 dollars worth—may have also influenced Croly.)[15] In March, Hoover heaped equal portions of scorn on the "reactionary" gangs in the Republican party and "radical" sects among the Democrats. Soon thereafter, Lippmann paid him a call to recommend that he bolt the Republican party if a reactionary was nominated. "He really wants to take a liberal line," Lippmann wrote Frankfurter, "but he does not know how to take hold. He knows that the liberal people and the progressives generally are slipping away from him."[16] It would have behooved Lippmann and Croly to find out why.

In the face of compelling evidence to the contrary, Lippmann and Croly steadfastly refused to discard their progressive image of

Hoover. "Every American must be grateful to him and admire him," Lippmann gushed.[17] Two of the United States' premier philosophers had done inferior homework. Hoover had grown up and spent most of his life in Britain where classic "liberalism" had an entirely different meaning from that practiced in the United States. In a broad discussion of Hoover and the issues, the two editors provided scant detail to exhibit their candidate's talents as a "realist, a devotee of politics that work," or, in the field of labor, a proponent of "fair play and neutrality." Hoover, they claimed, was "much too intelligent" to think otherwise.

Not all the men at *TNR* deluded themselves with such vague self-assurances. Washington editor Charles Merz wrote a letter to the correspondence column disassociating himself from the official editorial policy.[18] R. M. Lovett excoriated the temporary head of the American Relief Administration for handling negotiations with the Soviets ineptly and ignoring "death and mass starving in Volga."[19] George Soule, an economist and contributing editor, portrayed Hoover as an "excellent representative of the liberals' own shallow equivocation."[20] One month later, Hoover declared himself a Republican. Without ever renouncing the party's conservatism, he entered the California primary and lost. In June, Lippmann went to cover the Republican convention in Chicago where he contracted a serious case of hypocrisy. He simply did not understand how Hoover's supporters could promote their man "equipped with no issue, no votes and no threat" and "nothing to negotiate with except the undoubted excellence of Mr. Hoover."[21] Lippmann's original choice failed to garner a single vote. The decade began inauspiciously for *TNR*.

Neither of the major parties presented liberals with very appealing choices in the general election. The magazine considered the possible election of the Republican from Ohio, Warren Harding, as "nothing short of a calamity."[22] Hailing from a long tradition of McKinleyism, Harding to them, personified the worst aspects of Republican conservatism. His feeble grasp of issues and placid demeanor left him vulnerable to the magazine's sardonic wit: "If an optimist is a man who makes lemonade out of all the lemons that are handed to him, then Senator Harding is the greatest of all optimists."[23] The "utter lack of convictions, enthusiasms and ideas" in his "tea-cup mind," the editors warned, made him unfit to hold the office. The Democratic nominee, James Cox, had compiled a mildly progressive record as governor of Ohio, but, as New York governor Al Smith wryly remarked, in that year Democrats could not have won on a laundry ticket. In the editors' eyes, the party had been indelibly stained by the Treaty of Versailles, "the war with Russia" (Wilson sent an expedition to Vladivostok to rescue a Czech army from the Bolsheviks in 1918), and the "shameless destruction of American civil liberty."[24] "Defeat rather than victory," it was argued, would "teach the Democrats to take liberalism seriously." In turning down Croly's request to write a profile of Harding, the progressive newspaper editor William Allen White may have best captured the progressive malaise: "I am so low in my mind that I wouldn't laugh at Charles Chaplin throwing a whole custard pie at Cox or Harding or both."[25]

TNR's choices in the election stayed outside Democrats and Republicans, but a ballot cast for the Socialists meant "throwing one's vote away."[26] In 1916, Eugene Debs' protests against the war forced him to run his campaign from prison. He still ended up polling 915,000 votes, his largest amount ever. Yet neither the war's sad conclusion nor the government's continued harassment of Debs (he had yet to be released) altered the journal's opinion of his "pitying nature" and "absurd candidacy." The final option for independent progressives was the Farmer–Labor party led by the obscure Parley P. Christensen. The editors had never had any sentimental attachment to the two-party system. The magazine's founding editors, after all, had all been swept away in the spirit of Roosevelt's Bull Moose uprising eight years earlier. Once again, it was time to test the waters of a third-party movement. The organization's "tentative" and "inchoate" blend of populist and progressive programs appealed chiefly to the "independent farmer and agrarian tenant."[27] Nevertheless, the "minor" party afforded disaffected progressives a "pioneering" opportunity to build an "insurgent force." The meager 300,000 votes Christensen received did not dampen *TNR*'s spirit so much as the victory of Harding, a "hopeless reactionary."[28] The conservative triumph was complete, driving the magazine outside the U.S. mainstream for the rest of the decade.

In a pivotal essay aptly titled "The Eclipse of Progressivism," Croly subjected himself to intensive soul-searching.[29] The movement had collapsed, he concluded, because its "opinions were confused, scattered, distracted and impotent" and leaders not "willing to pay the price." Had the editor truly looked within himself, he would have discovered that *TNR*'s convoluted editorial policies may have contributed to this incoherence and failure to pay the price of intellectual integrity. In part, Croly absolved himself from complicity in progressivism's demise by shifting blame to demagogic, untrustworthy politicians. Roosevelt's band of followers in 1912 "included not only every shade of liberalism but almost every degree of conservatism," he lamented. In 1916, Woodrow Wilson "forced his progressive supporters to choose between loyalty to principles and loyalty to him"; it was little surprise which came out on top. Liberals repressed their qualms about Wilson and placed their precious "convictions" in the custody of a single man and his party. Thus, Croly learned from his affiliation, as well as his involvement in the Hoover venture, not to be beguiled by "party politicians" in power ever again. True to his word, he never did fall under the spell of another such leader as Roosevelt or Wilson.[30]

Despite his predicament, Croly avoided lapsing into inaction. With the channels of power closed, the challenge to liberals was to adapt "radical and realistic views of . . . agitation under the conditions of American democracy." While reaffirming his aversion to the "red flag of socialism['s] . . . call for blood," the moderate liberal was moving inexorably toward the left of the political spectrum. The only alternative to a restoration of the "wholesome balance of social and economic power," Croly warned, was an inevitable "violent class warfare." The incessant stream of Marxist jargon running through the piece revealed not a radical conversion, but Croly's apparent bewilderment. Organized labor would not progress very far in the fight for social justice until it was ready to be "aggressive and pugnacious." Toward that end, Croly hatched a scheme: the full-scale development of a farmer–labor party to unite industrial and agricultural workers. This, he declared, represented the ultimate "expression of liberal aspirations." The "collective class action" he envisioned required progressives to lay the crucial "educational groundwork." Where to begin? Croly refrained from hammering out a definite agenda because he himself seemed unsure of what he wanted.[31]

Two years later, at the mid-term elections, Croly still remained in a funk. He and his editors were clearly on the defensive. While union membership declined sharply, Harding covertly—and at times overtly—abetted business' ploy to break unions and preserve the open shop. Conservatives in the government ordered a wage slash in the railroad industry, leading to the walkout of 400,000 men. The attorney general responded with a sweeping injunction to break the strike. Farmers were victims of the worst agricultural conditions in 30 years. The steady drop in prices of their produce drove them off their farms in record numbers. "The sickness within the Republican party" brought about "one of the worst industrial depressions in American history," TNR reported in 1922.[32] All the while, Harding "vacillated between lethargy and muddled activity."[33] Both parties, however, got the blame. "Luckily for the politicians," the editors ruefully observed, "our disgust with Tweedledee this year causes us to forget the hatred we felt toward Tweedledum a few years ago."[34] Ironically enough, the reference "Tweedledee and Tweedledum" harked back to William Allen White's gibe against Wilson and Hughes in 1912—except that, a decade later, progressives no longer enjoyed the luxury of choosing between two candidates of their own ilk.[35] *TNR* waxed so melancholy over the state of affairs that it sat the election out.

In the political arena, the magazine wavered between direct confrontation and remote contemplation. Perhaps, an editor mused with a distinctly Crolian flavor, "the chief function of the wise liberal during the next generation . . . would be to . . . bring about an improved quality of human relations by other than political measures."[36] If it was impossible to "depend upon economic motives to bring about the social cohesion which political democracy had tried and failed to achieve," how then was change to be effected? By extraordinary political means. Heartened by farmers' increasing clout in the Midwest and victory of Farmer–Labor candidates in Minnesota, the editors welcomed the rebirth of progressivism and a "mandate to build economic and social agitation . . . [to] provide a better livelihood for the 'plain people.' " "Carry On," an advertisement in the magazine proselytized: "it is no time to lose hope, though all about you are faithless. What but faith ever moved such mountains as today block man's progress to the Promised Land?"[37] Another advertisement playfully enticed "New Republic people" to subscribe and save "Babbitt in spite of himself" with a free copy of Sinclair Lewis' popular novel.[38] *TNR* was preparing to mobilize its forces in anticipation of the 1924 campaign.

Before plotting strategy Croly wanted to explain to readers the exact purpose his journal would serve in the endeavor. A lengthy supplement grappled with the meaning of "The New Republic Idea." In one of the more memorable phrases he ever penned, the founding editor announced his magazine's goal "was less to inform or entertain its readers than to start little insurrections in the realm of their convictions." It was his duty, therefore, to alert readers to perils "threatening the future of civilizations" such as a "violent class warfare." Croly truly feared that the widening gap between the "ordinary American citizen who works with his hands" and those "who work with their brains" presaged a "long period of misery, poverty, and oppression." Such an outcome—the Great Depression—only magnified the importance of *TNR*'s unique brand of journalism. Yet Croly acknowledged the difficulty of "weekly publications with limited circulations" to act as the sole "spokesmen" of "vast and pretentious ideas." It would have behooved him to ask whether the audience he was addressing was comprised of men who worked with their hands or with their brains. The manual laborer and the intellectual, who actually read *TNR*, did not necessarily share similar assumptions. In fact, as Croly learned in 1924, the farmer preferred not to have the intellectual start "insurrections in his mind." The gap between these two groups was partially responsible for the loss of the election and highlighted a fundamental flaw in "The New Republic Idea."[39]

Early in the campaign of 1924, the magazine took aim at the Democrats. In March the editors advised Al Smith to withdraw from the race.[40] Few doubted that the probable nominee was "honest and able" as well as "democratic and progressive." His biggest handicap was his Catholicism, a religion that made the editors squirm. Polish and Italian immigrants, they warned, were increasing the "proportion of Catholics in the population both actually and potentially—potentially because of the superior fecundity of these peoples." Rarely had as patent a prejudice besmirched the magazine's pages. Nor did *TNR* distinguish itself by tormenting itself over the fallout of a Smith candidacy on "nativism and the KKK" and discord between "urban democracies" of the East; Protestants and Catholics; natives and "Nordics;" and cities and rural areas. In fact, Smith was the victim of religious intolerance, instead of the cause. Far from being a "grave embarrassment" or "fatal" threat to Democrats, Smith's ethnic baggage proved to be an invaluable asset when he was nominated four years later.[41] The urban masses embraced him as one of their own in the 1928 election. *TNR* failed to feel embarrassed for timidly ducking the religious issue, thereby conforming to Richard Hofstadter's descriptions of WASP "snobs of native stock . . . who looked down upon" Smith.[42] The middle-class reformers at the magazine brushed aside a hero for the immigrants.

The magazine all but wrote off the Democrats. The party had become a shadow of its former self since the bright days of Wilson. At the convention in Madison Square Garden, Bliven reported that "delegates cheered hysterically at the mention" of the late president's name, "hung his picture in the convention hall," and were "willing in fact to do anything for his memory's sake except perpetuate his policies."[43] The assembly of "neurotic recluses" preferred to draft a platform "just about half way between nothing at all and a genuine liberal progressive document" rather than to strike out on a bold course. From the convention deadlock between Smith and former Secretary of the Treasury William McAdoo emerged the Wall Street lawyer John Davis. Felix Frankfurter, a close friend of the editors, did not care much for the man. In one of the several anonymous editorials that he wrote during the mid-1920s, the Harvard law professor demonstrated how Davis' work while under retainer for the House of Morgan had shaped his reactionary positions on the regulation of trusts, fixing of railway rates, public utility control, and in the ever-constant conflict between capitalists and labor.[44] (According to this kind of guilt by association, a cynical reader might well have discounted the wisdom of a publication partially subsidized by a Wall Street fortune.) Further investigation of Davis' record revealed other conservative streaks in his "abstemious liberalism."[45] Unfortunately, the other party's candidate was even less appetizing.

For all intents and purposes, by 1924, Coolidge and the Republicans had become known as reactionaries. The party's determination to muzzle Robert La Follette's and Hiram Johnson's progressive voices at the convention repulsed *TNR*. Pandering to Chambers of Commerce and Rotary Clubs, the "business man's bloc" wrote a "disingenuous, cold and conservative" platform that worshipped the "divine right of industry." Republicans seemed not to care if the "whole community's interests were subordinated to those of big profits, big fortunes, and big business."[46] The magazine shed fewer tears upon the death of Harding in 1923 than at the rise of Calvin Coolidge, the new president. Bliven followed up a widely acclaimed series on the "Harding Gang" and the Teapot Dome Scandal with a pungent squib on "Silent Cal," entitled "Hail to the Accidental Chief."[47] Coolidge, he wrote, epitomized the decline of Yankee "stock in the 60 years since the Civil War":

> The best, most energetic and able members of each generation move away to take advantage of the opportunities for individual advancement to be found in New York or in the development and growth of the middle and far West.

"Most Americans are self-conscious, talk too much in consequence, and regard with veneration anyone with sufficient control to keep still," the managing editor observed. He was at a loss to understand the popularity of a "human slot-machine from which you never get more than one stick of gum for your penny." Indeed, Coolidge's renowned reticence only proved that "he has no small talk: a fact which is often stated as though it guaranteed that he has any quantity of big talk—which by no means necessarily follows." With this brief exception, *TNR*'s pages remained surprisingly free of lampoons of an innately ludicrous figure in U.S. politics.

Coolidge's personality posed less of a threat than his cruel policies. "Republican economics" had resulted in "colossal waste and terrible abuses," declining purchasing power, and the foreclosure of farm mortgages.[48] There seemed no relief in sight. The farmers' request for "bread", the editors wrote, had been answered with "stone." The mastermind of Coolidge prosperity, Secretary of Treasury Andrew Mellon, turned his back on the "smaller income taxpayer" and the downtrodden.[49] The virtual elimination of inheritance and estate taxes solidified the hereditary wealth of an entrenched plutocracy. The editors were never reluctant to engage in guerrilla sniping to press their case. Yet, in the face of a reactionary regime, they realized the need to resort to extraordinary tactics. If the Republicans and Democrats were permanently fixed in their positions, *TNR* intended to give them a jolt.

The formation of a third party promised progressives in 1924 a new age of politics. *TNR* cast the candidate, Robert La Follette, in a supporting role in his own campaign. Despite having pledged "The New Republic Idea" to purge himself of hero worship, Croly glorified the image of "fighting Bob" rather than the man himself. La Follette was a man "too uncompromising temperamentally to gain the confidence of the majority of the people," historian Charles Madison argues.[50] Throughout his career, he "was in a sense . . . the effective standardbearer of the discontented and class-conscious farmers and workers." In a special issue right before the election, Croly deigned to cite La Follette's qualifications for the office with a gentle salute to his talents as a "capable legislator and administrator."[51] To his enthusiastic supporters, he still symbolized the fire-breathing hero of the populist era. The magazine capitalized on this popularity with a promotional package that offered La Follette's biography and a year's subscription at a discount rate: "scores of requests already have come to us for a biography of the man who has chased both old parties up a stump," the advertisement declared.[52] He was leading a fight for the "rights of the common man to live in the kind of America this country was always supposed to be, special privilege for none and equal opportunity for all." In its revised form, "practical progressivism" was designed to act "chiefly as an instrument of resistance."[53] The superficial crusaders of 1912 had been too tempted by the lure of office to abide steadfastly by principles. Twelve years later, progressives suffered from no such illusions. The editors, in the company of John Dewey and Oswald Garrison Villard, were waging their campaign as an "experiment in agitation." They all fancied themselves the odd men outside the U.S. mainstream.

The task of knitting the different groups into a single, potent force proved more difficult than originally imagined. Down on the farm, trouble was brewing. With the exception of Alvin Johnson who hailed from Nebraska and Bruce Bliven from Iowa, the staff at *TNR* belonged to the traditional northeastern enclave of power and prestige. Though the farmers' broad agenda ranged from tariff reform to rural credit, *TNR* paid scant attention. The editors clung to their old notions of the group as a "symbol for everything resoundingly conservative in politics."[54] The popular McNary-Haugen bill, which provided federal subsidies to farmers, was labeled nothing short of "hazardous."[55] The "whims and snap judgments of the farm voters" on the tariff issue risked hurting the economy and their cause, *TNR* worried.[56]

The farmers and *TNR* diagnosed the same illness but prescribed dissimilar remedies. The "cards" would forever remain stacked against farmers unless they received comparable pay with those in commerce and industry.[57] They desperately needed cooperative organizations, agricultural credits, and fair tariffs to compensate them for the low prices of their commodities. At least industrial workers had their own world of "jobs, agreeable or disagreeable, under an employer to be cajoled or fought; a world of unemployed, of rising rent and exorbitant prices." By contrast, their rural counterparts' world combined all the "cares of the property owner and manager with those of the laborer." They did not even enjoy the advantage of organizing into a union to press for higher income. In late 1923, Bliven traveled to the Midwest to learn "Why the Farmer Sees Red."[58] In dark, haunting scenes that read like a Hamlin Garland short story, he told of farmers barely breaking even. Thousands were being driven off their lands because of delinquent mortgages and edging toward starvation.

In the course of the election year, *TNR*'s growing sympathies with farmers conveniently coincided with its rising enthusiasm for the La Follette candidacy. Society, it felt, was made of combustible material. A "rural population of peasants and peons, precariously . . . [supplied] cities overgrown and fermenting with proletarian discontent."[59] By the sheer force of statistics and graphic depiction, the editors sought to dispel the "farmer-capitalist myth."[60] The rural and urban proletarians remained mired in the same miseries and hopeless hardships. Bliven deplored the "wretched" living conditions of workers who were deprived of the right to own "decent houses at a fair price."[61] Employment and earnings in the coal, steel, cotton, and shoe industries were falling drastically.[62] An anti-labor administration kept unions constantly on the defensive. The ruling class' exclusive world of "country estates, running stables, high priced yachts, diamonds, expensive furs, and cabarets" was closed to the majority of people.[63] Only "specious psychological barriers" stood in the way of farmers and capitalists in their common struggle. With the educational aid of *TNR*, the editors believed they could handle such obstacles.

Built from the splintery planks of old progressive reforms, the La Follette platform augured poorly for the campaign. The magazine had no quarrels with the idea of heavy inheritance and excess profit taxes or public exposure of federal tax returns. The Versailles hangover still lingered in a declaration against the foreign policy of "financial imperialists, oil monopolists, and international bankers," and calls for new treaties to outlaw war and reduce armaments. The injunction and yellow-dog contracts would be outlawed and workers guaranteed the right to organize collectively. If not given the store, farmers were at least offered a large part of it. They could look forward to lower freight rates for their products and the nationalization of railroads and water power resources. Perhaps the platform did seem "one-sided" in the farmers' favor, the editors conceded, but this natural tilt resulted from too many years of an imbalance between agriculture and industry. The fate of progressivism hinged on the "balanced development" of "town and country." The campaign was being fought for nothing less than the realignment of the nation. Compared to the ephemeral movement of 1912, the editors believed 1924 offered the "disfavored" class a real chance to achieve lasting reforms.[64]

Walter Lippmann remained unconvinced. A week before the election, the former editor was invited back to the magazine to explain why he planned to vote for Davis.[65] "In this post-war world of fierce nationalism" Davis' "strong Jeffersonian bias against the concentration and exaggeration of government is more genuinely liberal than much that goes by the name of liberalism," he argued. This supernationalism misconstrued the U.S. party structure's federal character, which consisted of an "effective system" of national coalitions of state parties rather than a central party. La Follette's antitrust policy, he observed, was little more than a leftover from the rapacious individualism of the 1890s. Moreover, the third party's "irresponsible and isolationist" foreign policy proved that, in this domain, Davis was "more nearly on the right track than either of the two candidates."

Lippmann's accusation that *TNR* was "making a virtue of progressive ambiguities" rang slightly hollow. If anything, the platform was weighed down by an excess of specifics. He himself had found a wealth of details to discuss in his extensive critique. The increasingly conservative *New York World* editor was not simply bothered by La Follette's left-wing policies. He also dreaded the likelihood of the third party siphoning off votes from Davis and thereby ensuring the election of Coolidge. Lippmann rebuffed his close friend Felix Frankfurter by discontinuing publication of a plethora of anti-Davis letters on the *New York World*'s editorial page.[66] The move undoubtedly marked him as a team player at the avowedly Democratic *New York World*. "The farmers that are struggling and grouping behind La Follette are at least struggling and groping for a dream, for a different look at things in 1924," Frankfurter appealed to him, "that's why I am for them and in my small way want to help to give direction and definiteness to their dreams."[67] Lippmann refused to budge; he was reluctant to jeopardize his position at the paper by supporting a renegade.

Croly could not bear to see his sacred liberalism turned on its head. For Lippmann to oppose Hamiltonian centralization in deference to Jeffersonian states' rights contradicted much of Lippmann's own *Drift and Mastery* and more importantly, impudently struck at the core of *Promise of American Life* and all the theories Croly had spent a lifetime developing. The following week he responded. A short note in the front of the magazine took aim at Davis' so-called liberal friends. For the benefit of its former pupil, *TNR* reiterated the Jeffersonian idea in progressivism of a "national purpose."[68] The founding fathers' antiquated notions no longer applied. A few pages later in a piece entitled "Barriers to Progressivism" the editors identified the culprit: Walter Lippmann. The Democrats at their conventions behaved less like agents of reform than the "rattled father who goes to the club and gets fighting drunk in order to ease his apprehensions while the baby is being born," they sneered. Lippmann's archaic brand of federalism blurred such modern issues as "railroads, child labor, and the power of labor organizations," the editors reminded him. Their former colleague was obviously not reading the magazine closely. His dismissal of the third party's chances as a "hopeless gamble" misrepresented progressivism, which, in its then current phase, aimed to educate people rather than gain a foothold on power. In short, *TNR* angrily retorted, Lippmann's argument "proves more than a progressive can tolerate."[69] For Croly, the political arc the cofounding editor had traveled since his days at the magazine must have come close to treason.

For all the suspicion Lippmann's essay aroused about his own personal convictions, it scored a few telling points against *TNR*.

La Follette cared little about foreign policy. R. M. Lovett later recalled Hamilton Fish Armstrong's request for him to draft a statement on the subject for the progressives.[70] Lovett found the candidate "indifferent" in meetings and was given a free hand to write whatever he wished on the subject. The two men, after all, opposed the Versailles treaty for different reasons. La Follette represented the midwestern bloc of "irreconciliable" isolationists in the U.S. heartland. *TNR* was wary of repeating World War I's mistakes all over again but still conscious of the powerful role the United States could play in world affairs.

The issue of monopolies also fractured the facade of unanimity. By 1924, La Follette had lost none of his passion for trust busting. Every one of the 24 speeches he delivered during the campaign lashed out at the evils of corporate concentration, and no fewer than eight were solely devoted to the subject.[71] In the past, the magazine had belittled such "nostalgic rural toryism."[72] How could it reconcile this view with its own belief in the efficiency of trusts? Not very well. The editors usually sidestepped the troublesome topic. In "The Progressive Attack on Monopoly," for example, they simply recited the traditional litany of progressive economic reforms.[73] Most liberals agreed that laws should be passed to stop unfair competition and price fixing and bring about public ownership of railroads. The split arose over the use of combinations. Croly and the other editors had always argued that dismantling the trusts hampered useful cooperation between small enterprises and stunted economic growth:

> If we recognize and permit monopoly gains—as economic
> realism must force us to do—the logical complement to
> such a policy is to sequester a large part of such gains for
> the general good.[74]

This "economic realism" ran completely against the grain of La Follette's dream of the decentralized United States. Backing themselves into a corner, the editors fell back on their old recourse: when in doubt, call for a commission. In this case, it was "a qualified commission of socially-minded engineers and economists" to explore "conservation, transportation, inexpensive housing" and other pressing problems of the day. Such a meaningless proposal contributed little to the debate. La Follette's and *TNR*'s notions of government in the modern industrial society clashed, and the latter had no intention of abandoning one of its sacred articles of faith—even to create an illusion of unanimity among progressives.

Lippmann homed in on two glaring discrepancies between *TNR* and its presidential choice. In his search for particulars, however, he failed to fathom the rationale behind the third-party idea. The short-sighted voter could decide between Davis' "few and superficial changes" and Coolidge's "fatuous ignorance and essential absurdity." Informed progressives meant to "put the fear of God into the hearts of the businessmen and politicians." The magazine was repudiating the "process whereby wealth . . . was produced, distributed, and protected . . . to breed extravagent, shiftless, torpid, intolerant, unenlightened, self-satisfied and undeveloped American citizens." A curious reader, who ostensibly did not fit this unseemly description, wrote the magazine to find out what it exactly stood for. The editors printed the letter in its entirety and took time out to reflect on the function they served as "disinterested chroniclers and historians."[75] Their type of journalism provided readers with an "instrument" to enable them "to make up their minds." The heavy doses of the "acid of skepticism" were intended to "stimulate self-watchfulness." It hardly mattered whether the progressive agenda in the campaign was marred by inconsistencies. The underlying impulse of the La Follette candidacy recognized the harsh reality of the United States' lopsided wealth and pricked the public's conscience. In an imaginative piece of advertising gimmickry, bookmarks were inserted in books under the *TNR* imprint: "Cut the pages with this," the promotional material proclaimed, "and be reminded that *The New Republic* is a thorn in the side of complacency."[76]

On the day after the election, the editors were removing thorns from their own sides. The results came as a rude shock. Two weeks before, they had optimistically prepared contingency plans for the possibility of a deadlocked election being thrown into the House of Representatives and ran a long historical piece drawing parallels between the famous 1824 impasse and the probable one a century later.[77] The editors examined the wrong tea leaves. They wistfully predicted that crops would turn out a smaller yield than expected and, in the short term, would have to depend on other country's temporary poor crops for "salvation." The subsequent rise in foreign demand drove wheat prices up and the farmers' insurrectionary zeal down. The outcome thus confirmed the farmer's adage: "When corn is $1.00 a bushel . . . the farmer is a radical, when it's $1.50, he is progressive, and when it's $2.00 a bushel, he is conservative."[78] Kudos also went to Samuel Gompers for his half-hearted decision to break the AFL's long tradition of neutrality and enter the political fray on La Follette's side. When it came time to deliver the goods, however, it escaped *TNR*'s notice that the conservative union chief gave meager aid to the effort or that the United Mine Workers actually backed Coolidge.[79] The editors assigned much of the blame to La Follette who blithely assumed "progressive votes hung like ripe apples on a tree, and would fall into his lap just as soon as the tree was shaken."[80] No strategy La Follette plotted could have concealed his worst handicap, an empty treasure chest. His campaign neither laid the groundwork for an efficient organization nor raised sufficient money—difficulties that are endemic to all U.S. third-party efforts. Compared to Coolidge's 4,360,478,82 dollars, La Follette's forces spent only 221,856 dollars.[81] Under such trying circumstances, the minor party's 16.5 percent-share of the vote could be considered at least a partial victory.

The postmortems *TNR* performed on the dead party proved inconclusive. The editors were perplexed why the masses had ignored the progressive call in such vast numbers. "Millions of citizens were scared or fooled into voting," the magazine ruefully observed, for a government run "by and for business." By framing the debate in terms of "Coolidge or Chaos," the incumbents aroused fear in an extremely "suspicious, uneasy and skeptical" electorate. Given the choice between "jobs, wages and profits" and a radical "experiment," the overwhelming majority of workers innocently clung to the chimerical hope of a better tomorrow. The editors certainly had their work cut out for them if they expected to reeducate the one group least likely to heed their advice.[82]

Toward the end of 1924, the outlook of progressivism looked bleak indeed. "Those who are deliberating whether to continue the party," *TNR* counseled its brethren, "should weigh well, in light of the ascertained cost in money and effort, whether the game is worth the candle."[83] The collapse of the farmer–labor combination left the editors confused and lost. Looming large on the Democratic horizon, immigrant blemishes and all, was the politically unpalatable Al Smith.[84] In a rambling piece on the movement's misfortunes in December (probably authored by Croly), lines were cast across the Atlantic toward the nascent British Labour Party. According to the article, since U.S. liberals, for the time being, had little chance of winning legislative battles, they should concentrate on monitoring conservatives and precipitating "issues" and starting "ferment," *TNR* counselled. The paramount goal of a "radical party," should it emerge, would be to

> bring to existence a body of workers who do not consent
> to their existing inferiority of status and have equipped

themselves to take their appropriate share in a regenerated political and economic government. Their kingdom, if they are ever to possess a kingdom, must be established in the mind before it begins to subdue the unmanagable engine of political government to its purposes.

The "kingdom . . . in the mind" over which *TNR* presided encompassed a small realm. To fulfill his goals, Croly had to extend his sovereignty beyond his narrow readership and awaken the slumbering electorate with vibrant programs.[85]

In the aftermath of the election, *TNR* refused to retreat from the positions it had staked out during the campaign. The editors quickly resumed the offensive again. All the pent up frustrations with the AFL—"the best paid members of skilled trades, in the most conservative wing of American labor"—were released against its new director, William Green, a "rigid Conservative of the Gompers type."[86] The magazine outlined a federal child-labor amendment in great detail.[87] For "piling up huge fortunes for themselves," it threatened Mellon and company with heavier estate and surtaxes.[88] To prove that their interests were more than an ephemeral campaign ploy, *TNR* instructed farmers on every facet of their trade, from credit facilities to crop diversification.[89] It continued to mount scathing critiques against U.S. citizens, "the most royally wasteful people in the world," where spending sprees on "comforts and luxuries" could only be justified if they had "inexhaustible fortunes to live upon."[90] The economy appeared out of kilter. In a prophetic moment, the editors speculated on the deleterious effect of business' swelling purchases on credit and "fixed obligations" on the economy, if it ever ceased to expand.[91] At the peak of the roaring twenties' unbridled optimism, such dire warnings fell on deaf ears.

By the end of 1924, *TNR* found itself crying out in the U.S. political wilderness. While responsibility for La Follette's defeat ultimately rested with the candidate, the editors did not emerge from the ordeal as innocent bystanders. They had strugged to build their theoretical constructs on the flimsiest of foundations, papering over deep rifts between agrarian populists and urban progressives on trust-busting and other major issues. They had bent the campaign's harsh realities out of shape to fit idealized notions of the working class. Labor's successful political venture in Britain could not be easily transplanted to a nation in which the apathetic working class' imagination was permanently seized by the U.S. dream of upward mobility. On any day, bread and butter issues overrode fantasies about worker solidarity and the grandiose farmer–labor scheme. Croly and the others had every right to be disappointed, but not surprised.

Ironically, *TNR* ignored the lesson of defeat. The final election tally, it felt, was incidental to the campaign's primary purpose. As a "radical experiment" in U.S. politics, the effort had fulfilled the magazine's most sacred obligation to educate the public. La Follette's ambitious and imaginative platform placed progressives and the magazine far ahead of their times. Several of its proposals later resurfaced during the New Deal in the various forms of the Tennessee Valley Authority, "rapidly progressive" income and inheritance schedules, the Wagner Labor Relations Act, comprehensive aid to agriculture, the Securities Exchange, and the abolition of child labor. Croly had also kept his promise to "stimulate self-watchfulness." To his considerable dismay, most U.S. cititzens were all too eager to shove the progressive era's preoccupations on the back burner. The staunchest efforts of Croly and his Cassandra chorus to jolt the nation out of its smugness met the fiercest resistance. Only he, and a dwindling minority, seemed to realize that all that glittered was not gold.

. . . .

Two Dead
Men

· · · · · · · · ·
1925–28
· · · · · · · · ·

IN THE MIDST OF A CONSERVATIVE AGE, LIBERALS HAD trouble coping. Two of *TNR*'s founding parents, Croly and Dorothy Straight, began a process of soul-searching that was not always merely figurative. Until marrying Leonard Elmhirst, a wealthy Englishman in 1925, Dorothy was tormented by the loss of her dear, deceased Willard. In an effort to contact him, she held seances (a common practice at the time among war widows in Europe and the United States). "Is there anything valuable *The New Republic* can do?," she asked her husband's spirit. "Do not become too rabid," responded Willard from the Other Side.[1]

Croly, too, was exploring other dimensions. Fighting to rebound from his political losses, he felt tired and listless. "My vitality is ebbing slowly but inexorably," he lamented in a letter to Dorothy.[2] To revive his spirits and relieve his boredom with the state of events, he began to embark on long spiritual missions. His strong religious convictions surfaced in the form of rambling essays with such titles as "Christianity as a Way of Life" and "Christians, Beware!"[3] After work hours, he joined the mystical Orage cult, transplanted from Eastern Europe. As did Katherine Mansfield and Hart Crane, Croly embraced its ethereal teachings and partook in religious gymnastic exercises and diets. Managing Editor Bruce Bliven later compared these rituals to the experience of taking LSD.[4]

Croly also began to reexamine a magazine that afforded him fewer pleasures than it had in the past. Felix Frankfurter was not enamored with its quality and let his friend know it. The close relationship between the editors and Frankfurter occasionally became

81

strained. At one point, the law professor demanded to know whether Bliven remembered the principles on which *TNR* was founded: "the *NR* was dedicated to our numbers, not the 'man in the street,' " he reminded him.[5] On another occasion, Croly beseeched his old friend not to believe that "Willard's"original sense of the journal had been abandoned.[6] Privately, he harbored doubts about the magazine. For the past decade, he told Dorothy, he had worked hard "to reconstruct the personal intellectual architecture which the war destroyed and which . . . [he had] been trying ever since to recover."[7] This renovation started with *TNR*. Croly briefly toyed with the idea of converting it into a journal of literature, the arts, and moral philosophy.[8] But he thought better of the transformation and decided to preserve the magazine's traditional format.

Croly's consternation was more than intellectual. In fact, he feared for *TNR*'s life. A rapidly declining audience created severe financial hardship. According to his estimates, the nation's conservative mood had caused the magazine's circulation to fall from a wartime high of approximately 35,000 to a meager 14,000.[9] (The caustic Edmund Wilson believed Croly had only himself to blame for his troubles. "The magazine has become so dull," he joked to a friend, "that the editors themselves say they are unable to read and the subscribers are dying off like flies.")[10] By 1924, the magazine's cumulative debt had reached 800,000 dollars and the normally openhanded Dorothy began pulling in her purse strings.[11] In a particularly morose moment, Croly told her that he was even considering "murdering our costly and unruly youngster."[12] The payroll was cut back drastically—a painful process Croly explained to his employer, for an enterprise that already had enough problems keeping such talented men as Lippmann, Merz, and critic Stark Young who were "not satisfied with a college professor's standard of living." Fortunately, in a shrewd bit of bookkeeping, the magazine filed for bankruptcy and the company was reorganized, relieving its financial burdens and Croly's anxieties. He now looked forward to an "unimpeded vista of work ahead for several years."[13]

With the coffers temporarily replenished, the editorial and publishing offices attempted to breathe some life into their product to attract a wider audience. The famous TRB column was inaugurated in 1925. The origins of the mysterious signature at the bottom of a weekly feature called "Washington Notes" are open to question. Bliven claims to have coined the acronym while looking for a way to fill a line of copy en route to the printers on the BRT (Brooklyn Rapid Transit.)[14] He then, so his story went, simply reversed the letters. TRB may have also derived from a popular book series at the time, "The Wild Rover Boys."[15] In any event, the column soon became a success. Frequent advertisements appeared touting the "detachment and candor of the anonymous correspondent, who cannot endanger the confidential sources of his information by making public his identity."[16] The long succession of distinguished columnists—Frank Kent, Jonathan Mitchell, Kenneth Crawford, and Richard Strout—over the next 50 years usually lived up to this billing.

The back of the book or cultural section joined in the drive to generate publicity and cash. The magazine launched its own company to publish a catalogue of works on social and economic problems. These "dollar books" became so popular that, within a few years, 250,000 copies of some 40 different titles were sold annually.[17] Readers could also buy the books of other publishers by mail through *TNR*. In one of the more imaginative promotions ever conceived by the magazine, limited, signed prints of John Nash, Gwendolyn Raverat, and other notable artists of the period were offered for sale.[18] Customers were invited to the well stocked "New Republic Bookstore" on Fifth Avenue to make their purchases in person. They had to shop early, however. In the summer of 1928, the building in a high-rent area was torn down to make room for banks and beauty parlors; an apt sign of the times for the magazine and liberals in general.[19]

Several of the *TNR* principals were actively seeking additional outlets to promote their ideals. The idea for "The New School for Social Research" was originally hatched in the magazine's offices.[20] Patterned after the London School of Economics and the Ecole Libre des Sciences Politiques, the institution was designed to be free of normal academic pressures. Such regular contributors and associates of the magazine as Charles Beard, John Dewey, and Harold Laski agreed to serve on the faculty. Dorothy Straight provided much of the financial backing, and editor Alvin Johnson left *TNR* to head the school. The project signaled the progressive movement's determination to broaden its base beyond politics to the deep roots of the U.S. educational system.

In many respects, the famed Sacco-Vanzetti case, which *TNR* covered closely, served a similar purpose of stimulating public awareness about social problems. The two Italian anarchists were charged with robbing and murdering a shoe-factory paymaster and his guard on very sketchy evidence. Their misfortunes rapidly became the progressive cause celebre of the period. Bliven dubbed it "America's Dreyfus affair."[21] No event so crystallized society's distribution of power and privilege. The issue "aroused keener and more interest," the editors announced, than any "since *NR* began publication."[22] The fight for Sacco and Vanzetti brought back memories of the fierce battle over the Brandeis nomination in 1916, except that this time the editors were less sensitive about their terminology. The conservatives' dogged persistence, they maintained, was "chiefly a matter of pathological class consciousness." The two immigrants' ethnicity and unconventional politics, as did Brandeis' Judaism and progressivism, touched the "Back Bay on its tenderest and most vulnerable spot."[23] The trial judge, Webster Thayer, boasted to a golf-club crony of doing in "those anarchist bastards."[24]

Liberals were enraged. Students, writers, lawyers, newspapermen, and labor officials organized protests and sent out appeals. *TNR* published 40 articles, some two dozen editorials, countless poems, notices of protest meetings, and important documents in the case.[25] Dorothy Straight contributed generously to the cause. Appeals for donations to defense funds appeared regularly, and the magazine took out a full-page advertisement in the *New York Times* to solicit more money.[26] Just before the execution, Bliven visited the inmates in their prison cell.[27] Speaking eloquently and with a heavy Italian accent, Vanzetti thanked him and his friends for their kindness but said that it had been useless—that he and Sacco were "dead men." "When you are free," the condemned man told the editor as he was departing, "you will perhaps go back to Italy and drink again the lacrimae Christi?"

Although they had prepared themselves for the worst, the case's sad outcome devastated the staff at *TNR*. In a letter to Dorothy's new husband, Leonard Elmhirst, Croly privately mourned it as an "unmitigated tragedy." The man, usually stoic, could not restrain himself and unleashed his fury, in an unsigned editorial, at the "intolerant self-righteousness" of the "dominant class of businessmen in America."[28] With one quick stroke of his pen he demolished *Promise*'s patriotic premise: "Americans are likely to wake up some morning and find that the liberty of expression which the fathers valued so highly is buried in a common grave with the aspirations of economic independence and equality of the early American pioneer." Croly came short of advocating a class struggle. But his "methodical curiosity" obliged him "to face the fact," for the first time, that society might well "be torn to pieces." On the night of the execution, Bliven tended to his sorrows by walking the streets with colleagues from the magazine for hours until they were exhausted and went home to bed to go to sleep. A few years later, in *Exile's Return*, Malcolm Cowley described how the Sacco-Vanzetti defeat drove the intellectual "back into his personal isolation."[29]

To a large extent, progressives were responsible for their own exhaustion and loneliness. The brutal travesty of justice certainly warranted their irate response. Sacco and Vanzetti's plight drew attention to the age's pressing social problems: ethnic discrimination, violation of civil liberties, and class oppression. Progressives found their ideal martyrs in the two immigrants. Such strategy, however, posed dangers. By raising the stakes so high, the movement's leaders seemed to lie prostrate before, as one wag called them, the "dago christs". Intellectuals appeared remote and aloof from such daily concerns as housing and minimum hours and wages, which had fueled the 1924 battle. *TNR*'s political posturing placed it even further outside the U.S. mainstream.

The trend away from practical politics continued through the next presidential campaign. The magazine decided to exploit the occasion to settle the issue of religious bigotry, the most nagging social issue nationwide and at *TNR*. The cruel rallying cry of nativists against Smith, "Rum, Romanism and Rebellion," exposed the deepening schisms between urban and rural United States and between Catholics and Protestants. Whatever fondness the editors had for the candidate was tempered by this "notorious" and "fatal disqualification."[30] Smith, they believed, had a lot of questions to answer about his affiliation with the church. How, for instance, did his dual allegiance to a foreign pontificate, the Pope, square with the U.S. principle of nondenominational public law and schools? "Considering the special nature of their traditions, education, and organizations," the editors worried, it was "not unreasonable to watch Catholic candidates for Presidents with unusual care" and monitor the way their "culture" made "them excessively deferential to the political influence of their ecclesiastical superiors." *TNR* insisted, in a bout with ambivalence, it was not trying to aid and abet the fanatical fundamental forces or shore up the "Protestant middle-class burgher." The problem centered on the serious handicaps of the "one thorough-going progressive" in the race.[31] Liberals had to remove a glaring stigma from their candidate to help him reach the White House.

The socialist option was promptly discarded. In 1916, Croly refused to give the fire-breathing Debs his due because he was too radical. Ironically, 12 years later, *TNR* ignored the same party because it appeared too conservative and no longer enjoyed the working class' support. Norman Thomas, the handsome Princeton graduate and Presbyterian minister, took the correct stands on issues and was "a man of high character and unusual intelligence."[32] He was, perhaps, too intelligent. The main grievance lodged against him concerned his intellectualism. His party was too "overbalanced" with practitioners of this mental capacity, the editors complained, to make "headway" among union members and farmers.[33] "Middle-class intellectuals like Mr. Thomas himself, like most of the Socialist agitators, like his adherents in college faculties and like so many progressives" (including editors of NR), they were wont to concede, "are not the stuff out of which a dynamic party of radical opposition can be wrought."[34] The editors backed away from the Socialists precisely because they mirrored themselves and did not wish to watch a command performance of the campaign four years earlier—even if it meant disparaging the very power of ideas and agitation for which the magazine supposedly stood. Practical politics took precedence over visionary progressivism in 1928.

Herbert Hoover's candidacy compounded *TNR*'s quandary. Croly had yet to recover from his brief fling with the "unconventional politician" in the 1920 campaign.[35] The statesman, technician, and engineer possessed the "restless, alert, progressive, and dynamic" traits of Croly's mythical "saint and hero" in *Promise*. No number of tributes to Hoover's integrity and intelligence could alter the fact that, as historian John Hicks argues, he "well reflected" business, "the single-interest domination under which the Republican party had fallen."[36] Republicans' free-market economics and hostility to all government intervention on the wage earner's behalf placed them far to the right of *TNR*. Their standard-bearer, for all purposes, spouted the "most dreary Coolidgisms" around the worst "selfish economic motives of individuals."[37] Handcuffed by a reactionary party, Hoover could not possibly meet any of the progressive qualifications.

Stranded without a candidate, the editors decided to take a closer look at Smith and his record. Working his way up from the lower-east-side slums through the Tammany Hall machine, he never forgot the immigrant brethren he left behind and always commanded their allegiance. A heavy New York accent and large brown derby were trademarks of the most colorful character on the national political scene. As governor of New York, he earned liberal accolades for programs establishing minimum wage for women and minors; extending rent control and promoting low-cost housing; and passing health and safety labor laws. His successful efforts to streamline state agencies and expand the state prison system cast him in the classic progressive mold of the efficient, good-government reformer. Yet, underneath it all, he too was essentially a conservative man who feared class conflict and preferred to let big business look after itself. The platform on which he stood differed only slightly from the Republicans', and the chairman of his campaign, John J. Raskob, was a top official at General Motors and, until that year, a Coolidge Republican. From the General Motors building, where the party headquarters was relocated, the business tycoon energetically solicited the support of bankers and corporation officials.

TNR'S original reservations about Smith's personal flaws spread to his policies as well. Croly informed Dorothy Elmhirst of his difficulty in choosing the next president "in almost a complete intellectual and moral vacuum."[38] The editors initially dismissed Smith as an "accomplice rather than a positive alternative to Republican rule."[39] "The primrose path for him," they continued, "will be to decline his allegiance to Jeffersonian principles, his abhorrence of federal centralization and his faith in some variation of what Mr. Wilson used to call the 'New Freedom.' " Government's subordination to business under Republican rule squandered the opportunity to channel the nation's wealth toward social ends. The U.S. orgy of stockmarket speculation and extravagant consumption wasted valuable resources. Although no official records were kept, private studies estimated that the jobless rates had risen to 10 percent and that structural unemployment remained at intolerably high levels.[40] "No crusader," Smith deftly sidestepped these crucial issues.[41] His "silent game," Croly wrote Dorothy, gave *TNR* nothing to "get a hold of."[42]

If the magazine could not defeat Smith, it would join him. What the editors previously considered to be, in the current jargon, an image problem was suddenly transformed into an asset. Smith's religion and ethnicity set him apart from the rest of the pack. He alone represented the "unpedigreed foreign-born, city-bred, many tongued . . . synthetic Americans."[43] In a remarkable reversal, the politician's affiliation with the notorious, vice-ridden Tammany organization became a virtue. Setting aside its obvious failings, the editors pointed out that the machine had always "taken good care of its own people, who for the most part, belon[ged] to the class of the underdog." Perhaps, they mused, Tammany politics could be translated into "national economic and social policy." The best advertisement for Smith, of course, was Smith himself—a hero to his people. That a man from his humble surroundings could lift himself "up by his own boot-straps" held out hope for the toiling masses of a "genuinely equalitarian political society."[44]

Croly labored to build the Al Smith legend, but aired his suspicions first. "As a nursling both of Tammany and the Catholic Church," Croly feared, "he is accustomed to depend on too much authority."[45] His main immigrant supporters were "mercurial, suspicious, credulous, avid of the good things in American life and only superficially rooted in American soil." They were "connected" across the country "with one another by hyphens" (a contemporary figure of speech to describe immigrants' foreign names). Without the faintest trace of self-consciousness, Croly was spinning a litany of nativist falsehoods about the Church, family, and so-called alien character. His perception of Smith was still colored by the same waspish elitism of the last election. Despite his skepticism, Croly really wanted to applaud the "superb actor [on] . . . the political stage," and give whatever assistance he could. He even supplied the candidate with memoranda written by *TNR* editors to use in his acceptance speech for the nomination.[46] No one, after all, could deny the fellow's "lively intelligence, abundant good will and large generosity of impulse" or his appeal to immigrants. Croly was unable to bring himself to embrace him wholeheartedly. In their tepid endorsement of Smith, the editors whimsically beheld "the bridegroom of a better Democracy."[47]

The magazine's undulating responses to Republicans and Democrats reflected the utter disarray of progressivism. University of Chicago Professor (and future U.S. Senator) Paul Douglas recruited disenchanted progressives to the "Independent Committee for Thomas." In a rebuttal to *TNR*'s Smith endorsement, Douglas laid out the socialist agenda—which bore a strong resemblance to LaFollette's farmer–labor platform—and lamented the "sorry pass" to which the liberal "intelligentsia" had come.[48] In the same issue, his committee took out a full-page advertisement to offer *TNR* condolences for its "pathetically quixotic" efforts to rehabilitate the Democratic party.[49] The sponsors included Fola La Follette and Bertha Poole Weyl (the widows of Robert and Walter, respectively), *TNR* editor R. M. Lovett, Upton Sinclair, and W. E. B. DuBois. Norman Thomas, for his part, dashed off an angry letter to the magazine attacking Smith and comparing the differences between the two major parties to "the pot and the kettle." Croly generally agreed. In the course of the campaign, he laced several Smith stories with equally pungent phrases. The parties, he sneered, were fighting a "boxing exhibition with soft gloves" and resembled "stagnant pools of muddy political vegetation."[50] Outside the magazine's page, in a letter to

Leonard Elmhirst, Croly expressed his frustration with the silent campaign.[51] Unable to raise the decibel level, he admitted to him that the whole affair was a "wash" for the magazine and he was powerless to do much about it.

The strains of an indifferent decade exacted a heavy toll on Croly. In the fall of 1928, he collapsed in the bathroom of his apartment from a massive stroke. He and his wife then moved to a rented house in Santa Barbara, California, to begin a long and valiant march toward recovery. Dorothy sent large sums of money to pay for the expensive, and ultimately ineffective, treatments. Croly died two years later, deprived of the chance to see many of his most cherished reforms enacted in the New Deal.[52]

Within a year after Hoover's victory, the stock market crash marked the end of the roaring twenties. *TNR* departed the era somewhat chastened and utterly baffled. The Sacco–Vanzetti tragedy had left liberals too numb to recover and gather their forces in time for the 1928 election. Torn between activism and apathy, the editors gained neither the rewards of victory nor the moral satisfaction of the 1924 crusade. They surrendered before the battle even began. Capitalists were gently prodded to be social-minded with their wealth rather than attacked for foolishly endangering the economy. In presenting Al Smith with all his crudeness as a political version of a Horatio Alger success story, *TNR* thus accepted the primacy of business and acquiesced to its most alluring myths. The liberals' submission to a materialistic culture topped off the conservative triumph.

Liberalism withered but survived. The idea of social justice was still embedded in its tentative tenets of reform. *TNR*'s decision not to ally itself with the Socialists and to work within the system through the Democratic party was to create new possibilities. What idealistic purity was lost from the farmer–labor bid four years earlier was restored through the realism of practical politics. Tripping over Smith, the editors unwittingly knocked into the future of liberalism; the growing support for Smith's party among Italian, Irish, Jewish, and other urban ethnic blocs presaged the development of the New Deal coalition. The magazine, however tenuously, was finally connecting with—to borrow Frankfurter's phrase—"the man on the street," the interests of whom the magazine, in large part, was defending.

The prosperity bubble was waiting to burst, and the worker would bear the main brunt of the explosion. In the late 1920s, a Brookings Institution report indicated that inequality of income was rising while the majority of wage earners were falling below the minimum standard of living. Using modern quantitative methods nearly a half century later, historians estimated the unemployment rate then to have been about 13 percent (higher than *TNR*'s figure of 10 percent).[53] The nation's labor force, moreover, remained stuck at the bottom of the social ladder. Although *TNR* could not press its points with such statistical precision nor predict the terrible nature of the impending disaster with any certainty, it kept unpopular issues alive in the nation's background. "Tired" or not, radicals and other members of the Cassandra chorus were the ones best prepared to meet the awesome challenges that lay ahead.

. . . .

Herbert Croly, *The New Republic*'s editor from 1914 to 1930

Willard Straight, and his wife Dorothy, founded *The New Republic* in 1914 (Cornell University Libraries)

The elegant editors' dining room at the old headquarters.

A young Walter Lippmann at work, 1915

Edmund Wilson served off and on as literary editor from 1928 to 1931 and contributed frequently thereafter

Bruce Bliven, editor from 1930 to 1941

Malcolm Cowley, literary editor from 1930 to 1941

Paper Politics:
· · · · · · · · ·
1929–32
· · · · · · · · ·

EDMUND WILSON WAS A PENSIVE MAN. EVEN AT AN early age, he developed a reputation as a stalwart intellectual. By young adulthood, he had already mastered more than half a dozen languages. After serving in World War I as a private, hospital attendant in France and member of the Intelligence Corps he became *Vanity Fair*'s managing editor from 1920–21. He joined *TNR* in 1926 and served as an associate editor and chief book reviewer for five years. Colleagues were intimidated by his patrician airs and dyspeptic disposition. His character was as "hard as a diamond," remarked copy editor Elizabeth Huling. Underneath a stodgy exterior bristled a brilliant mind of extraordinary scope and depth. He excelled as a novelist, short-story writer, playwright, poet, and essayist. Published in 1931, his *Axel's Castle* trenchantly analyzed the works of Yeats, Eliot, Pound, and Joyce in terms of the French symbolist movement. Wilson's equally original and provocative appraisals of such contemporaries as F. Scott Fitzgerald, William Faulkner, Katherine Anne Porter, and Dorothy Parker enhanced their literary statures immeasurably. In 1930, the "radical independent," as literary critic Daniel Aaron has dubbed him, turned his Promethean talents to politics and, in the process, forever altered the face of progressivism.[1]

Unlike the eclectic Wilson, George Soule spend his time immersed in the minutia of a few important subjects. After graduating from Yale University with a dual degree in economics and literature, he traveled to Gary, Indiana, in 1919 to investigate the great steel strike. There the erratic behavior of William Z. Foster, a union organizer and soon-to-be communist, permanently drove him away from ideological crusades. A year later Soule helped found the Labor Bureau, Incorporated—a think tank to conduct technical research for professional workers and labor organizations. After serving as director of the National Bureau of Economic Research, he began a 20-year career at *TNR* as a junior editor in 1922. Soule quickly and resolutely filled a niche as the staff's economics writer. Colleagues were struck by his steady productivity, a natural complement to his placid personality and demeanor. Each week, with uncompromising regularity, he ground out long, involute treatises on the virtues of restricting the United States' grossly inefficient form of capitalism. "The prose was simple, logical, and clear," Malcolm Cowley (a copy editor at the time) later recalled, "but somewhat lacking in heat, like a steam generated in a vacuum." The crash came as no shock to Soule, since it reinforced his deepest convictions and fulfilled many of the magazine's pet prophecies. Undaunted by the intense trauma all around him, he calmly set about drafting comprehensive plans to reconstruct a shattered society.[2]

The Great Depression overwhelmed the United States. In 1929, the bottom of the economy fell out, sending the nation into a tailspin. From large banks in Chicago to local neighborhood grocery stores in New York, businesses across the country went bankrupt in record numbers. Farmers reaped the dust bowl's bitter harvests. Those fortunate enough to be still employed had their wages slashed to subsistence levels. By 1933, at the Depression's peak, 12 million people were without jobs—over 25 percent of the labor force. Affirming his faith in the traditional values of voluntarism and the free market, President Hoover shunned major federal initiatives in the belief that the ailment would run its course. Local charities and relief agencies proved sadly unequipped to shoulder the heavy burden. While hobos traveled by foot and rail through the countryside, whole families in cities moved into shacks and shanties called Hoovervilles. When not standing on breadlines or waiting in soup kitchens, the hungry and dispossessed took to the streets to vent their rage through large and often violent demonstrations. The United States appeared on the verge of a social collapse.

One had hardly to look further than the magazine's offices to see just how hard times were. The few dozen pages in each issue could not begin to accommodate the indigent writers begging for work. Malcolm Cowley, who was then literary editor, started a fund from the sale of unreviewed books for the needier cases. Every kind of crank, from self-help enthusiasts to millenarian fruit-juice drinkers, visited *TNR* to peddle some panacea for the nation's woes.

One crazed woman marched into the building demanding that her manuscript be read in the editors' presence: "I know you editors. You'd steal my ideas and print them under a different name. You'd steal the pennies from a dead man's eyes."[3]

The editors' awakenings took place outside the magazine's offices. *TNR* transformed itself overnight to meet the new circumstances. Its normally desk-bound writers journeyed into the field to investigate the rumblings of discontent. Literary editor Edmund Wilson (who alternated with Cowley in the position) combined his impressive skills as a critic with the methods of a journalist to study the complex U.S. text. In 1930 and 1931, in perhaps the best reportage of the period, he traveled throughout the United States to document the growing unrest. "The Social Fact"—as one historian terms the genre—had countless imitators, but, with the possible exception of the writing of James Agee, few equals.[4] Wilson later compiled his articles in a book entitled *The American Jitters.*

The "grey" and "dismal" town of Lawrence, Massachusetts mirrored the spirits of its striking textile workers. A "gruesome, groaning and booing crowd" of hungry men milled about the "half-sleepy" streets, wondering what would happen once they wore out their "last heelless pair of shoes" and consumed their "last bag of bread." They knew full well that their "feeble and diseased children" and "slattern-looking string haired" wives were consigned for the rest of their lives to being on the "wrong side of the social wall."[5] From Detroit, Wilson detailed the process of melting down cars as a metaphor for the scrapping of human beings. "Black coupes; blue town sedans; maroon tudors; buff roadsters; green trucks" and undernourished, laid-off workers were all interchangeable parts and disposable commodities.[6] Carey McWilliams (later editor of *The Nation*) served as Wilson's tour guide in San Diego, where he studied the coroners' records. Bankers, architects, and other members of the middle class would "go into their back sheds or back kitchens and swallow Lysol or ant-paste . . . drive their cars into dark alleys and shoot themselves in the back seat . . . hang themselves in hotel bedrooms . . . take overdoses of sulphur or barbiturates . . . [7] stab themselves on the municipal golf-course." Their individual suicides were microcosms of a civilization in its death throes.

Wilson's two-part series on "Hull House in 1932" memorably reproduced the squalor of abject poverty. The settlement house, a powerful symbol during the progressive era of well intentioned reform, now resembled an Elizabethan poorhouse. The place was "fused in the stagnant smell of humanity; they eat chickenfeed and slum amid the deafening clank of trays." An "old man" was "dying of a tumor, with no heat in the house on a cold day, his pale bones of arms like bent pins." "Welcome to Hoover's Hotel," someone had chalked on the wall. Having lost their "independence" and "personality," its inhabitants were degraded to the "primal, neutral, undifferentiated city grayness, depriving them of even the glow of life which sets them off from the pavements and the factories and the old newspaper and the fog, rubbing them down to nothing." For once, the unflappable Jane Addams, Hull House director and its matriarchial figure, appeared to Wilson to be bewildered and out of place in the sordid setting. When a communist paid her a visit, she listened intently and asked pointed questions that digressed from his "regular line." Miss Addams and the party apparatchik spoke different languages, and the meeting was closed.[8]

The first-hand observation of these scenes drove Wilson to escape the United States and seek refuge in other cultures. As "the best possible antidote to New York," Wilson wrote friend Maxwell Perkins, he decided to journey to New Mexico.[9] As spectacular as he found "landscapes" and "forests," Wilson wrote the famed Scribners editor, he was particularly curious about the "communistic Indian villages—said to be models of good government." *TNR* published his impressions in an essay entitled "The Enchanted Forest," one of his most haunting works. The dark shades of dense forests and "slopes of the mythological green valleys" invited the reader into a surrealistic world where people only intruded. Pete Ferguson, the frustrated owner of a shut-down labor mill, was worried about socialist talk among the unemployed men. *TNR*'s onlooker evinced little sympathy for him. Since the first settlers' arrival, cattle grazing and the lumbering and mining industries had despoiled this Arcadian setting. The indigenous population of Indians, by contrast, lived harmoniously with the environment. Their jerry-built houses on the cliffs' terraces blended in with the terrain. This "communal race of people . . . [which] survived the centuries from alien races . . . [was] narrow, unbusinesslike, incurious, illiterate, unhygenic, unscientific." Far from New York cosmopolitanism, Wilson happened upon the noble savage. Surveying the scene, an old-timer compared his experiences with whites and Indians: "The Indian's religion and government are the same thing and they fit him like a glove—where our laws don't fit us anywhere—nor our religion either!" Amidst the United States' advanced chaos rested the uncivilized tranquility of an ancient society.[10]

Each editor left the office to try his hand at reportage. In February 1930—"this winter of Hoover Prosperity"—Bliven poked around the Bowery.[11] Many of the "down-and-outs," he discovered, were professionals who were unemployed for the first time. Outside a lodging house and YMCA, long lines of them wound around the block in a "grey-black human snake." George Soule visited Rhode Island to explore the possibility of "class war" by studying laid-off textile workers. His encounters with tired and hungry men shattered all his illusions about a potential revolution in the United States. The workers were too dejected and apathetic to search for their next meal, let alone for answers from communism. "How can anyone seriously believe" this inert mass was capable of overthrowing the government, Soule asked.[12]

Malcolm Cowley drew different conclusions from trips to the nation's capital. He watched the U.S. cavalry rout the ragamuffin Bonus Army (a force of some 12,000 homeless and unemployed World War I soldiers) with drawn sabers, tanks, and infantry.[13] Dodging tear-gas bombs and bayonets, hordes of veterans, women, and children, "waking from sleep to cough and whimper" from the noxious fumes, fled in terror. "I used to be a hundred-percenter," one protester yelled, "but now I'm a Red radical. I had an American flag, but the damn tin soldiers burned it. Now I don't ever want to see a flag again." At the end of 1932, Cowley returned to Washington to view a "red hunger march" sponsored by the Communist party. The police's "absurd display of force against unarmed people" disgusted him. *TNR*'s editor left the scene with the first bars of the "Internationale" still ringing in his ears.

Cowley was not content to remain a spectator. At a meeting of novelists, critics, liberal editors, and crusading journalists in Theodore Dreiser's New York apartment, he joined John Dos Passos and Sherwood Anderson in drafting an appeal to "Professional Writers" to form a communion between "muscle workers" and "brain workers." In the winter of 1932, Dreiser led a delegation of writers, including Cowley, to Kentucky's infamous Harlan County to render service to the coal miners in their struggle against ruthless coal operators and their goons. The "brutal subjugation and oppression" of workers and their wretched living conditions convinced Cowley that the class struggle was "inevitable." The literary allies' efforts to deliver food to the beleaguered miners and their families were quickly halted by jack-booted deputies with a pronounced distaste for "Bolshies." The group was put in jail for a couple of hours for "criminal charges," herded into police cars, and deposited at the state border. Cowley later recalled one of the driver's conversations with a friend on the way: "You sure would have plugged that miner today, John, if you got a fair shot at him. It was a pity he got away in the crowd." Waldo Frank, a contributing editor to *TNR*, and a lawyer were roughed up. "If they beat me I'll scream. It's about the only hope of stopping them," Cowley said to himself.[14]

Back at the magazine, the editors were thrashing out proposals to deliver the United States from its crisis. The field of economics gained new prominence as experts and laymen frantically searched for solutions. Classical theories were heaved out with abandon. "Do you still Believe in Lazy-Fairies?," *Business Week* asked its readers.[15] The popular economist and journalist Stuart Chase wondered why "Russians . . . [should] have all the fun of remaking the world?"[16] *TNR*'s Soule, in full agreement, scolded social reformers for having "no dependable technique for bringing fundamental change into being."[17] This was his chance to set his ideas in motion.

In 1931, he wrote a major book, *A Planned Society*, to promote his policies for overhauling the nation's economy and socializing capitalism. He presented a complex blueprint that eliminated unemployment by balancing production and consumption. At the height of the Great Depression, the task of managing society was too important to be left to private enterprise. Citing the successful example of planning during World War I, Soule suggested that government once again mobilize and coordinate the nation's resources. The other example he had in mind was the Soviet Union where, various reports indicated, planning and collective cooperation were creating unprecedented comfort for its beleaguered population. Deep differences between the two societies, he admitted, obviously precluded U.S. adoption of the Soviet model. Instead, Soule called for the president—with the Senate's advice and consent—to form a "National Economic Board" composed of "economists, statisticians, engineers, and accountants." Once assembled, the staff would correlate various plans among industries; devise productive tax and spending policies; and nationalize factories, railroads, hills, mines, and the land. Armed with his expert knowledge, the great "organizing man" would achieve "victory after victory" in the war to "organize society" and put it back on a sound footing. The "organizing man" became the updated version of Croly's much vaunted "saint and hero."[18]

Soule had trouble convincing other progressives, though not for want of effort. Excerpts from his book and long articles on such topics as "Chaos and Control" (interchangeable with "planning and order") appeared with monotonous frequency in the magazine. "I have insisted *ad nauseam* on more concreteness in *NR*," Frankfurter snapped at Bliven, "instead of repetition of general talk about a planned society."[19] John Dos Passos suggested to Wilson that *TNR* print "THIS IS ALL BULLSHIT" at the bottom of each page and stop using so many "whoopee-words." Soule, he complained, was "stuttering on ponsasinorum" and was incapable of making a "definite pronouncement because the statistics aren't all in yet."[20] Although they probably overstated their cases, Frankfurter and Dos Passos had good reason for frustration. Without clearer guidelines, any government administrator examining Soule's tangled network of government agencies and councils would have been at a loss to fully comprehend his suggestions, or even figure out how to implement them. *TNR*'s former publisher Robert Hallowell accused Soule of flinging a "crystal globe into the air."[21] The economics writer called for "more vigorous steps." "Hell! What are they? Define them. *No, take them!*" he demanded. Hallowell had a point. The economist's work also lacked a soul. His systematic approach and didactic discourses on the glories of technological efficiency removed reform from the emotional, human world of politics. Leaden abstractions and formulas were not going to capture the imaginations of Soule's countrymen.

Edmund Wilson, for one, paid scant attention to his colleague's work. The "scenes of privation and misery" he so vividly described in his reportage incited him to rebel. Leaving his associate's work back on his bookshelf, Edmund Wilson resolved to redefine completely U.S. liberalism. Early in 1931, *TNR* printed his famous call to arms, "An Appeal to Progressives." No one, he lectured his brethren, should "be afraid to dynamite the old shibboleths and conceptions and substitute new ones as shocking as possible." The Crolian faith, as expressed in *Promise*, in capitalism's capacity to reform itself was thoroughly misguided. The restoration of society's "weak" morale and "idealism" required the outright rejection of liberals' "middle class psychology" and "bourgeois solidarity." In the face of such a grave crisis, they could ill afford to "fall back on" cliches about greater government or organizing labor. Social planning, Wilson argued, meant pure, unadulterated socialism and the concomitant abolition of capitalism. Toward that end, the United States needed to import the Soviet Union's successful economic models, which had "all the qualities that Americans glorify—the extreme of efficiency and economy combined with the ideal of a herculean feat to be accomplished by common action in an atmosphere of enthusiastic boosting—like a Liberty Loan drive—the idea of putting over something big in five years." Wilson envisaged a domestic adaptation with all the spirit of the original communist doctrine and none of the party's rigid dogma. He exhorted his radical and progressive brethren: We "must take Communism away from the Communists, and take it without ambiguities or reservations. . . . " This battle cry would ring out through leftist circles for a decade.[22]

Wilson's passion for communism inspired him to spread the gospel. Karl Marx would be "turning in his grave with glee" if he could see his "prophecy . . . being fulfilled," he ecstatically wrote a friend.[23] "The liberals whom *TNR* represented had never been willing to accept Marx's assumption" that capitalism was on the verge of extinction, he told another acquaintance.[24] In subsequent articles, Wilson fired a steady barrage of invectives at Stuart Chase, Charles Beard, and other mild-mannered reformers. Their "middle class acceptance of the status quo," he sneered, bespoke "mediocre . . . political thinking."[25] At the root of the nation's malaise, Wilson probed a flaccid psyche; an ailment he decided to treat in *TNR*'s pages. While Malcolm Cowley (with whom he shared literary duties) was away for a brief period in 1930, the critic dipped mischievously into the magazine's barrel of manuscripts and plucked out an attack on Thornton Wilder by Marxist polemicist Mike Gold. Much to Cowley's dismay, the crude review of the popular novelist's *The Bridge of San Luis Rey* (which the other editor printed in its rawest form) touched off what soon became known as the "literary class war." Gold's broadside against "the prophet of the genteel Christ" signaled a wider war against the whole middle class and a society rotten to the core.[26]

Wilson, adding ammunition to the side's arsenal, followed up with a series of signed and anonymous defenses of Gold. Wilder's sentimental trash, he claimed, was a "sedative for sick Americans" obsessed with "the activities—advertising, salesmanship, manufacturing—of a precarious economic system, the condition for whose success is that they must swindle their neighbors and each other." The "bourgeois'" crass commercialism had to be destroyed and replaced with a higher system of beliefs. Wilson's feeble entreaty to the proletariat for new art forms emerged out of loyalty to his radical principles. In his heart, he really wanted "scientists, philosophers, artists, engineers" and other members of the "intelligensia" (including, no doubt, *TNR* readers, to whom his manifestos were primarily addressed) to become U.S. "brokers and pioneers." Their active "intellectual-tool making" spelled the difference between a continuing slide toward cultural inferiority and civilization's renaissance.[27]

The momentum of Wilson's arguments forced him into a corner. For all his revolutionary lingo, he revealed a remarkable disdain for the strategy and tactics of building a genuine political movement. Wilson paid lip service to the notion of a proletariat because he viewed the masses in the abstract. Their tragic stories in his reportage took an illusory appearance, as though the individuals were characters in an epic novel. After arriving in Harlan County with the Dreiser delegation to assist the miners in person, he confronted the reality of a treacherous group of party organizers and quit in a huff for being "used."[28] The radical independent privately expressed his frustrations with the conventional communist formulas with Dreiser and Waldo Frank before the trip began. A revolution, he insisted, depended on the support of white-collar workers and the identity of the "petty bourgeois with the proletariat rather than the possible class dictatorship of the proletariat over the bourgeois." [29] Having turned the classic Marxist strategy completely inside out, he boldly put forward "An Appeal to Desk Workers." In fact, Wilson's pronouncements passed judgment less on a legitimate revolution than on the disarray of the U.S. intelligentsia and his own efforts to foment unrest among its leaders.

Wilson's manifestos drew swift and furious responses. His naïveté astounded Robert Hallowell: "We don't need anyone to sell communism to America: we need *TNR* to sell America to America."[30] Stuart Chase resented his detractor's shallow sloganeering: "Well, I'll tell you, Mr. Edmund Wilson.[31] While you were dissecting Proust and other literary gentlemen—and a very pretty job you did—I was dissecting the industrial structure." Planners, Chase immodestly stated, had "found a new analysis to fit the American scene, the American temperament." Socialists had a field day. Norman Thomas was gratified to see someone else also dwell on the inadequacies of "old style progressivism."[32] Novelist, and long-time socialist, Upton Sinclair joyfully welcomed "comrade Edmund Wilson" to the fold. The acceptance of the socialist program by an "exalted high-brow editor of *The New Republic*" was an event for which he "longed, but hardly dared hope."[33] Sinclair's salutations aside, Wilson's leftward leaning by no means completed the rest of the staff's conversion to his viewpoint.

George Soule continued to hold out. In an oracular essay, "Hard-Boiled Radicals," he endeavored to extinguish Wilson's inflammatory rhetoric. His colleague's certitude about the inevitability of collapse was transporting him to an "imaginary heaven" or a "dream world." Who, he incredulously asked his colleague, would lead the "violent overthrow" and what would be its outcome? Daily reports of "hardships and repressions" from the Soviet Union cast long shadows on its great experiments. If progressives intended to advance their program,

Soule cautioned, they would have to forego their fantastic utopianism and push for changes in a "piecemeal fashion" by
stimulating "social learning." The stakes were too high to indulge in
the sort of "intensive paper activity" that was thrilling to read, but
detracted from the fundamental debate about economic reform.
Soule's warnings in "Hard-Boiled Radicals" would return to haunt
him and the magazine for years to come.[34]

Amid the fracas, the upcoming presidential election ranked low
as a priority. The editors viewed the whole affair with revulsion.
"Humpty Dumpty Hoover," they feared, was "so broken beyond
repair" that nothing could put him back together.[35] Felix
Frankfurter, in an angry letter to Bliven, labeled the magazine's
sparse coverage of the administration's abysmal policies "rotten
journalism." "As far as I know," the managing editor explained, "all
intelligent people assume the stupidity and incompetence of most
persons in high office who are directing our national activities," and
that fact was "no news."[36] For four grueling years, Hoover blindly
clung to his faith in sturdy self-reliance and adamantly opposed
federal relief for the destitute and most measures to ameliorate
their suffering. He appeared to preside over his ramshackle regime
with complete equanimity. "Even Republicans intensely dislike
him," the editors wrote, "and the campaign is guided by the
philosophy of 'don't change barrels while going over the Niagara!'"[37]

Franklin D. Roosevelt could fool no one at *TNR* either. The
editors cared little for him or his policies. Following in the footsteps
of Smith, the New York governor expanded the state's social responsibilities to fund public works, employment insurance, and the
distribution of food to the hungry. In his acceptance speech, the
nominee promised to duplicate his New York successes in
Washington and (probably borrowing the phrase from a series
Stuart Chase wrote for *TNR* by that name) he called for a "New
Deal" for U.S. citizens.[38] On the campaign trail, he spoke eloquently
about "the forgotten man at the bottom of the economic pyramid."
Had the election taken place 15 years ago, *TNR* noted, the "liberal
minded" candidate would surely have received its endorsement.[39]
Unfortunately, in a different context, Roosevelt's "liberalistic
meliorisms" barely dented the surface of a civilization in desperate
need of extensive "remodeling." The radical sound of the
Democratic platform did not hide the fact that the party was a "feeble echo of the Republicans" and had not undergone any change of
its conservative "heart" since the days of Wilson.[40]

Roosevelt, the man, still remained a mystery to the magazine.
He had, Wilson wrote, the "ambiguity of shadows."[41] Bliven thought

him "intelligent" and "personally honest" and believed his election would "be no calamity to the American people."[42] Yet, echoing a widely held view in the press at the time (Lippmann, in an oft-quoted observation, slighted Roosevelt as a "pleasant man who, without any important qualifications for the office, would very much like to be president"), Bliven dismissed him as an "untried jockey on a very lame horse."[43] Roosevelt's wealthy background roused considerable suspicion. "The Hudson River Progressive['s] . . . flaccid patrician upbringing," Wilson speculated, boded poorly for the underclass.[44] As a "son of wealth," Bliven argued, he instinctively "condescends" toward the "forgotten man"—for whom he "is no spokesman . . . by any blood brotherhood"—and gains his knowledge of "the people" only from "books."[45] Perhaps, TNR sounded the loudest note of insincerity whenever it hypocritically impugned the motives of affluent reformers or politicians. No one at the magazine ever challenged Woodrow Wilson or Theodore Roosevelt because of their wealth. For all their mythologizing about the proletariat, the editors' salaries were still being paid by wealth every bit as patrician as Roosevelt's. During these periodic outbursts of proletarianization, they chose to vilify the upper class instead of seeking common ground with the lower class.

The editors left themselves with no other choice but the dreaded Socialists. When the League for Independent Political Action—a group headed by such liberal intellectuals as Paul Douglas, John Dewey, and The Nation's Oswald Garrison Villard—abandoned efforts to form a farmer–labor party and endorsed Thomas, TNR reluctantly followed its example. The "record number of Americans," readers were advised, "who wish to register their disillusionment and disgust with both Republican Dee and Democratic Dum . . . [should] vote for a candidate who is pledged to fundamental economic reform."[46] A self-conscious editorial responded to criticism of the journal's "indecision" during the election.[47] It was true that the Socialist platform best represented the set of social programs for which TNR had fought since its founding. As in 1928, the editors' reservations centered on the dubious tactics of supporting an "agitational minority" largely comprised of middle-class, college-educated do-gooders. The Socialist party provided "an easy way for intellectuals to escape the necessity for action" and organize labor, white-collar workers, farmers, and technicians.[48] No movement, in short, was going to grow on the narrow base of TNR's readership. Faced with their quadrennial dilemma of whether to sacrifice their principles for political expediency, TNR decided to stand its ground, and, as Bliven served notice, "wait for . . . the New Party of 1936!"[49]

In the back of the editors' minds lurked an audacious alternative to the temperate Thomas. When novelist Sherwood Anderson once asked John Dos Passos to explain the difference between communists and socialists, he responded, "the communists mean it!"[50] In an extraordinarily long, 3,800-word article, a few weeks before election day, Soule lavished considerable affection on William Z. Foster, who had been an object of the editor's derision since the 1919 steel strike and the magazine's in his previous bids for the presidency.[51] Foster combined the Yankee qualities of Thoreau and Emerson, Soule argued, with the "common sense" of Henry Ford. He had the "flexible, ingenious, and practical mind" of the quintessential "engineer." The communist thus met each of his exacting qualifications to take charge of the United States.

Outside *TNR*'s pages, Cowley and Wilson joined Dos Passos, Anderson, Dreiser, and 48 other artists and intellectuals in the "League of Professional Groups for Foster and Ford."[52] Social critic and contributing editor Lewis Mumford chastised Wilson and Cowley for being involved in "so transparently opportunistic" an organization. "We must have something better than the official Communist Party in this country," he wrote in a letter sent to the two men, "even if you and I have to take off our shirts and create it."[53] Cowley was not overly eager to heed his call. "We had the feeling in those days that history and the future and the Russian Revolution were all on our side," he later reflected, "and that the little assignments we carried out were bathed in, as it were, supernal light."[54] Cowley did his part by writing "Culture and the Crisis," a campaign pamphlet addressed to U.S. "professional workers." A doctrinaire party hack rehashed his original copy so as to read like a predictable piece of propaganda. Cowley, normally a stickler for style and good grammar, swallowed his personal pride in this, the only campaign in which he ever participated, for the good of the greater cause.

The results of the 1932 election understandably baffled *TNR*. Roosevelt's sweeping victory occurred, the editors reasoned, only because the majority of citizens wished to register their dissatisfaction with Hoover. The Socialists' "distinctly disappointing" showing of some 800,000 votes confirmed their doubts about the party's popularity.[55] "Stealing Votes from the Reds" proclaimed a headline above a story on the mysterious loss of voting machine rolls in several of the nation's largest cities.[56] Vote jiggering only explained a small part of the Communists' 100,000 tally. The editors' false expectations about the leftists' performance derived from their own inaccurate reading of the political climate. "Again, for the nth time in American history," observes historian David Shannon, "radicals and reactionaries were mistaken in their predictions as to how the American people would meet the adversity."[57] Regardless of the extent of its radicalism, *TNR* realized that the winds of change were not blowing nearly so hard as first forecast.

The editors simply could not comprehend why their theories about revolution were not borne out in practice. On returning from their reportage trips, they pondered the United States' pervasive apathy. Bliven wrote about Boston:

> The most striking thing about the depression is that many of its victims are so completely without any resentment for what has happened to them—not all, of course, but thousands and thousands of them regard it as a natural calamity, beyond human control, probably beyond human rectification. . . . Now, they must blow on their hands, grin sheepishly, and go on doing the best they can.[58]

The violence Cowley observed at the Bonus Army march in Washington impressed on him the dispossessed's impotence. "No, if any revolution" occurs, he predicted, "it will come from the government itself . . . [through] a fascist movement."[59] In his reply to Wilson's manifesto, Soule asked him what sort of revolution he envisioned. As long as the "great masses of people are not being starved into revolt . . . [and] production and consumption are still going on" capitalism would not collapse, he concluded.[60] "We cannot have a revolution," he wrote in *Planned Society*, "just because a few people want it."[61] United States citizens demonstrated their resistance to "it" by not storming the White House to have off with Hoover's head nor, at the very least, casting their ballots for the radicals in November. For *TNR* to wield any influence on the national agenda whatsoever, the editors slowly began to realize that they had to recognize the precise ideological lines of demarcation the electorate had drawn.

Wilson preferred to straggle outside the liberal discourse. As a progagandist on the outer fringes of the Communist party, he felt almost no compunction about banishing himself to the radical wilderness. The telling criticism leveled against his battle cries by Chase, Mumford, and others rolled off him. Wilson, wrote Cowley, was "an innocent in politics, because he never bothered to understand how people act in groups."[62] Ever the rugged individualist, he obdurately refused to tie himself to any organized party or official dogma. His "appeals" consisted mainly of shock tactics to keep other intellectuals honest and to force them to defend their own convictions. His ranting and raving and involvement in front organizations were intended for effect. This type of paper politics, to paraphrase Soule, bordered on irrelevance. Discussions of imminent apocalypse and uprisings were used as shock tactics to raise the hackles of other intellectuals and force them to defend and reevaluate their own beliefs. His hysteria was divorced from the reality of a numb populace. Far from acting as the vanguard of the proletariat, Wilson was on the verge of forming a dictatorship of the dilettantes.

Soule suffered from a different dilemma. He had mastered many of the controversy's fine points without understanding the larger topic. The economist's fascination with the efficiency of the machine, industrialism, and technology came at the expense of political considerations. "The government of man," St.-Simon once predicted, "will be replaced by the administration of things." Outside the laboratories of his books, Soule's economic democracy could only take root in the political arena of ideas. *TNR*'s hostility toward all four parties and aloofness from the election in general hampered efforts to frame the debate and ensure the eventual enactment of Soule's agenda. With the incoming Roosevelt administration, the editors had to decide how distant they would remain from the world of practical politics.

. . . .

A Good
Radio Voice

· · · · · · · · ·
1933–36
· · · · · · · · ·

BRUCE BLIVEN DID NOT CONFORM TO THE *TNR* MOLD. He boasted neither Soule's technical knowledge nor Lippmann's and Croly's philosophical training. He found his calling in journalism early. No other editor in the magazine's history joined the staff with as much experience in the trade. Born in Emmetsburg, Iowa, he worked his way through Stanford University as a campus correspondent for *The San Francisco Bulletin* and held a regular summer job there as a cub reporter. After working as a freelance magazine writer in California, Bliven moved to New York in 1919 and started work for the *New York Globe*. While there, he broke a major story on the housing shortage in the city, which prompted Governor Smith to speed up the process of construction of new apartments. *TNR* hired Bliven as managing editor in 1923. Croly considered him a "trustworthy and able" editor whose signed articles were occasionally "very good." His "editorial work," however, he told Dorothy Elmhirst, "lacks intellectual distinction and drive." On Croly's death in 1930, Bliven took control of the magazine with Soule and assumed the bulk of editorial responsibilities and kept to a seven-day workweek. Uninterrupted, he later remembered, the two editors could produce "acceptable copy at the rate of a thousand words an hour." At times, the huge volume of work precluded the leisurely contemplation Bliven desired, and needed, to stay apace with the rush of events.[1]

The gravity of the times injected a sudden sense of urgency in *TNR*. Circulation more than doubled, from an all-time low of 12,000 in 1930 to 25,000 the next year, and slowly edged upward to 30,000 by the end of the decade. Money, as always, was tight. Although salaries remained at the same level, an annual deficit of some 10,000 dollars forced the magazine to keep close tabs on expenses.[2] (After the editors lost a book for a review, Charles Beard, in an act of supreme generosity, told them to buy a new one and deduct the cost from his payment![3])

Even at the lean rate of 2 cents per word, the back of the magazine in the late 1920s and early 1930s easily attracted the prime talent in the English language. At various points, *TNR*'s pages were graced by the poetry of W. B. Yeats, Robert Penn Warren, James Joyce, E. E. Cummings, and Archibald MacLeish. Stellar essays featured E. M. Forster on Ibsen the romantic; T. S. Eliot on the idealism of Julian Benda; and F. Scott Fitzgerald on Ring Lardner. Malcolm Cowley enjoyed the discovery of a rising star as much as a contribution from an established writer. In the middle of the decade, he befriended a severely depressed James Thurber, who had recently separated from his first wife and was living alone at the Hotel Algonquin and roaming the city in night-long taxi rides. Thurber paid back gratitude with two articles, including a whimsical remembrance of his childhood love affair with the fantasies of *The Wizard of Oz*.[4] Cowley accepted a manuscript, "Expelled from Prep School," from a young man in New England and sent a few of his fictional pieces to *The New Yorker*. Thus began John Cheever's remarkable career.[5] Another figure taken under Cowley's wing was William Faulkner, whose reputation he rehabilitated. He put together parts of the novelist's work, wrote new introductions, and brought them back into print. The subsequent reputation and Nobel prize Faulkner earned testified to *TNR*'s prominent position in U.S. culture as a principal arbiter of literary taste.

One historian has hailed the New Deal as the "second American revolution." During his first term, Franklin Roosevelt grasped the reins of government and instituted sweeping reforms on an unprecedented scale. The National Recovery Administration (NRA), Civilian Conservation Corps (CCC), Works Progress Administration (WPA), Civil Works Administration (CWA), Agriculture Adjustment Administration (AAA) and the rest of the long litany of programs and agencies typified, Arthur Schlesinger maintains, Roosevelt's monumental acts of "social mindedness." In a massive effort to humanize capitalism, the alphabet soup of reforms reached out to the unemployed, workers, farmers, the old, and children. The New Deal, William Leuchtenberg notes, "drew on a thousand books" —with particular emphasis on such theorists of new nationalism as Walter Weyl, Herbert Croly, and the Walter Lippmann of *Drift and*

Mastery. Soule's work on planning also belongs on the list. The day of reckoning for *TNR* had finally arrived. A president appeared to see the light of twentieth century liberalism and employed the full force of the state to eliminate poverty and provide all U.S. citizens with a decent standard of living.[6]

In fact, it took a long while for Roosevelt to win the hearts of most liberals. While he described himself as "a little to the left of center," he carefully avoided any political labels or ideologies that might constrain him. Roosevelt was an incorrigible experimentalist and improviser. When asked to choose between two contradictory tariff statements during the 1932 campaign, the candidate told an adviser to "weave the two together." On fiscal policy, for instance, he might well have incorporated the suggestions of budget balancers and deficit spenders into a final proposal. Roosevelt's "unsystematic" views, explains James MacGregor Burns, produced a government of the "middle way," which lurched back and forth and invariably failed to meet the left's own strict guidelines. He had neither a master plan nor a commitment to deep structural reforms. In the end, the trials and tribulations of the Roosevelt presidency reflected on the soundness of *TNR*'s own philosophy and the purpose of the magazine itself.[7]

A residue of skepticism still lingered from the campaign among the editors. "People are seeking a Messiah, some mystic and powerful savior who will put everything right," they wrote.[8] The "people" were bound to be disappointed by the president's cures for an "extremely sick civilization." Roosevelt was "the doctor called in to prescribe for the symptoms while most members of the household feverishly hope that he will not touch the underlying malady." His first and foremost tasks were to rectify the maldistribution of income, restructure the financial system, and end starvation among the unemployed. He could do no less. Every move he made was closely monitored with the knowledge that history was being made. On a visit to Washington early in the administration, an "intelligent observer" explained the following to Bliven:

> Two things to remember. First, that what is now being done can never be undone. If the New Deal succeeds we can't go back; if it fails, we can't—no matter who wants to or how much. The command is forward, from now on, and the movement is certainly toward the left.[9]

The pendulum was not swinging, the editor soon learned, as far to the left as originally anticipated. The epithet—"recovery without reconstruction"—summed up *TNR*'s grievances against the New Deal.[10] Capitalism was too broken, they relentlessly argued, to be patched up with shallow reforms.

The National Recovery Agency's short, unhappy life exposed the pitfalls of the New Deal and the magazine's interpretation of it. In 1933, the much-ballyhooed experiment drew up some 750 codes to promote fair competition for business, bring about orderly prices, and guarantee a reasonable work week and a living wage to labor. Section 7a of the bill granted workers the right to organize and bargain collectively. With great fanfare, the NRA's director Hugh Johnson, a former cavalry man, permitted employers who cooperated to display the blue eagle—the NRA emblem—in every conceivable place from store windows to cereal boxes. Gigantic blue eagle parades were sponsored to whip up enthusiasm. The NRA accomplished much of what it set out to do: it gave 2 million jobs to workers, stopped deflation, established a national pattern of maximum hours and minimum wages, and abolished child labor and sweatshops. On the whole, however, its disorganization and carelessness proved to be its undoing. The exercise in self-government gave large industries disproportionate control to the detriment of small businesses and relied primarily on the good faith of employers to enforce the labor provisions, rendering them ineffectual. By the end of its two-year tenure in 1934, the NRA was engulfed in a storm of protest from the right and left. Before Congress and the president could extend it, the Supreme Court declared the agency unconstitutional, and it went out of existence.

TNR assailed the NRA from the outset. The blue bird adorning the upper right corner of its cover did not deter the editors from assailing the "half-hearted" fiasco.[11] Poorly designed and hastily conveived, the melange of policies surrendered "economic life of the country" to "reactionary profiteers."[12] Watching the "Washington Kaleidoscope" go round, Bliven lamented the way the NRA was "working at cross-purposes." Soule reiterated his concern, while recommending a large volume of total production and stepped-up purchasing power as the best remedies.[13] Labor also received short shrift. As long as the toothless section 7a remained open to flagrant violation by antiunion capitalists, Bliven argued, the recovery program would "go down in history as a fraud and failure."[14]

As the chief of the NRA, the volatile Hugh Johnson sat atop a powder keg. Bliven, for one, thought him the wrong man for the wrong job: "All the church-boy methods of the patriotic 'drive,' with window-stickers," he reported from Washington, "four-minute speeches, patriotic boycotts of slackers, and all the rest. General Johnson hears the time bomb ticking, even in his sleep."[15] Frustrated by their inabilities to organize, workers went on strike in major industries in 1934. Johnson's sweeping accusations of subversion and treason against the participants removed any of *TNR*'s doubts that he was a "fascist." The state's subjugation of the labor movement at the hands of "profit-making employers" bore a frighteningly close resemblance, the editors reminded readers, to the abhorrent tactics of Hitler and Mussolini. "Crack Down on the General," they urged in a piece calling for his dismissal.[16] If the irony of lowering the boom on the general was not lost on them, the editors kept it a secret. Unbeknownst to them, the downfall of NRA and Johnson had serious repercussions for liberals.

TNR was caught in the classic progressive conundrum. The editors were still striving to resolve the Crolian dilemma between Hamiltonian means and Jeffersonian ends. The NRA's corporatism and resistance toward organized labor actually approximated Mussolini's fascism (and, ironically enough, the proposals Croly outlined in *Promise* for bringing unruly unions under government control). And yet, liberals had not enjoyed such an opportunity to harness the state's power since World War I. Soule, of all people, should have appreciated the NRA's efforts, albeit haphazard, at coordination and planning. He also remembered the war's darker side. The patriotic hoopla of NRA parades conjured up memories of virulent nationalism. When it came time to put a diluted version of Soule's ideas into action, he hesitated out of respect for the liberties that were suppressed in the postwar clampdown. In the wrong hands, government could just as easily become a tool of political oppression as economic freedom—particularly in such turbulent times.

TNR actually feared seeing its policies carried out by the wrong people. "Without the 'thin red line' of experts who have at heart the welfare of labor and consumer," the New Deal flirted with a potential disaster on the magnitude of "the old anarchy" or a "capitalist dictatorship."[17] After the NRA's expiration, the editors demanded that government (presumably under the executive branch) ignore the Supreme Court's ruling, take matters into its own hands, and do its own lawmaking. An obituary, with a heavy scent of Soule, called for a corps of "experts" to establish a "Supreme Planning Council" to direct the nation's social and economic management. Its regulations would "be imposed and supported . . . by the economic power of the organized masses."[18] The uneven power flow between the masses and experts tested his allegiance to the democratic values he was, in principle, promoting. The ideas he so cherished on paper posed formidable risks.

Unemployment continued to weigh heavily on the magazine's "mind." By 1933, 12 million still did not have jobs. "The unemployed are still human beings," the editors insisted. Either the administration had to find an "intelligent method" of helping "workless men and women" or let them degenerate into "pauperism."[19] The magazine assessed the administration's relief policies with a mixture of sympathy and exasperation. In late 1933, Bliven reported from Boston on the "complete and unqualified success" of the Civilian Works Administration and marveled at the new airports, schools, and muncipal golf courses.[20] The creation of 4 million jobs in minor construction finally heralded the government's intention to intervene in the private economy and start providing work. What nettled Bliven was the "temporary stop-gap" nature of these measures. Only a mammoth federal public works program could possibly save all the "down and out." Roosevelt was generally in favor of humanitarian assistance, but, on the termination of the CWA in 1935, he backed off, fearing that a class of reliefers on the government payroll might "become a habit with the country" and suggest a "permanent depression."[21]

TNR did not treat such "stupidity and blindness" lightly. Roosevelt's relief projects, such as the Civilian Conservation Corps, Federal Relief Administration, and Public Works Administration, showed how irresponsibly he was "muddling through" the issue of the unemployed.[22] Essential relief was being clogged in a sea of red tape. The U.S. failure to adopt a national plan for unemployment insurance, as practically every other industrialized nation had done, prevented a full-scale recovery. The president had to jettison his training in the classical economics of budget balancing and take a lesson in the new Keynesian school of pump priming. Huge public works, the editors explained, validated the debt by stimulating the economy and creating additional jobs.[23] After two conferences between Roosevelt and the British economist in the spring of 1934, TRB, in his Washington Notes column, expected to see future "preachments" on the dangers of debts go out "the White House Window."[24] Perhaps then the government could bring back prosperity once and for all.

Midway through the first term, the magazine vented its rage at the New Deal's "dismal" record.[25] Roosevelt, for his efforts, was compared to a "football quarterback who decides each play on the impulse of the moment." He deserved credit for skillfully weaning "influential businessmen away from their more nonsensical obsessions," aiding farmers with payments through the Agricultural Adjustment Act, and creating the CWA to prevent people from starving.[26] He deserved abuse for practically everything else. Responsibility for a "pitifully low standard of life for many millions of Americans" rested with the president. "Left, Right, Left,'" he stumbled, vainly trying to appease all factions instead of pursuing bolder taxing and spending policies.[27] Taxes on incomes and corporate profits could be channeled into such social purposes as financing CWA and other public works the administration had allowed to peter out. The "millions" of farmers, laborers, and consumers "left in poverty" required immediate attention. Even a "halfway program of social insurance, a certain amount of government subsidy in housing, [and] a trade union movement" would put the United States on a par with most other industrial nations. Roosevelt's lukewarm "liberal capitalism" allowed the United States to lag far behind the rest of the civilized world's advanced socialism.[28] The editors were growing restless.

In 1934, George Soule released his pent-up frustrations in an odd book, *The Coming American Revolution*. By handing the "system back to the old rulers," he predicted, the New Deal was sowing the seeds of its own destruction. A "prolonged period of turmoil and scarcity" would ensue, he wrote in probably the most impassioned prose of his life, followed by "terrible disconfort . . . and meanness. . . . This will not be Utopia." Soule sifted through the Communist party, the scattered fascist movements across the nation, and all the "raw materials lying about" for a logical sequence of events, climaxing in the collapse of the ruling class, but came up empty-handed. In truth, he expected and envisioned a revolution of another, peaceful sort. Capitalism would have to "surrender to social planning." Just as feudalism inevitably became extinct, so "capitalism must in the end give way to the life of working classes and socialism." Social planning, under the auspices of a "stronger central government," could collectivize the "important powers of business" and mobilize workers, farmers, professors, and white-collar workers. Despite the radical tinge of his arguments, the specific components of his programs for a planned society (which he outlined in his previous book and each week in the magazine) differed slightly, in toto, from the basic thrust of the New Deal. Soule only wished, for the good of U.S. social welfare, that the president would take bolder action and resolutely lead the nation on a straighter course. Soule's "new society," he poignantly concluded his book, would consist of "men and women in a new bond of comradeship setting forth on still another voyage to the unknown."[29] The uncertainty of the editor's own destination portended ominously for liberal theorists. The substitution of irate rhetoric for substantive proposals provided the nation no new direction and permitted the president to follow his own course.

Bliven also seemed lost at sea at the time. In a 20-year *TNR* anthology, he paid tribute to the "one million words Croly wrote "during his association with the paper" but deigned to print only a few—an inconsequential piece on the Russian Revolution, which, at best, was a minor footnote in the founding editor's catalogue.[30] "Most of his articles," Bliven apologized, "are already so dated that their reproduction here is inappropriate." Despite this slight, the editors were not yet prepared to consign one of the pioneers of modern U.S. liberalism to the dustbin of history. Much of his wisdom was resurrected for reflections on "Liberalism Twenty Years After," a special note in 1935. In light of the troubled times, Croly's faith in the "precious human values" of democracy and "dignity of the individual" was worth bearing in mind. The essence of political and economic liberty in the twentieth-century industrial state, as he stressed, had evolved from a Smithian and Millsian hands-off philosophy to a powerful interventionism. "Absolute liberty" in all societies, however, was "impossible." Because U.S. citizens lived in neither a "Greek city-state or New England town meeting," they had to be willing to delegate considerably more political authority than they were traditionally accustomed to delegating in exchange for guarantees of economic security. This goal would only be reached with extreme care. Unchecked, social planning concentrated excessive power in a board or body of political executives to "such an extent that virtual dictatorship" might be "established." In recognition of the pitfalls of Soule's theories, the magazine, in these rare moments, appeared at odds with itself. Moreover, it noted, liberals might ponder the gradual, complex process of social change throughout U.S. history and not place all their hopes in the single basket of Roosevelt Democrats, the progressive Republicans, the Socialists, the Communists, the Workers' Party, or an incipient farmer–labor organization. The virtue of a "transvalued liberalism," a new term the editors coined to mark this occasion of hand-wringi..g, lay in its tolerance for the vast array of opinion among those who were "moving toward a collective society."[31] Tied to no group or set of doctrines, *TNR* was toeing its own independent line that increasingly isolated it from other liberals in and outside the administration.

Each successive phase of the New Deal failed to pass the magazine's exacting muster. The handling of unemployment continued to draw the heaviest fire. Bliven lashed out at Interior

Secretary Harold Ickes for his unsteady direction of the Public Works Administration. Rather than testing Keynesian policy and embarking on a vast public works program to speed up the recovery, Ickes played "magical hocus-pocus."[32] By the beginning of 1935, 10 million were unemployed and barely eked out an existence. "It is a confused makeshift, a minim to stave off mass starvation while the government waits for old-fashioned revival by old-fashioned capitalisms," the editors despaired of "Roosevelt's new order."[33] The new-fangled economics they had in mind required drastic refurbishing of the economy and the adaptation of socialist measures.

In 1935, the president underwent a change of heart and launched the "Second New Deal," which included the most ambitious public employment program in history. The Works Progress Administration created some 3.5 million jobs building parks, schools, and hospitals. A man's "morale" must be preserved and "hunger is not debatable" were two favorite dictums of Harry Hopkins, the head of WPA.[34] *TNR*, never a journal to shy away from a good fight, wanted to debate. The unemployed's self-esteem and hunger were not the sole issues. In less than a year, the editors demanded the liquidation of "the scandalous WPA." The "mess" was becoming "more malodorous every day."[35] Reports trickled in from every part of the country of "outrageous squandering of money, of graft, and political favoritism." The "erratic" behavior of the disorganized agencies often prevented the aid from reaching the victims, thus depriving millions of the humane standard of living to which they were entitled. Less than 6 percent of the projects were for white-collar workers, "despite the desperate need of many persons in this group." The WPA was just a "bad idea." The editors, not surprisingly, claimed they had some better ones. A "national planning commission" would establish an "economy of abundance" by coordinating reports, objectives, and specific measures. In addition, a permanent, nationwide employment service (a plan that had been floating around since *TNR*'s first issue) might be founded to match jobs with the unemployed. The wisest policy of all, however, would enable the federal government to bear a larger burden of relief out of taxes and thereby "uniformly" distribute the country's wealth and earning power.[36] Once again, the improvisatory nature of the New Deal conflicted with *TNR*'s rational, orderly blueprints.

Readers might well have benefited from adding to their knowledge of the public works squabble by reading other publications. The WPA's numerous defects were readily apparent. It cared for only 3 out of the 10 million unemployed and let many aged, crippled, and sick fall through the cracks.[37] Interminable delays and boondoggles hampered relief in heavily stricken regions. The administration's refusal to reallocate the national income through sharp tax increases wasted a propitious opportunity. Yet the melancholy chapters *TNR* presented comprised only part of the book about relief. On a purely practical level, the WPA harnessed the nation's vast human resources for productive enterprises and mitigated the sufferings of millions formerly on the dole. The wretched breadlines and soup kitchens Wilson and Bliven described a few years earlier had all but disappeared. The WPA's psychological successes could not be measured solely in numbers. The United States' sagging spirits received a sorely needed lift from the government's tacit promise to provide the downtrodden the "stake in society" Weyl and Lippmann (in his earliest books) deemed so noble. The surge in pride and general sense of esprit de corps among participants in many of these programs accounted for their overwhelming public support and continuance throughout the 1930s. The president "saved my home" and "gave me a job," declared a typical beneficiary.[38] On the rare occasion that they broached the subject of the nation's changing sense of itself, the editors grudgingly admitted the widespread enthusiasm for the Civilian Conservation Corps and National Youth Administration (early domestic versions of the Peace Corps for young men and women). Few programs, in fact, helped heal the nation's wounded pysche as effectively. But praise at the magazine was kept to a minimum for fear, apparently, that it might be misconstrued as wholesale endorsement of the New Deal.

TNR seemed in no mood to compromise its agenda. From afar, the Social Security Act of 1935, which Roosevelt regarded as the "supreme achievement" of the New Deal, marked a "definite advance" toward the "collective responsibility" for the "aged, widows and orphans and the blind."[39] On closer inspection, Soule correctly pointed out, the inadequate apparatus was the only welfare system in the "civilized" world that took funds out of workers' earnings—as in the form of a compulsory saving scheme—instead of taxing the wealthy and established no set of national standards for unemployment insurance. Twenty percent of the labor force, including farm workers and domestics, received no coverage at all. In due course, the system was liberalized to extend benefits to a larger share of people. Looking back several decades later, Cowley hailed Social Security, for all its faults, as "the most important, and revolutionary, of all the new measures."[40] During the period, the term "revolution" was rarely used in the context of the New Deal at *TNR*. If any revolution were to occur, it had to follow *TNR*'s design.

The patchwork of reforms fell far short of the editors' grandiose plans for a social democracy. Their affection for the British model had hardly diminished since Croly's Anglophile days. Each piecemeal program in the United States failed to measure up to its sterling counterpart overseas. Britain, for all its shortcomings, at least offered a humane nationalized system for health insurance and medicine.[41] In the United States, meanwhile, the PWA authorized a tiny fraction of the 1 million houses built in Britain. The whole notion of "security for Americans," Soule argued, hinged on "idle dreams" of a comprehensive social program and attendant recovery.[42] The magazine's continual quest for paradises elsewhere led it toward foreign problems and away from the real problems back home.

One of the magazine's primary aspirations actually had a chance of being fulfilled. The NRA, though an utter fiasco, ultimately redeemed itself by planting the seeds for a rapid growth in unions. The New Deal's "most valuable and permanent contribution," the editors wrote in its initial stages, "might turn out to be a strong labor movement."[43] Purely as an exercise in "education," the government's encouragement raised workers' consciousness and stirred them to act.[44] Troops were called out in 16 states and several men were killed during a outbreak of strikes in 1934 and 1935. Minneapolis witnessed a bloody altercation between an armed police convoy and city truck drivers, which resulted in the shooting of 67 men, 2 of whom died. Dock workers called a general strike in San Francisco and engaged in savage battles with authorities. By the time the last bricks, stones, clubs, and tear gas fell on the streets at the end of "Bloody Thursday," two strikers had lost their lives and scores of others were injured. In Toledo, the "Little Detroit," the manufacturers of autos and auto parts slashed wages and workforce and refused to bargain with employees. The moment a phalanx of armed company guards erected a roadblock around the plant, violence erupted. Rioters overturned cars and set them on fire, providing an excuse for the Ohio National Guard to intervene and put their tear gas bombs, firehoses, and rifles to use. Two strikers died and 25 were injured. *TNR* viewed the "civil war" and was aghast: "The sorry American scene in Toledo finds its setting in broken promises of the New Deal."[45]

The passage of the Wagner Act of 1935 rekindled hopes for labor. Workers were finally given protection against discrimination for joining or belonging to a union. Employers were ordered to recognize and deal with labor representatives and faithfully engage in collective bargaining. The law also prohibited businesses from instituting such "unfair" practices as company unions (an old ruse to trick workers into believing they had protection), the blacklist, and yellow-dog contracts. A permanent independent agency, the National Labor Relations Board, provided the tools for enforcement. "Heaven knows" it was "not a revolution," the editors patiently explained. But "rulers of industry" beware, they warned. "To them, the social world does not change," they noted. "Dictatorship by capital is the only formula they understand, they all cling to it, though the old order crashes about their ears."[46] This crashing slowly began to reverberate through *TNR*'s pages.

Labor's struggle crystallized the dominant theme of the times. It was a battle, the magazine announced, for power between "working men and women" and the capitalists' "limited monarchy."[47] The rapid rise in membership of the mining, clothing, and garment trades attested to the industrial unions' massive appeal among the unorganized. Their inalienable right to collective bargaining and the open shop—the instruments of leverage against their employers—had been championed in the magazine and the editors' books since the dawning of the progressive era. The social tumult of the Great Depression magnified the importance of unions in redressing age-old imbalances under capitalism. At long last, a generally sympathetic government and public created the perfect climate for sliding the weights on the proverbial scale of justice from the plutocracy (to use Weyl's favorite term of two decades before) to the workers. The editors hailed labor's right to organize and bargain collectively as the "Roosevelt Doctrine."[48] Of all the New Deal reforms, the government's mobilization of "the political power of the masses" promoted the purest progressive ideals. "The fight against economic royalists is the real issue in 1936," *TNR* proclaimed.[49] The real issue in the campaign year emerged as the paramount one through the remainder of the decade. Organized labor held the key to any type of "industrial democracy."

TNR eagerly plunged into the battle against the reactionary opposition to social reform. The nature of this beast the editors relentlessly flogged assumed a variety of shapes and sizes besides those of capitalists. Bliven labeled Father Charles Coughlin, the Roman Catholic radio priest and ferocious foe of what he called the "Pagan Deal," a "demagogue."[50] "Full of sound and fury," Coughlin's denunciations of socialism and communism and empty populist rhetoric channeled "off the hopes and resentments of the citizens into a foggy cloud of words." At first glance, Senator Huey Long's flamboyant dress—white flannels, pink neck tie, and orange handkerchief—and roguish behavior—a fondness for earthy humor and his sobriquet "Kingfish"—might prompt an amused observer to dismiss him, as the editors put it, as a "clown" or "jester."[51] Likewise, his seemingly ludicrous "Share Our Wealth" scheme had to be the brainchild, in Bliven's words, of a "naive utopian." Long could not be disregarded quite so simply. For, he, as did Coughlin, excelled at manipulating the fears of the aggrieved; namely the lower-middle class of poor farmers, small merchants, and skilled white working men. Many of them bought the goods the Louisiana senator was selling. Herein lay the danger of demagogues so hungry for power and Roosevelt's job that they would stop at nothing and, Bliven speculated, "spearhead . . . a fascist movement that would seek to preserve capitalism in its dying struggle by enslaving the working masses of the people as they would have been enslaved in Germany and Italy."[52] *TNR* shed nary a tear on the assassination of Long, this proponent of "Hitlerism" in 1935, but mourned over the "turmoil" he so successfully exploited.

Aside from rabble-rousers, Roosevelt had to fend off assaults from *TNR*'s brethren in the press. Bliven called the scurrilous stories about the president "one of the great national phenomenon of modern times."[53] The predominantly Republican publishers and editors in the business hated "FDR not on patriotic grounds, but pocketbook reasons."[54] Bliven drafted an open letter to William Randolph Hearst, the czar of a long chain of newspapers, suggesting he retire from "active journalism. Why not turn over the reins to someone else and enjoy the sunset years? You might relax and travel a little, look at the world's most expensive pieces of art and perhaps buy a few?"[55] The "cruel" anti-Rooseveltism Hearst disseminated disgraced his profession. "Fascism" appeared in the unlikeliest places in papers—even the funnies! A lengthy, thoughtful editorial appeared in 1935 exposing "Hooverism" in the "Little Orphan Annie" comic strip.[56] Daddy Warbucks, Annie's guardian, was made a "mouthpiece of extreme reactionary doctrines" and "virulent" attacks on the labor movement and the New Deal. The "great, big, lovable . . . benevolent capitalist" was having a terrible time controlling a cabal of union organizers named Claude Claptrap, Horatio Jack, and Ronald Renegade. To Daddy and his loyal employees' relief, a group of workers, "in a burst of grateful pride," beat up the union leaders and tarred and feathered them. The story's patent moral concerned the administration's reform legislation to promote unions and thereby "ruin capitalism." Published in over 100 papers nationwide, the comic strip was no laughing matter. With a circulation of some 25,000, *TNR* could not easily counter "propaganda" that went into millions of U.S. homes.

Conservatives arrayed against Roosevelt with well stocked arsenals. Loud "thunder on the right" emanated from such traditional "legions of unregenerate capitalists," the editors wrote, as the National Association of Manufacturers and the U.S. Chamber of Commerce.[57] Equipped with full coffers and extensive organizations, they set out to sabotage the New Deal at every turn in the road. Al Smith, who felt personally betrayed by Roosevelt, and other conservative Democrats teamed up with Du Pont and General Motors executives to found the American Liberty League in an effort to revive the classic value of self-reliance and combat the "imported, autocratic, Asiatic, Socialist party of Karl Marx and FDR."[58] In a three-part series, Soule peered behind the facade at the menace posed by this consortium of big-business interests.[59] Roosevelt's fiercest detractors, of course, used the Republican party as the permanent base of their operations. The "GOP Bourbons," *TNR's* favorite term of derision, had become "the happy hunting ground for special privilege" and vanguard of the Darwinian philosophy of "making the rich so much richer . . . that the poor will get more crumbs from the table."[60] The Republicans' inveterate hostility to federal government and subservience to unrepentant capitalists foredoomed its obsolescence in the modern age. In 1936, the magazine politely excused Alf Landon and his party for "automatically cross[ing]" themselves out at election time.[61]

TNR's indictment of Roosevelt's implacable enemies glossed over a salient point. He gained handsome political capital playing off them. A genuine "Roosevelt revolution" could not be judged by the self-serving "scum and froth" among members of "country clubs, businesses and banking executives."[62] The editors stewed in their frustrations watching conservatives in a state of frenzy over reforms that, in the long term, preserved capitalism and protected the "ruling economic powers." Thus, the ostensibly radical rhetoric of Roosevelt's 1936 state of the union speech—replete with references to the "resplendent economic aristocracy" and "entrenched greed"—rankled the editors no end. Roosevelt—the consummate politician—once explained to an aide, Bliven later recalled, that he "welcomed critical comments to prove to right-wing nemeses that he was no mere tool of the left."[63] This adroit posturing allowed him to push for programs in the relative security of the middle ground and offend as few people as possible.

The editors despised the frivolous game of politics because it constrained them. Roosevelt's uncanny ability to elude simultaneously the pressures of the right and left, and convincingly emerge as the president of all the people, was the secret of his political genius.

The loss of a sacred liberal cause or two in the shuffle hardly cost him at all, except at such places as *TNR* where political purity counted the most. Even if he had subscribed to *TNR*'s philosophy, the reactionary onslaught he continually faced would have tugged him back toward the center. Early in the magazine's history, Croly's brush with the socialist watchdog Ogden Mills and his National Civic Federation demonstrated the difficulties of veering too far toward the left. The same Mills reappeared again in the 1930s to render his special services to the Liberty League. The high decibel of Mills' and the Republicans' censures, of course, reached the White House. These conservative coalitions against Roosevelt were a force to be reckoned with, and an inescapable reality of U.S. political life. *TNR* preferred to ignore it rather than modify its proposals.

Instead of rallying to the Democrats' defense at election time, the editors plotted yet another scheme to create a new party to their own liking. In mid-1935, they employed flowery Crolian language of "brotherhood . . . companionship and mutuality" to add some passion to an otherwise bland call for a "movement" to achieve "collective ownership and management" and a planned economy.[64] Workers, it was reasoned, would not stand for a president who threw "bones to . . . [them] and pieces of meat to employers."[65] "Surely," there was a "void to be filled by a populist socialist or labor party . . . [of] workers . . . farmers, teachers, technicians, white collar workers."[66] Their confidence was short-lived. When midwestern progressives decided to back Roosevelt and no such organization materalized, *TNR* dejectedly assessed the sorry state of affairs and looked foward to 1938 and 1940. By then, the "millions of workers" union leaders had hoodwinked into voting Democratic would grow disgusted with their static conditions and desert the party in droves. At that juncture, the editors reasoned, in a typical fit of wishful thinking, that perpetual "pleading for a realignment" based on a farmer–labor party would finally bear fruit. In the meantime, they decided to content themselves with waiting out the imminent Democratic victory. Living in the future complicated their decisions in the present.[67]

Ironically, *TNR* enjoyed fairly close ties to the administration. Several members of Roosevelt's brain trust, an informal council of academic aides and architects for New Deal programs, had collaborated with the magazine before going to Washington.[68] In 1928, at the behest of Croly, Rexford Tugwell, later one of the most important and liberal New Dealers, became a contributing editor and wrote editorial comments—an honor he likened to "accession to the college of Cardinals."[69] Two of F.D.R.'s biggest power brokers,

Harry Hopkins and Harold Ickes, read *TNR* religiously and borrowed ideas from it freely.[70] Their elaborate rationales for administration policies periodically appeared as letters and articles. Tugwell wrote eloquently about "the meaning of the Greenbelt towns," the administration's innovative pilot projects in low-cost housing.[71] "Ours is a venturesome and experimental habit of mind," he wrote in an article on national planning and critique of the magazine's "naive approaches to public policy."[72] "I have neither the time nor the inclination to make replies to all the irresponsible" critics of the PWA, Ickes told the editors in response to that week's attack on his agency. Three months later, he managed to find a few idle moments to answer the "feet-on-desk critics" of his federal housing program, proving how seriously New Dealers did take the magazine.[73] In one advertisement, the magazine even boasted that visitors to the White House noticed copies of *TNR* on Roosevelt's desk.[74] In light of his reputation in its pages, the invocation of the president's name for promotional purposes showed the extent of the magazine's willingness to exploit his popularity for the sake of a few extra subscriptions. Business was business.

At the risk of losing friends in high places, the editors kept a safe distance from the administration. Soule was offered several posts in the New Deal, but he declined all of them.[75] The brain trust would have appeared to match the "scientifically trained minds of impartial experts" perfectly.[76] Whatever liberal advice the president received from the prestigious group, *TNR* gathered, was canceled out by its conservative members, such as Bernard Baruch. Had such a mythical board of like-minded liberals existed, Roosevelt would probably have "ignored" them anyway. The editors had upheld a different set of journalistic principles from the time of Wilson's presidency when Lippmann and Croly periodically hobnobbed with Colonel House and his boss. In retrospect, the Versailles debacle and Red Scare had compelled them to reappraise the wisdom of that relationship. Some 15 years later, Bliven and Soule scrupulously placed a higher premium on their intellectual independence than access to the White House. At cocktail parties, Roosevelt's principle troubleshooter, Tommy "the Cork" Corcoran, bitterly objected to the magazine's unfavorable coverage of the New Deal.[77] Ickes, in a letter sent to various newspapers and *TNR* columnist Heywood Broun, expressed his exasperation with the "failure" of "progressive commentators to bestow a few compliments . . . [on] a liberal administration." "Whenever a liberal editor wants to reassure himself of his own liberalism," he drolly noted, "he searches for a fly-speck upon the record of one of the few liberals in public office and proceeds to magnify it until it is as big as the side of a barn."[78]

No matter how staunchly his lieutenants defended him, *TNR* could not bring itself to endorse Roosevelt or his policies in 1936. In a "Balance Sheet of the New Deal," the liabilities far offset the assets.[79] The president deserved credit for reducing much of the Depression's misery and keeping Republicans and fellow reactionaries at bay. He earned the editors' enmity for failing to maintain a "secure abundance and rais[e] the material and cultural well-being of the people." His "inconsistent" policies had not increased the real incomes of farmers and wage earners nor boosted production and employment. As an "accident of leadership," he pretended to "please everybody" without doing much for anyone. The New Deal was a "reasonable start" but was marred by "promises and pretensions" and outright "blundering." By contrast, the socialists' and communists' sweeping social agenda proved, the editors noted (paraphrasing Sinclair Lewis), they "undoubtedly mean what they say."[80] Teetering on a tangled tightrope, *TNR* advised readers to cast their ballots for the president in close states and pull the lever for Norman Thomas or communist Earl Browder in states leaning toward Roosevelt. On the local and congressional level, *TNR* also advised that voters might consider bypassing the two major parties to send Washington a signal. Such token protests, it was hoped, would send the president a message and possibly pave the way for the eventual formation of a third party in 1940. *TNR*'s idiosyncratic notion of ticket splitting succinctly captured the essence of the editors' ambivalence about Roosevelt and the New Deal.

The magazine's general contempt for his programs colored its views of the man. The editors felt uneasy about warming up to him largely because he was not one of their own. His "staccato" intellectual habits, biographer James MacGregor Burns maintains, consisted of skimming the newspapers.[81] He instinctively trusted his common sense, historian Paul Conkin concurs, and rebelled against "formal thought" or the sort of "coherent set of ideas" Woodrow Wilson postulated.[82] *TNR* regularly disparaged Roosevelt's mental capacities as shallow and wondered what all the fuss was about. His enormous popularity among U.S. citizens never ceased to amaze the editors. Two months after the president's inauguration, Bliven traveled south to evaluate the New Deal's impact on "the land of cotton." While there, he was thunderstruck by Roosevelt's "hold on the affection of the commonwealth and the feeling that he is concerned for poor people, his geniality. The excellent appearance he makes—the talking newsreels and, above all, his fine radio voice and simplicity and friendliness with which he has on so many occasions talked over national affairs with the whole population in a neighborly way.[83]

Through the balance of Roosevelt's first term, no one at the magazine ever elaborated on this theme again or sought to explain the phenomenon. TRB, in a forgettable "Washington Notes" column, paid homage to the president's "effective" adaptation of "the many devices available to the White House occupant for the nursing and nourishment of a favorable popular sentiment." The secret to Roosevelt's success was not attributable to simply an adroit public relations strategy, however.

The magazine had fallen victim to its own history. The chastening experience with Wilson left a bitter residue in its pages for two generations. By the peak of the Great Depression, liberal intellectuals had trouble regaining their composure sufficiently to understand the urge, as Bliven described it in 1932, for a "savior." The horrifying spectacle of Mussolini and Hitler reinforced their fears of the cult of personality and *TNR*'s resolve to avoid becoming, as Bliven later boasted, a "hero worshipper."[84] Carried to its extreme, this independence tended to warp the magazine's outlook on politics by completely removing it from the human realm of politics and artifically separating the man from his acts. (Twenty-four years before, the vibrant Bull Moose movement had coalesced around a dynamic leader—with whom *TNR* also had a falling out—with the same name and attributes.) On a purely personal level, the abundant affability and charisma Franklin projected in soothing fireside chats and heartwarming speeches translated into support from millions of U.S. citizens, which gained him intangible, but significant, political rewards. He, in large measure, personified Croly's "saint and a hero" and accounted for the New Deal's enormous public approval.

The nation's ailing condition at the close of the first term confirmed many of *TNR*'s worst fears about the New Deal. The magazine's cherished "economy of abundance" had yet to materialize. Eight million U.S. citizens were still without jobs and construction continued to lag. The New Deal's patchwork of reforms, as the editors argued repeatedly, bolstered the conservative status quo and foreclosed the possibility of replacing an archaic and inefficient capitalist system with an advanced social democracy. The ideas of a collectivist society or planned economy, William Leuchtenberg wrote, "had never been in the cards."[85] Roosevelt faltered between one set of stopgap measures and another, as *TNR* explained, rather than adopting a bolder strategy to renovate thoroughly a dilapidated system. The editors rightfully condemned him for not taking stronger action to achieve a full economic recovery. The "transvalued liberalism" they propagated hewed to no party line nor doctrine, giving them the freedom to form their judgments about the effectiveness of Roosevelt's program and advance their own.

TNR preserved its rigorous objectivity at a high cost. At times, editors appeared too skeptical even to admit the accomplishments of the New Deal. Since 1933, unemployment had dropped by about 4 million, and 6 million jobs had been created. Business activity and corporate profits had risen and industrial failures decreased. Harking back to the period several decades afterwards, Cowley wished he had perceived the nation's changing mood.[86] Had Bliven made additional trips to the hinterlands to do additional reportage pieces after 1933, he would have seen that the sense of a "common we" felt between U.S. citizens and their president extended to other regions besides the South. Edmund Wilson or another gifted practitioner of the genre might well have pondered the significance of coal miners' carrying F.D.R.'s picture on the picketline and hanging it in their homes.[87] He failed to understand the phenomenon for the same reason apocalyptic reportage pieces became unfashionable by the mid-1930s and ceased to appear in *TNR*. Why did the people vote for a "pleasant smile and a good radio voice?" the editors asked after Roosevelt's landslide victory.[88] Roosevelt was reelected handily because the electorate instinctively blocked out fears of impending doom and lapped up his dulcet messages. The editors' crude condescension reflected poorly not only on their political acumen and instincts, but also on their views of human nature. The vast realignment of labor, farmers, and the professional class that *TNR* had envisioned for so long within the framework of a third party finally occurred in the form of the New Deal coalition—and the editors missed it. Their celestial aloofness during the election distanced them further than ever from the secular world of politics. At some point, they had to discontinue carping from afar and work with what they were given.

. . . .

Half a Loaf

. . . .

1937–40

. . . .

IN THE MIDDLE OF THE DEPRESSION, *TNR* LOST A DEAR friend. Dorothy Straight Elmhirst decided to move the magazine out of the fabled brownstone in Chelsea to consolidate it with three other publications she and Leonard Elmhirst owned—*Asia, Antiques*, and *Theater Arts*— under one roof. Etienne and Lucie, the butler and cook, retired to Italy, and the platform tennis courts in the backyard, where the staff had spent summer afternoons drinking Tom Collinses, were torn down. The nicked and scratched Windsor chairs, threadbare carpets, and old lazy Susan Croly had used to spin manuscripts around the conference table to other editors were discarded. The new modern offices designed by the architect William Lescaze were furnished with sleek leather and mahogany furniture, resembling, Cowley recalled, "the tourist-class lounge of an ocean liner." A party was thrown to celebrate the change of venue. The boisterous festivities were capped by John Dewey's collision with a table—and the sound of 50 glasses crashing to the floor—and an artist who vomited in the bathroom while his wife held his shoulders. Toasting the future, the staff drowned itself in a sea of spirits in remembrance of things past. The magazine's last link to the light-hearted, carefree Greenwich Village days was severed. "After spending so many years downtown among rebels," Cowley reflected with a pang of nostalgia, he felt alien in his subdued environs in the upper reaches of Manhattan. Their revels now ended, the editors soberly confronted the day's grim realities.[1]

On the heels of his tremendous victory, Roosevelt resumed his duties with renewed vigor and purpose. In his inaugural speech on

January 20 and annual message of February 6, 1937, he sounded a clarion call to aid "one third of a nation ill-housed, ill-clad, ill-nourished" and continue the New Deal's unfinished business. The administration acted resolutely to expand public housing, assist tenant farmers, and broaden social security coverage. Labor was awarded a comprehensive wages and hours bill, a hallmark of social reform in U.S. history. The slow climb out of the Depression was abruptly delayed in late 1937 when a deep recession again wreaked havoc on the nation and put millions more out of work. Once more, the government poured vast sums into the WPA, CCC, and similar public works projects to relieve the distress and fuel a recovery. Additional social reforms were enacted to provide vital services to the neediest in the poorest urban and rural areas. By 1939, constant wrangling in Congress and within his own party and the dire events overseas diverted Roosevelt's attention from the domestic front to the international arena. His administration, he announced, would take up no new reform legislation. The New Deal was thereby consummated and, for all intents and purposes, the modern welfare state firmly set into place.

In the aftermath of Roosevelt's stunning reelection and encouraging inaugural speech, *TNR* revised its strategy. The editors' new tunes began to contain New Deal melodies. "The horizon seems to be calm and hopeful again," Soule chirped during the presentation of a variation on his old battle cry "recovery without reconstruction."[2] His protests against "recovery without reform" reaffirmed a commitment to a more substantial set of programs than the New Deal offered, but he realistically set his sights shorter than the "planned society" he had embraced in the past. "Fundamental reform" had to be postponed, he advised liberals, until "the appropriate time arrives" and the necessary "social forces" were marshaled. The Roosevelt coalition of labor, farmers, and professional groups augured well for transforming the Democratic party into the "sort of people's front" *TNR* had always dreamed about. Suddenly, the magazine stood by him as never before. His "fighting" speeches publicizing the plight of the nation's "one third" and call to arms against poverty and injustice instilled hope in "every American" who believed in the possibility of "peace, happiness, and security."[3] Armed with a mandate by "the people," Roosevelt was striving to "carry out the aims of the New Deal," and, for the first time, *TNR* was on his side.

The president needed help. The editors gamely took the offensive against his archnemeses in the press. "I am getting a little tired of the Cassandra racket," Bliven wrote in a stinging indictment of columnists Walter Lippmann, Frank Kent, and Dorothy Thompson. These widely read journalists' unrelenting spate of articles on Roosevelt's fascist tendencies and about creeping socialism in the federal government seemed to mask their true motive of turning the "clock back" to the prehistoric era of laissez-faire and self-reliance.⁴ In 1937, *TNR* ran a three-part series, "The Press and the Public," exposing the bias of several of the nation's largest and most influential newspapers, including the *Chicago Tribune* and *Los Angeles Times.* "TUGWELL HAS HIS BRIGHT YOUTH/SO HAS STALIN," read one headline in the insidious red-baiting campaign Hearst and his cohorts were waging against the New Deal. The daily falsification of news in these publications, the editors argued, betrayed the public interest and reduced the sacred idea of "freedom of the press" to a hollow slogan. To combat this menace and to bring back "truthful reporting and truthful news," *TNR* urged a mass boycott of the worst papers.⁵ If all else failed, citizens could always pick up the latest issue of the United States' foremost progressive journal of opinion to gain a fair balance.

The heaviest blows Roosevelt parried, of course, came from other branches of the government. His aborted attempt to "pack" the Supreme Court with liberal justices received *TNR*'s enthusiastic support. (In keeping with Croly and Charles Beard's tradition, liberals paid minimal deference to the Constitution's archaic strictures.) The "hysterical fury" that ensued ranked as one of the "nonissues" of 1937.⁶ Surely, the editors reasoned, no one opposed "a more efficient" operation of our "democracy." By the end of the year, the Court came around and supported the New Deal. With this major obstruction to reform removed, Roosevelt shelved his plan and the furor died down. Roosevelt had a harder time wrestling with the southern conservative Democrats' opposition to antilynching and wages-and-hours measures in 1938. These "saboteurs under the President's banner," *TNR* warned, threatened to rend the party asunder and undermine "the consistent program or set of principles" of liberalism. Indeed, the New Deal's ultimate "aspiration for the remaking of American life" transcended "the traditional policies" of old-style politics.⁷ *TNR* thus congratulated Roosevelt for "sticking to his reform guns" during a frenzy of politicking at the midterm election aimed at purging the party of his tormentors.⁸ The editors' spirited defense of Roosevelt marked a radical turning point for the magazine and the start of a new realism. The self-righteous disdain for politics receded in the face of a formidable conservative counteroffensive. The shift in "balance of power . . . from special privilege to the masses of people," *TNR* patiently explained, depended on the survival and growth of the New Deal.

The balance of power continued to sway back and forth in the widening war between labor and management. *TNR* watched the birth of the Committee for Industrial Organization (CIO) with keen interest. As a craft union, the AFL had historically been organized by the skills workers possessed and the tools they used. When John Lewis, the CIO's founder and leader, challenged this rigid hierarchy, *TNR* gave him four pages to argue his case for the organization of unskilled workers in steel, automobile, rubber, and other mass production industries.[9] "The President wants you to join a union," said one worker, thus enunciating what *TNR* termed the "Roosevelt Doctrine."[10] Bliven described the CIO's emergence and stunning series of victories from 1936 through 1938 as "the most encouraging single development in American labor history." "No issue has ever been plainer," he wrote, "than the fight between property and people now raging in these United States, with its outcome still in doubt."[11] Like war correspondents at a front, the editors donned their helmets, dove into the trenches, and covered labor's battles every week in vivid and often gory detail. The moment of truth for an industrial democracy had finally arrived.

In late 1936, labor launched its first major offensive in the auto industry. Long a stronghold of the closed shop, General Motors reserved the right to pay pitiful wages and hire and fire at will. Employees were often laid off during model changes and rehired later at their starting rates. Resorting to the increasingly popular "sit-down strike," disgruntled workers in Flint, Michigan, occupied their plant to prevent operation of its machinery. Reporting from the scene, Bliven expressed great admiration for the discipline and determination of the 1,500 men who lived in the building for two weeks, kept tidy quarters, and damaged no property. "The newly completed car bodies . . . were as clean as they would be in the salesroom with glass and metal shining." (Five years earlier, in his funereal essay from Detroit, Edmund Wilson treated these objects with far less reverence.) On January 11, police tried blocking the delivery of food and cutting off the heat, thereby inciting a full-scale riot. After repelling a barrage of tear-gas bombs, clubs, and bullets, the strikers fortified their position and held out for a settlement. Bliven closely observed the United Auto Workers' (UAW) leaders, Victor, Roy, and Walter Reuther, and went away in awe of the "new . . . strongly, responsibly led labor unions" developing across the United States.[12] In February, a weary GM management still adamantly opposed the open shop but agreed to recognize the union as the sole bargaining agent for the workers and permit collective bargaining. Within three years, the UAW successfully organized the Chrysler corporation and, in a protracted and bitter struggle, even prevailed against the oldest bastion of antiunionism, the Ford Motor Company. Onward labor march, *TNR* proclaimed.

While the steel industry's major barons resolved their differences with the CIO peacefully, their junior colleagues refused to surrender without a struggle. In March 1937, U.S. Steel signed a momentous contract acknowledging the union and granting a 40-hour week and increase in wages. Soule, on the heels of the recent GM victory, saluted management's good sense in appreciating the energy of a vital "social force" and eagerly anticipated the "movement spreading like a prairie fire."[13] Little Steel, a collection of such small producers as Republican Steel, intended to douse the flames. Tom Girdler, the incarnation of a diehard and ruthless capitalist, engaged in espionage, used armed guards, and suppressed freedom of speech among employees—a form of "old-fashioned strike breaking," the editors lamented, which was "essentially similar to the tactics of Mussolini and Hitler."[14] A savage clash between heavily armed police and strikers in South Chicago on Memorial Day, 1937, ended in the deaths of 10 men and injuries to 168 others.[15] Labor seemed at a crossroads. The senseless bloodshed drove Soule, in an essay on the "panic over labor," to remind readers that a "real strike . . . [was] no strawberry festival." "The deep social stirrings of the depression, followed by the New Deal's promises," *TNR* eulogized, "brought a new determination and new hope for the industrial workers."[16] Their hopes were ultimately fulfilled in 1941, thanks to the government's friendly and forceful intervention through the Wagner Act. The steel workers, as a result, received unprecedented wages, job security, and—above all—the power and weapons to stand up to their employers. The evil industrial oligarchy, an eternal object of *TNR*'s hate, slowly collapsed in a relatively bloodless revolution (compared to the tumult in Europe at the time). The idea of an industrial democracy had matured from a Crolian abstraction to a tangible fact of U.S. life.

Union troubles hit home at *TNR*. Early in its history, Croly once discontinued publication for four issues during a printers' strike rather than have a nonunion shop print the magazine.[17] Under Bliven's reign, the militant and then communist-dominated American Newspaper Guild drove very hard bargains. Bliven was a card-carrying member of editorial unions from his newspaper years, but long, tedious meetings with surly representatives exhausted his patience. The eventual organization of the staff by another union did little to reduce tensions. The Book and Magazine Guild not only filed a grievance with the National Labor Relations Board, but also threatened a nationwide boycott of *TNR*. Conciliatory efforts by both sides brought about an agreement, and the magazine was unionized, allowing Bliven and his band of liberals at last to practice what they preached.[18]

The editors, to be sure, had no intention of closing the book on the New Deal and declaring it an unqualified success. In late 1937, credit restrictions and reduced federal expenditures precipitated a severe slump. Within a year, unemployment soared from 6 to 7 to 11 million, and major economic indices plummeted to frightening lows. In a tragic encore performance, the deepening depression revived nightmares of those who would have preferred to forget it had happened at all. Scenes of families scavenging through garbage and reports of starvation in the South refreshed the nation's short memory. "The Depression Marches On," read the headline of a *TNR* editorial on the crisis.[19] "If people are not to starve, Mr. President, and you have assured us that they shall not, the federal government must shoulder the burden again," Bliven wrote Roosevelt in an open letter.[20] Despite the desperate sound of his plea, the magazine remained surprisingly temperate. Rather than taking up arms against the administration or firing warning shots about the collapse of capitalism as they had a few years before, the editors calmly got down to the thorny business of helping the president find a way out of this predicament.

TNR's growing sympathies for Roosevelt heavily influenced its economic reporting for the duration of the Depression. Soule appeared with three leading economists in a lengthy and turgid supplement to grapple with the vexing question, "What Has Happened—And Whose Fault Is It?" He concluded his excruciatingly arcane essay by refusing to place blame "exclusively either on government or on business."[21] Bliven, for his part, winced at the "anguished howls of businessmen" who, in a spree of Wall Street speculation, had brought their current spate of troubles on themselves.[22] "One of the great mysteries that historians of the future will puzzle over is why . . . [the New Deal has] aroused such bitter animosity," he mused and why businessmen did not bless it for rescuing them from "the brink of chaos." Even though the New Deal had not ended the Depression, *TNR* explained, "those who blame . . . [Roosevelt] for the depression, like those who blamed Hoover for the previous one, are barking up the wrong tree."[23] In fact, some of the president's severest critics were yapping up the right tree.

A significant part of the current economic malady lay with Roosevelt's capricious policies. Deep cuts in the WPA and PWA and the collection of social security taxes, which took the money out of circulation, satisfied his wish to balance the budget but took the air out of the economy. Meanwhile he adopted, notes Leuchtenburg, "Hooverism" and kept a tight hand on relief expenditures.[24] Finally, in April 1938, he approved a 3-billion-dollar program. "Roosevelt had tried rigid economy," Burns argues, "then heavy spending, then restriction of spending again. He had shifted back and forth from spending on direct relief to spending on public works."[25] TNR could and probably should have commented on the president's weak grasp of economics and taken him to task for his irresolute remedies. That it withheld a scathing critique of Roosevelt underscored the magazine's desire to become his partner instead of adversary.

In this rather sudden role reversal, TNR began showing increasing appreciation for the New Deal's successes. The president, the editors admitted, had a "better record" than any president during previous depressions.[26] Their weekly paeans to the WPA could have been released from Harry Hopkins' office as press releases. "What Uncle Sam got for his money," they convincingly demonstrated, was bridges, dams, and a vast array of other civic improvements. In addition, work relief "salvaged millions of persons, kept their skills intact," and "prevented the moral and mental breakdown" of civilization. The growing importance of public work projects to TNR derived, in large part, from the new school of economics it embraced in the mid-1930s. Although no one claimed Keynesian policies to be a panacea, they seemed to provide the most effective means of accelerating a recovery. In the late 1930s, TNR editorials began to resemble a textbook on the subject and overflowed with short chapters on such theories as the "multiplier principle" (whereby indirect effects and public expenditures would increase beneficial forces several times over.)[27] By 1939, Soule received a diploma from the Keynesian school. "The ups and downs of business activity since 1933," he maintained in an essay on the "legacy" of the New Deal, "may be almost exactly paralleled by the increases and decreases of government spending,"[28] The editors' stress on the efficacy of pump priming and deficit financing reflected a heightened awareness of the inadequacy of the brand of liberalism they heretofore had espoused. Idle discussions of planned and collectivized societies vanished from TNR's pages. Before the economy could ever operate with "social efficiency" (a synonymous, but more polite, term for planning), the government had to stimulate a recovery by pouring subsidies into productive and worthwhile public works.[29] To promote such programs, TNR realized it had better tone down its rhetoric and play by Roosevelt's rules.

The editors rushed to defend the New Deal for pragmatic reasons, as well. Toward decade's end, the reforms appeared in such a state of siege that the editors felt compelled to launch a rescue mission of their own. Emboldened by the defeat of prominent liberals in the midterm elections and the president's slide in popularity, conservative Democrats and Republicans combined forces in 1939 to slash relief funds and dismantle major social programs. Outmaneuvered and out-numbered, Roosevelt showed little inclination to put up a stiff resistance and turned his attention to international issues. *TNR* roared. "Even from the most selfish viewpoint," it chastised an ungrateful nation, "every American" should have thanked the WPA for water facilities and sanitation; parks and playgrounds; and dams and reservoirs."[30] Millions had been taught to read and write and had received medical and dental care at clinics. Over 100 million hot lunches were served to hungry children in schools by housewives who depended on their work from the WPA. Nevertheless, the United States, Harry Hopkins perspicaciously explained, had simp-ly become "bored with the poor, the unemployed and the insecure."[31] *TNR*, aware of the changing mood, wanted to get its last licks in before the era of reform ended.

The fate of many of the editors' pet WPA programs hung in the balance. In the past, they had hardly seemed to notice the Federal Arts and Writers Project, which employed actors, painters, writers, and other white-collar workers. The rich body of work the program generated included T. S. Eliot's *Murder in the Cathedral* and Sinclair Lewis' *It Can't Happen Here,*[32] as well as the famed regional guides and fiction by John Cheever. When faced with extinction, however, the editors tearfully responded with tender tributes to these projects' "aesthetic and social significance" and stood up for the state sponsorship of the arts.[33] We have been "accused of a cer-tain quality of aloofness from the facts we prepare," the editors con-fessed in a rare moment of self-reflection in the summer of 1939.[34] For once, they intended to do something about it. In an uncommon display of civic duty, the editors summoned their intellectual reserves and urged readers to send telegrams to the president (who, for some strange reason, was "smiling" a lot lately) and selected members of Congress to demand the restoration of appropriations to the WPA. As if to punctuate the seriousness of this plea, a note ap-peared at the bottom: "*signed editors of NR.*" This extraordinary lobbying campaign, in effect, showcased the editors' metamor-phosis from skeptics to outright New Dealers.

TNR appeared considerably agitated about the prospects for completing the welfare state. The editors praised the administration for being the "first to make any real attempt" to deal with "the grave shortage of housing all over the United States," a constant concern of the magazine's over the years.[35] The Home Owners Loan Corporation (HOLC) helped millions of city dwellers and farmers from losing their homes because of mortgage foreclosure. The Federal Housing Administration issued beneficial mortgage terms to promote private construction. Of special note for *TNR* was the U.S. Housing Authority (USHA), which sponsored slum-clearance projects and low-cost housing. "The Slums Begin to Fall," exclaimed the headline of an editorial.[36] The USHA, the magazine maintained in a subsequent issue, destroyed

> some of the worst slums in the US . . . and . . . moved . . . inhabitants . . . into new buildings which in comparison are palaces and are literally, in regard to light and air and open space, far better than the dwellings for which wealthy people on New York's Park Avenue pay $20,000 or $30,000 a year for rent.

The grass indeed appeared greener to the editors on the other side of the fence. The New Deal still had a long way to go before meeting the housing demand. During the 1938 recession, the HOLC dispossessed some 100,000 homeowners for failure to make payment on their mortgages.[37] By 1940, the USHA had built only 180,000 units, a number far short of its original goals.[38] *TNR* wished the administration had spent "more money" on housing but, overall, was satisfied that it had "done a good job."[39] A few years earlier, it probably would have vilified Harold Ickes for such unsatisfactory results. In the second term, the editors muted their criticism and bestowed generous compliments on the administration. Liberals, they believed, stood to gain more from working with the administration than against it.

Down on the farm, a whole new world waited to be discovered for *TNR*. With the exception of the Iowan Bliven, the predominantly northeastern, urban staff at the magazine usually ranked rural issues as a low priority. Even during the La Follette campaign, the farmers' ideas were routinely ridiculed. Every four years, the man with the plough conveniently surfaced as the other half of the farmer–labor coalition. In 1933, reports on violent strikes in the "corn-belt" sporadically appeared, featuring angry "men armed with pitch forks patrolling the roads which lead to town."[40] In a review of John Steinbeck's classic *The Grapes of Wrath*, Malcolm Cowley bewailed the "American tragedy" of the "friendless, homeless, and therefore voteless" migrant farmworkers "with fewer rights than medieval serfs."[41] Aside from these sentimental—and infrequent—odes to rural rebels and oppressed Okies, *TNR* devoted a relatively minor amount of space to the subject of agriculture. The editors summarily dismissed the central piece of farm legislation during the first term, the Agriculture Adjustment Act (a complex scheme by which farmers received subsidies for reducing their acreage), as too inefficient, costly, and as another forgery of real economic planning. "We hope that before long the farmers will stop fooling around with economic patent medicines and old-party politicians," they grumbled, "and will join city labor and do the job from the subsoil."[42] Had the rural population taken *TNR*'s advice and migrated en masse to economically devastated cities, they probably would have found fewer opportunities than back in the country. Who, for that matter, would have stayed behind to tend the nation's food basket? The editors evidently had not given the farm question much thought. Their casual sociology and patronizing air effectively eroded the magazine's credibility on the issue.

Thus, *TNR* could quietly slide over to the administration's side while still feigning firm objectivity. Roosevelt's set of agricultural policies "are nowhere nearly adequate to rescue the stricken farm policy," they noted in a fit of equivocation, "but it has done something and without it conditions would have been infinitely worse."[43] The Surplus Market Administration (as part of a newly passed AAA in 1938) received high marks for providing surplus foodstuffs to families on relief. It encouraged abundance rather than scarcity and made an attempt to resolve the age-old paradox of want in the midst of plenty. The editors hailed the Rural Electric Administration's drive to light up the countryside as "one of the most special successes for the New Deal." In addition, the planting of millions of trees in "shelter belts" saved thousands of acres of land that would have otherwise disappeared in the Dust Bowl. One rural group did not fare so well as a result of Roosevelt's agricultural policies. The removal of large tracts of land from production under the AAA imposed especially heavy burdens on 3 million tenant farmers and sharecroppers.[44] *TNR* considered the distressing loss of their livelihoods as probably the biggest blotch on the New Deal record. Yet the editors did not try to examine the underlying social changes occurring at the time and inevitable disappearance of an outmoded class of workers, or propose any substantial reforms. They merely proposed, in the short term, augmenting various federal aid packages to bring quick relief to the victims. In the long term, on this issue and the whole farm agenda, *TNR* followed the administration's lead.

As the decade drew to a close, *TNR* frantically raced from one wall to the next to fill in the cracks of the New Deal. It closely monitored the programs to modify social security and enlarge its benefits. The final version lowered burdens on low-income groups, provided retirement insurance for people at age 65, and provided payments for needy widows and domestic farmers. The United States had finally overcome its "outmoded frontier psychology," *TNR* announced, and saved millions from the "ragged edge of starvation."[45] Soule held out hope for a national comprehensive health plan to, among other things, reduce the infant mortality rate and expand services for children and the mentally ill.[46] It, he wrote, remained the "last important item of unfinished business in the New Deal programs of social legislation." Prior to 1939, Soule disputed whether the New Deal had even started any meaningful business. Now he discussed finishing it. The apparent satisfaction Soule felt from completing Roosevelt's agenda indicated just how deeply *TNR* had reconciled its fundamental differences with him.

The magazine's evolution involved more than a set of social programs. The march of events in Europe forced liberals to reevaluate their relationship with their government and country. After Germany's conquest of Austria in 1938, *TNR* began to consider foreign policy seriously for the first time since Versailles. (The subject will be covered in greater depth in the next chapter.) While still attached to the isolationism of the 1920s, the editors began to look at their own backyard in a broader, international context. With Western democracies in mortal danger, it became less fashionable to harp on U.S. faults and welcome the imminent apocalypse or "revolution" as Wilson and Soule once did. The foreign bogies of Hitler and Mussolini *TNR* conveniently used in the past as shorthand to vilify Hugh Johnson or Tom Girdler seemed perversely exaggerated in the context of domestic politics. The ruthless New Dealer and conservative capitalist paled in comparison to the genuine articles. Likewise, Nazi Germany represented the "fatally sick society" against which the editors had railed during Hoover's reign. At election time in 1940, the "Biggest Issue" for *TNR* was democracy itself, the editors announced in a "Voter's Handbook," and Roosevelt's stature as a "world figure, in whom the masses everywhere" were "ready to repose their faith." The president stood as a "symbol of democratic security in the present world hurricane, no matter what the minor issues" were. "Dr. New Deal," as the popular slogan went at the time, became "Dr. Win-the-War."[47] But many of these "minor issues" constituted the better part of a decade's worth of editorials. Surely the magazine—even for the sake of national unity—could not blithely brush aside its most sacred causes. The task of enthusiastically endorsing the president for a third term while remaining true to its principles proved somewhat taxing.

The delicate compromise that *TNR* reached separated the man from his deeds. Though it refused to become a "devoted follower of FDR" and always distrusted him for "not moving strongly or resolutely enough," the magazine knew it needed him badly.[48] He alone commanded the loyal support of low-income blacks, farmers, and the professional class—the people whom *TNR* had sought to mobilize under one banner for 20 years. Members of the New Deal coalition placed their deepest faith in the United States' "assertion of universal brotherhood, its aspirations for equality of opportunity."[49] The editors might as well have reprinted one of Croly's old soulful essays to complete the benediction. Liberals confidently assumed they could settle their differences with the president over particulars after November. In the meantime, they had to ensure his reelection.

The magazine's stance required it to change its traditional campaign game plan. Its alliance with the Democrats naturally snuffed out the possibility of a third-party challenge. "Half a loaf is better than no bread," the editors explained in a sharp departure from *TNR*'s historical precedents.[50] Their rationale represented pragmatic politics, pure and simple. Liberals could wield more "influence" on future legislation by joining the president instead of fighting him. *TNR* gamely leaped into the unfamiliar foray of partisan politics. Wendell Willkie, a moderate businessman and supporter of many New Deal reforms, received a merciless—and perhaps unfair—drubbing at the hands of the pugnacious editors. The Republican candidate was thrashed, in an emblematic editorial, as a "bumptious small boy with a tin whistle" whose career and views consistently upheld the "supremacy of private business for private gain!"[51] For the first time in its history, the magazine devoted a special supplement to "one man," Willkie. (The presses worked 23 shifts to meet the demand of a total edition of 700,000.)[52] The lavishly detailed exposé of the "big corporation president's" shady deals harked back to *TNR*'s ferocious muckraking journalism directed at John Davis during the 1924 election. No stones were left unturned. Barely a week elapsed without a stinging editorial about "Willkie and Wealth"; "Willkie . . . Slipping"; "Mr. Willkie Plead[ing] Guilty"; and why "Mr. Willkie . . . [was] Wrong!"[53] It did not seem to matter whether the magazine blew the case against arguably the least conservative Republican candidate since Theodore Roosevelt out of proportion. In the conversion of their journal of opinion into an instrument of the Democratic party, the editors were not at all reluctant to use their entire arsenal to obliterate the few remaining pockets of resistance toward the modern welfare state.

By decade's end, *TNR* recognized the necessity of coming to terms with the New Deal. Although the reforms failed to cure the nation's major social ills, they were "groping in the right direction" and offered hope.[54] The legal support of collective bargaining, protection of minimum wages and maximum hours, the Social Security Act, and the federal housing program constituted Roosevelt's crowning achievements. What the editors truly wanted was more of the same and the president to accelerate the "pace of the New Deal." Rather than rejecting his solutions, the seemingly intractable problem of unemployment (10 million still had no jobs in 1940) called for the state to "pick up the slack" in bad times and step up spending on housing and other public investments. George Soule hailed the sound debunking of the myth of private enterprise and "free" economy and celebrated the advent of "partial planning." The spreading horror of fascism in Europe sensitized him to the dangers of "dictatorial" bodies in government and the importance of decentralizing authority for final economic decisions. Such a mechanism, he took care to explain, promised economic efficiency through genuine "democratic planning." The revolutionary jargon that filled his book *Coming American Revolution* disappeared. Corporations and the wealthy need not have feared any sort of upheaval. Soule only demanded that the government dig deeper into their coffers and "equalize the tax burden" for social purposes. The "next step after" the New Deal, the editor suggested, was the expansion of the "production and consumption of useful goods and services and larger incomes for consumers." In other words, a full economic recovery would straighten out the business cycle, create "abundant and stable prosperity," and end the Depression. Soule's circular reasoning exposed the thinness of his own proposals. His abstract and complicated hodgepodge of schemes for adjusting the "valves of the economic system" and coordinating costs, prices, and wages showed the value of existing programs. The editor's cryptic discussion obscured his profound allegiance to the core of the New Deal.[55]

Bliven had a harder time reconciling himself with the popular perception of Roosevelt's reforms than his colleague. "The New Deal has a fine story of achievement and there is no reason why it should not be told," he wrote before the campaign.[56] The nation's apathy baffled him. The average voter appeared to have forgotten about the Depression and relief measures and taken for granted such programs as social security. "People are not very logical in political affairs," he complained in a characteristic burst of frustration with the imperfect U.S. political system. The task fell on New Dealers to halt the country's conservative drift and "sell" their "principles . . . all over again." Bliven, an arbiter of independent liberalism, thus found himself in the curious position of pleading with the administration to abide by its own principles. To observe the magazine's twenty-fifth anniversary, he stepped back to jot down some "notes" on the United States' "character." He wondered why the "American dream" exercised such a "compelling force upon vast numbers of people" when it conflicted with so "many of the known facts." Satisfied with their basic material and spiritual desire for a "job, home, children, health and security," a majority of citizens contented themselves with their rewarding lives and prosperous futures. On the track's other side, the "poorest" group of people in the United States remained permanently "isolated in the prison of their poverty." These "victims of oppression" included millions of individuals who were "half-starving" or on the public dole, unemployed and unskilled workers, and sharecroppers in the South trapped in worse living conditions than "cattle on a prosperous farm." The editors considered the strain of democracy in the United States too strong to ever permit shouts of "Duce!" or "Sieg Heil!" down Main Street. But economic and political freedom, like New Deal programs, did not occur automatically. The "large minority" of people who read progressive weeklies and participated in protest movements had their work cut out for them. For the "price of liberty," Bliven warned, was "eternal vigilance." He realized how carefully he had to tread this line of reasoning. *TNR*, in accord with public activists and its socially conscious readers, occasionally felt the urge to vent its anger at the apathetic populace and try to awaken the slumbering body politic. Its constant challenge was to maintain the "vigilance" without losing faith in democracy or, as the United States prepared for a possible war, denying the swelling sense of patriotism and respect for traditional ideals.[57]

Malcolm Cowley began his analyses where his colleagues left off.[58] Soule, the economics specialist, and Bliven, the seasoned journalist, lacked the literary editor's imagination to gain an understanding of U.S. culture. A sampling of contemporary popular taste in literature reinforced Cowley's static notion of the American dream. The readers of Carl Sandburg's mythological *Abe Lincoln of Illinois* or viewers of the romantic *Gone with the Wind* sought refuge from the Depression's tormenting uncertainties in a "glorious past."

Fearing change, they held on a "fixed place in the community" and satisfied themselves with life's "amenities" such as cooking, gardening, bridge, and croquet. The middle class, in short, entertained no higher aspirations than to enjoy leisure activities and become full-fledged participants in the consumer culture. Perhaps Cowley could not have found more convincing evidence to press his case than in *TNR* itself, which ran the public service advertisements of General Electric. The Norman Rockwellian depictions of the United States glorified capitalism in its fullest splendor. Each week, the entire cast of stock characters, from pipe-smoking grandpa to the apron-clad housewife, were paraded out to salute "the highest standard of living known in any country." While mother enjoyed the convenience of her "electric refrigerator," father installed "sanitary plumbing and central heating." In one advertisement, General Electric presented a stark piece of social realism to dramatize the quiet revolution that was taking place. "Who is the mystery man?" it asked in reference to a blue-collar worker holding a lightning bolt. He was the man who could "have more and work less" by saving up the wages he earned during his 40-hour week. He could even buy a car in four and a half months.[59] The political pendulum had swung a long way in a short time. That such a titan of industry as GE not only recognized labor's new status, but trumpeted it in its promotional materials proved how deeply the New Deal had become ingrained in society. The mutual faith of labor and management in capitalism and its bountiful treasures was the stuff of the American dream, and a source of consternation among the editors. For it, in effect, removed the impetus for future reform.

TNR underestimated the United States' capacity to heal itself. Although the New Deal failed to cure the Great Depression completely and left a large reservoir of unemployed in its wake, most people viewed it as a success. At the Depression's peak, the lethargy of the unemployed and starving had baffled the editors. Several years thereafter, their immutable faith in U.S. progress still confounded Bliven. The people clung to the president as a symbol of stability and cared not a whit whether he had a master plan or that he had achieved neither complete recovery nor reconstruction. The welfare state would tend to the forgotten few. Roosevelt's reluctance to seize the initiative for deeper reforms stemmed as much from his own moderate and unsystematic beliefs as the constraints society imposed on him. At every turn in the road to reform, a conservative ambush awaited him in Congress, the press, and from such ad hoc groups as the Liberty League. Under the circumstances, even *TNR* had to admit that social security and the emergence of an "industrial democracy" (to use the magazine's favorite terminology) under the Wagner Act constituted a quasi-revolution. Much of the New Deal fell short of this mark. Ultimately, the editors' willingness to concede that "half a loaf was better than no bread at all" drew them into Roosevelt's corner where they had less room to maneuver but greater impact on the debate. In the process of rubber-stamping the New Deal, *TNR* came to show a keener appreciation of the heart of the welfare state as hastily conceived during the Depression. Since replacing Herbert Hoover, the president had completely redefined the purpose and goal of government. Ironically, upon the New Deal's completion, Bliven awkwardly reminded U.S. citizens of this quantum leap and urged the administration to continue its march down the same path. Rooseveltian liberalism had taken hold. The magazine celebrated the development by defending the status quo.

. . . .

Hoping for
Utopia

1932–40

MALCOLM COWLEY STOOD TALL AS THE GUARDIAN OF his breed. Since he had been a young man, *TNR*'s literary editor had kept a close vigil on the stirrings of his fellow intellectuals. In World War I, he served in the ambulance corps in France with the likes of John Dos Passos, E. E. Cummings, and Dashiell Hammett. Traumatized by the senseless carnage, he, along with his compatriots, turned away from political affairs and joined the "lost generation" during the following decade. He memorably chronicled his adventures in the famed *Exile's Return*, which originally appeared in *TNR*. The "pathos and absurdity" of modern life drove writers, painters, composers, and philosophers to eschew all forms of politics and explore their individual ideas of artistic "self-expression" on the left bank in Paris and in the "haunts of affectation" in Greenwich Village bohemia. Uprooted from the United States, they retreated even further into their own remote world of arts and letters and settled in a region of "uneasiness and isolation." As the Depression forced intellectuals to reevaluate their roles in society and their "empty" political beliefs, Cowley took over the back of the book after Edmund Wilson in 1931. The space previously reserved for fiction, drama criticism, and poetry then devoted much more attention to political issues. Initially, the pipe-smoking editor with a fondness for seersucker suits practiced the book reviewer's trade with his usual placid demeanor. After work, he fraternized with his cohorts in the liberal New York intellegentsia. The genteel civility and camaraderie did not last long. Within a few short years, the battle lines were sharply drawn. Cowley fought so fiercely for his side that he would carry mental scars with him for the rest of his life. Looking back at the era, he regretted committing such "sins of silence, self-protectiveness, inadequacy, and something close to moral cowardice."[1]

The "Red Decade" consumed liberals. Edmund Wilson's "Appeal to Progressives" in 1931, the formation of such front organizations as the "League of Professional Writers" to aid Harlan County's miners, and William Z. Foster in his presidential bid conferred a new aura of respectability upon communism. It became quite fashionable during this "era of primitive faith and enthusiasm," Cowley recalls, for liberals to sympathize with the radical fringe party and occasionally contribute their literary talents. In the company of many other writers and the editors of *The Nation*, Cowley became a fellow traveler. Though no one at *TNR* ever joined the party or subscribed to its Marxist dogma, the editors generally shared the radical party's disenchantment with capitalism in its current form and, according to Cowley, the "high purposes and dreams" of building a "better society."[2] Except for its token gesture in the 1932 campaign, *TNR*'s empathy for the communists rarely extended beyond spiritual, abstract equalitarianism and the romantic aim of eradicating injustice. On the domestic front, the hues of utopianism lightly shaded a faint form of democratic socialism that was impervious to theories of dialectical materialism and inevitable revolutions. The Communist party figured in none of the magazine's political plans. Throughout the thirties, *TNR* revealed a split personality. At the same time that it courted the Democratic party to promote its agenda at home, its unabashed romance with the Soviet Union attached it firmly to the party line in the international sphere. At no other point in its history did the organ of liberalism come so perilously close to sacrificing its preeminent value of thoughtful independence.

Each editor during the early 1930s looked toward the motherland for inspiration. Cowley bestowed his blessings on Anne Louise Strong, the renowned propagandist for the Soviet government.[3] In a review of one of her books, he praised her admiration for Stalin and "deep respect" for

> a system—which Miss Strong describes more intelligibly than any of the writers on Russia—[that] seems tyrannical to people on the outside, whereas to those millions who help to formulate policies, it seems the most democratic system that ever existed. One can easily understand why Miss Strong did not seriously think of become a Communist until she had seen the system from the inside and had actually taken a part in planning the party line.

Following in the footsteps of Bertrand Russell and John Maynard Keynes, Bliven and Soule made their own pilgrimages to the New Jerusalem. In late 1931, Bliven examined the Five Year Plan in person and declared it a "heroic enterprise."[4] In contrast with the United States, the Soviet Union provided services for the old and infirm and superior housing and recreational opportunities. Bliven cared for neither communist fanaticism, a "neo-Cromwellianism," nor the "discomforts" the population had to undergo. "But one's suffering is mitigated when one knows," he explained, "that everyone else is cold and hungry too, that a better day is coming and that this better day is in fact made possible by present sacrifices."

Does socialism work? asked Soule in a three-part series after returning from a visit.[5] He answered his question with a resounding yes. It was "downright nonsense," he maintained, to think that officials were "in the business of putting on a show" for the thousands of tourists entering the Soviet Union to marvel at the sights. Despite a shortage of consumer goods, the "young and hopeful" nation kept its citizens well fed with a cornucopia of fresh meat and dairy products. The widespread enjoyment of these material comforts and extensive social services allowed "everybody" to lead carefree lives and pursue such leisurely activities as reading. "One should not take this great question of liberty lightly," Soule argued. Indeed, "much" did strike him as "out of place" in the Soviet Union. Yet, "as a partically informed tourist," he had no reason to think that the "masses, who have made the revolution, felt any lack of freedom, or were governed by fear." In May 1936, articles from what was to become Edmund Wilson's *Travels in Two Democracies* first appeared in *TNR*.[6] Although life was not "easy" and a large number of unfortunate souls were "slaving away" in construction camps, the Soviets seemed perfectly willing to accept hardships for the greater good of socialism and the security of being fed and clothed. "You feel in the Soviet Union that you are on the moral top of the world," Wilson proclaimed.

TNR's paeans to the Soviet Union strained its deepest sensibilities. "Soule and I were unforgivably slow to realize what was happening," wrote Bliven in his autobiography. "I cannot in retrospect condone it."[7] What was happening was the national collectivization of farms, resulting in the starvation of millions of peasants. Cowley later lamented that Stalin turned out to be the "enemy" rather than embodiment of "ideals."[8] In all fairness, only vague and scattered reports of the horrors trickled into the United States at the time, and other publications than liberal journals also became susceptible to Soviet propaganda. (The conservative *New York Times* hailed the Five Year Plan as "the most extraordinary enterprise in the economic history of the world.")[9] *TNR*, however, carried its coverage one step further by converting the object of its affection into a cause. The editors' estrangement from the United States drove them to project their own dreams and wishes on Soviet culture, and derive a vicarious pleasure from its so-called successes. Soule viewed the model factories and collective farms that he saw during his manipulated tours as vindication of the Five Year Plan and his own proposals for achieving economic efficiency. Bliven and Cowley exalted the ideals of community and mutual sacrifice as contrasts to the selfish inequalities of capitalism. To Wilson, the rising socialist state presented a comparison to a declining democracy. The Soviets were boldly seizing the future. *TNR*'s justifications for the repression contradicted the very meaning of liberalism: liberty itself. The tenuous distinction drawn between economic and political freedom was predicated on the assumption that the ends justified the means and that the Soviet Union was evolving from an economic democracy to a political democracy. By any reasonable Western standard, of course, economic and political freedom were contingent on each other. Joseph Schumpeter's famous analysis explored the intense urge dynamic capitalism fostered among elites to criticize society. *TNR*'s primary concern with U.S. economic failings and social injustices during the Depression, and hazy inattention to the realities of the international situation distorted its whole political outlook. The willful enactment of fantasies thousands of miles away took for granted democratic luxuries back home.

TNR's sentimentalization of the Soviet Union formed the backbone of its popular front strategy. Liberals, socialists, and communists forged the alliance as a bulwark against fascism. For once, leftists put aside their differences and joined hands in a common struggle. Cowley, its most enthusiastic proponent at *TNR*, wrote to Edmund Wilson in 1935 that theirs was the only publication that could "honestly stand for a united left movement."[10] The editors envisioned using it not only as a weapon against Hitler, but also to combat the forces of reaction in the United States. This latter cabal encompassed big business, the Ku Klux Klan, the American Legion, professional patriots, and conservative publications.[11] Faced with this menace, one could not afford to be too meticulous about one's friends. "It is better to win with the aid of people, some of whom we don't like," the editors argued in 1936, "than to lose and come under the iron-fisted control of people all of whom we dislike a great deal more."[12] Two years later, in an attempt to attract additional converts, the U.S. Communist party positioned itself in the center and wrapped itself in the red-white-and-blue rhetoric of Jefferson, Paine, Jackson, and Lincoln. *TNR* heartily applauded its commitment to the "worthy cause[s]" of civil liberties, union principles and social legislation. When Max Eastman, the disillusioned former communist, accused the "Stalinist organ" of misleading its "gullible readers," *TNR* maintained its innocence and reaffirmed its support for the communist "goal" of the popular front.[13] With the help of their strange bedfellows, liberals thought they could remake the world.

The magazine's advertisements reflected its changing complexion. In any given issue, vacationers could select from half a dozen tours to the Soviet Union, where they might marvel at the "outburst of enthusiasm" for the "successful collectivization of national farms." Candy could be ordered "direct from Moscow," with a genuine label from Leningrad. Closer to home, the festive were invited to a "Red Indian Dance" ("in a real Indian Village") at the Manhattan Opera House sponsored by the New York State Communist party. Afterward, they could show their allegiance to the popular front by catching the late-night show of "Confessions of a Nazi Spy," starring Edward G. Robinson—the first movie promotion ever to run in *TNR*. There were not many others.[14]

In those balmy days of fellow traveling in the late 1930s the magazine offered conservatives a tempting target. Henry Luce, a scourge of liberals, was no admirer. After the magazine celebrated its twenty-fifth anniversary, an article appeared in *Time* about the "pinko weekly" of which the liberals were described as "dismayed, confused, unhopeful, stoic."[15] On the far right, Elizabeth Dilling, the queen of witch hunters, collected data on file cards to pillory hundreds of every political stripe, from Albert Einstein to Eleanor Roosevelt.[16] The troop at *TNR* received decorations for spreading pernicious doctrine against the United States. Witnesses before the odious Dies Committee, a precursor to the House Un-American Activities Committee, lashed out at the magazine's "Communist" subversion. Bliven filed a sworn statement with the committee denying its allegations that the magazine was a communist weekly.[17] Back at the office, the editors were on the lookout for trouble. Communist infiltrators posing as liberals were lurking about. The impersonators' dour natures and Marxist rhetoric tended to give them away, and they were promptly shown the door.[18] Unfortunately, the magazine did not remain totally immune to their ideology.

In 1937 and 1938, the Moscow show trials tested the depths of the editors' convictions. Each week, they closely followed the arraignment and execution of the old Bolsheviks charged with conspiring against the revolution. It was later learned that, by the finish of Stalin's reign of terror, perhaps 1 million persons had lost their lives and countless others had been banished to the Gulag Archipelago. As a contemporary observer, however, "it hardly mattered," Cowley admitted afterwards, whether he or the other editors "believed the evidence: false or true it painted a terrifying picture of the workers' fatherland."[19] Relying exclusively on the official accounts of the trials, he wrote lengthy essays condemning the defendants' plots to side with Trotsky and "destroy the Soviet state which they helped to build."[20] Rather than presenting the confessions as a "clumsy frame-up," Cowley accepted them at face value. The elaborate schemes for espionage, sabotage, and terrorism were reviewed in vivid detail. "Most of them were guilty almost exactly as charged," he wrote Wilson. "Trotsky himself walks on eggs when it comes to discussing the guilty or the accused." Stalin, after all, had to break a few eggs to protect the revolution and had to engage in "political repression."[21] By May 1938, Cowley began to reconsider his views in private. After the third major trial, he and 150 other "American Progressives" signed a statement justifying the trials.[22] The letter, he acknowledged to Wilson, was "about three-quarters straight." That one quarter of doubt returned to haunt him.

In the front of the book, Bliven and Soule generally seconded their colleagues' notions with only a few minor reservations. By consistently hemming and hawing, they too effectively whitewashed the trials. It was "impossible" to arrive at a consistent editorial policy, Bliven informed Cowley in early 1937, and "on the basis of present information to comment authoritatively on what has happened in the USSR."[23] Yet, he still planned a lead editorial stressing "the harm that is being done by the controversy in this country." His main concern centered on the enormous "blow" the adverse publicity dealt "to the prestige of the Soviet Union," not the validity of the evidence.[24] In truth, for all the editorials that claimed to suspend judgment until the "facts" came in, *TNR* published an "enormous accumulation of evidence" proving the conspirators' complicity.[25] The suspicious holes in most of the cases and violation of basic political liberties could also be rationalized. The "historical" nature of Soviet institutions ran contrary to the different tradition of "Western safeguards of judicial procedure."[26] The "travesty of justice" perpetuated against Sacco and Vanzetti in the United States, for example, was documented through extensive records. If only the Soviet government, the editors maintained, could adopt such customs and "move more rapidly toward democracy," it could regain the respect that it had lost in world public opinion. The editors betrayed their ulterior motives by acting as Stalin's apologists.

TNR placed the Soviet Union and popular front above its democratic principles. The purges forced the editors to explain a multitude of atrocities committed in the name of progress. "Stalin, with all his faults and virtues, represents the communist revolution . . . [and] the new society . . . and [a] promise for the future,"[27] wrote Cowley. Therefore, the man and his methods had to be defended at all costs. Perhaps the "rapid" collectivization of peasants and tempo of the Five Year Plan caused excessive "human suffering." "Nobody can say that life is perfect in a country that let two or three million of its own citizens starve to death," he wrote Wilson.[28] But the Soviet Union was still "the most progressive force in the world," Cowley advised readers, and to it "we owe our loyalty."[29] In 1938, Bliven wrote Stalin an open letter pleading with him to stop the purges and institute procedures "compatible with that of the countries under the Anglo-Saxon or Roman law tradition."[30] The "real tragedy" involved the increasing hostility of critics who lumped together "Hitler, Stalin, and Mussolini." "The Soviets are not only a country but an idea, and it is entirely the ultimate hope that it will spread throughout the entire world," he wrote. The editors clutched their illusory "idea" for all it was worth. By bending the truth to conform to their idealized view of the promised land, they could casually dismiss the evils as aberrations and temporary hardships in the longer struggle. To have admitted the full extent of the horrors would have amounted to surrender.

In the war for the Soviet Union's worldwide standing, *TNR* refused to take any prisoners. Throughout this period of what Alfred Kazin has described as "sheer savagery," the magazine turned into a battleground for anti-Hitler and anti-Stalin factions.[31] Cowley "swallows the whole Stalinist interpretation," wrote Dwight Mac-Donald, editor of *Partisan Review*, the political and literary journal.[32] The object of this vituperation lashed out at his "sneering and superficial" detractors and their "tone-deafness."[33] The *Partisan Review* responded in kind with a denunciation of Cowley's "political commitments to the Communist party."[34] In May 1939, the Committee for Cultural Freedom—an organization headed by John Dewey, Charles Beard, and Sydney Hook—published a statement declaring its opposition to all forms of totalitarianism on the right and left in *The Nation*. *TNR* declined to print it.[35] The editors roundly condemned the statement's comparison of political freedom in the Soviet Union and the United States, advising the committee to "go into a Southern textile town . . . and preach unionism, and to see a prompt instance of Hitlerism in action." In response, one of the committee's directors accused *TNR* of giving "aid and comfort to the agents of Stalinism" in the United States.[36] The "slightest" trace of communism, the editors replied, drove the anti-Stalinists to "apply the Red smear" and split the "Progressive movement" in half.[37]

TNR ultimately fell victim to its own political paranoia. The intense animosity it had felt so long toward the "plutocracy" in Croly's day and the "fascist" in Bliven's became a reflexive response. Beleaguered liberals instinctively identified all critics of socialism and communism with the forces of reaction. "A great deal can be said for conservatism, so long as it sails under its own colors," Cowley wrote Wilson in reference to the editors of *Partisan Review*.[38] It appalled him to hear this group of supposedly lapsed liberals still call themselves "Marxists and revolutionists." The "extremists" were so "obsessed with hatred of Stalin" that they searched for him "under every bed." Most of the obsessions actually belonged to Cowley. Although the committee and *Partisan Review* staff undoubtedly contained fallen Trotskyites with old scores to settle and a few individuals of an increasingly conservative bent, their message rang truer than *TNR*'s rigid "anti-anti-attitude," to borrow Arthur Koestler's term, toward opponents of communism.[39] Cowley invariably mistook his friends for foes. As the committee pointed out, any defense of the Soviet government's "draconian policies" played into the hands of sanctimonious reactionaries who were able to seize the moral high ground.[40] In retrospect, Cowley wished he had heeded the anti-Stalinists' warnings. Unfortunately, he later regretted, "no one was willing to listen" back then.[41]

No student of Stalinism seemed capable of swaying the editors. Articles by Beard and Dewey appeared in *TNR*, equating Soviet monstrosities with those of Germany. In 1939, Vincent Sheehan wrote a two-part article entitled "Brumaire: The Soviet Union as a Fascist State."[42] Perhaps Edmund Wilson touched the tenderest nerve of all. While Cowley continued to romanticize about the Soviet Union, the former *TNR* editor gradually began to desert the camp of fellow travelers. In a brief manifesto, "Complaints: The Literary Left," published in the magazine in 1937, he dwelt at length on the "tightening of terrorism" under the Stalinist "dictatorship."[43] After reading Cowley's essay on the Moscow trials, Wilson fired off a petulant note in which he upbraided his friend for being "misled" by "cooked up . . . government propaganda intended to provide scapegoats and divert attention from more fundamental troubles."[44] Meanwhile, Wilson came to grips with his own understanding of Marxism in *To the Finland Station*, a study of the revolutionary tradition in Europe and the rise of socialism, which was excerpted in *TNR* and *Partisan Review*. He concluded the book by repudiating the Marxist formulas for eradicating class privilege and establishing an egalitarian society. No matter how noble their intentions appeared, dictatorships guaranteed the "happiness" of nobody "but the dictators themselves."[45] As did his British counterpart George Orwell, Wilson followed a political odyssey during the decade consistent with his ideals. He abhorred the economic oppression under wanton capitalism in 1931 and the political authoritarianism under Stalinism in 1939 with equal passion.

In the midst of all the intellectual ferment, the logic of Wilson's argument escaped the editors. Several years after he retired from *TNR* in the mid-1950s, Cowley wrote periodic essays to confess his gnawing "sense of guilt" and atone for his sins. "I was not a political theorist," he admitted, "and I had a tendency to simplify matters for clear exposition."[46] Cowley found rereading his essays on the trials many years later a "painful" experience. *TNR*'s interpretations of events in the Soviet Union foundered on a number of erroneous assumptions. The application of U.S. legal standards to the Soviet system placed the two cultures' democratic traditions on comparable footing. Yet, the Soviet Union maintained its respect for the nuances between innocence and guilt and for the reliability of the evidence only so far as it served the interests of the state. In the Soviet Union, Sacco and Vanzetti, to use the editors' example, would have disappeared without a trace, let alone become a public symbol of injustice. In addition, the editors contrived a dubious double standard whereby the domestic persecution of a union buster, such as Tom Girdler at U.S. Steel, raised the hues and cries of "fascism," while the deaths of millions of peasants and systematic terrorizing of an entire population signaled a leap forward in the liberation of the "human spirit." The hypocritical acceptance of Stalin's brutalities effectively crippled many liberals' credibility. They had no right excusing repression in either country.

The popular front mentality limited debate to only one side of an argument. Although Cowley denied any intention of ever becoming a "propagandist," he held on to his doctrines with the conviction of a proselytizer.[47] John Dos Passos, a good friend of Cowley's, broke earlier with communist front organizations than most in his circle. "I'm through with writing these lousy statements," he told Cowley in 1935. "We have all got to hang together or we will hang separately," came Cowley's response.[48] Four years later, the editor tied a noose around the novelist's neck when he went to Spain to cover the civil war. The Soviet Union, the only nation to supply arms to the republicans, earned the accolades of liberals for fighting fascism. Cowley rejected Dos Passos' articles in favor of the "superficial" reporting of Ernest Hemingway, as Bliven described in his autobiography.[49] Dos Passos' worst suspicions about Soviet infiltration in the republican ranks were confirmed when Jose Robles, an old friend and professor of Spanish literature at Johns Hopkins University, was executed by Stalinist agents, despite his opposition to Franco.[50] Dos Passos chronicled his disillusionment with communism and the Soviet Union in *Adventures of a Young Man*. In a generally unfavorable review of the semiautobiographical novel, Cowley greeted the erstwhile radical's descent "from the high mountains of idealism" with mild annoyance.[51] Dos Passos wrote a vitriolic reply, taking direct aim at: "American communist sympathizers" and, echoing the exact sentiments of Orwell, conveying his horror at the "vast butchery that was the Spanish civil war ... [and] the bloody tangle of ruined lives that underly the hurray-for-our-side aspects." There was no use in arguing with Cowley, Dos Passos told Dwight MacDonald—"his deductions are all wet."[52] The republican cause, as did the Soviet Union itself, represented an article of faith to the editors. Dos Passos and Wilson, two longtime friends and comrades in the heyday of fellow traveling, could not persuade them to shed their illusions, but a shocking series of events in 1939 did.

The Nazi–Soviet Pact demolished the popular front and *TNR*'s dreams. On August 23, the nefarious nonaggression treaty between Stalin and Hitler was signed. According to secret clauses, the Soviet Union was rewarded with rights to Finland and certain Eastern European countries in exchange for German occupation of most of Poland. On that very date, in a fitting piece of irony, the editors parried another blow from the Committee for Cultural Freedom with a refutation of the "fantastic falsehood that the USSR and the totalitarian states are basically alike" and reiterated a long, predictable litany of the motherland's socialist miracles.[53] The virtues of this "bulwark" against fascism and militarism pointed to the necessity of "continued friendship between the US and the Soviet Union." The thought that "the steamroller of totalitarianism" might crush democracy with Stalin in the driver's seat never occurred to *TNR*.[54] The move caught it off guard. The treaty's rationales rested on a shaky concept of realpolitik. Having temporarily mollified Hitler, the Soviet Union bought itself the same "isolation" the United States enjoyed and time, just in case, to prepare. Without any knowledge of the pact's unpublished provisions, the editors based their rosy prediction of Poland's security and autonomy on the Soviet

Union's honorable "record of . . . past performances." Stalin earned their esteem for "serving the interests of his country rather than observing a non-existent international morality."[55] On the heels of the unexpected bargain with the incarnation of evil, the editors, in keeping with tradition, left it up to the Soviet Union to shape its perceptions of morality and put the best face on matters.

The Soviet occupation of Poland fractured the core of *TNR*'s beliefs, and the invasion of Finland broke it. The "communist imperialism" obliterated the popular front's "cherished democratic ideals" and lowered the Soviet Union to the abysmal level of other members of the "Fascist bloc."[56] The editors shed as many tears over the death of their beloved cause as Stalin's "criminal folly" in Finland. His aggression against the small nation thrilled "every Tory in the world" bent on destroying communism "and all its works."[57] What probably hurt *TNR* the most was the knowledge that the conservatives, and liberal anti-Stalinists, had been right all along. The tyrant, *TNR* reluctantly admitted three years after the first trials began, had resorted to "ugly repression" and "mowed down a succession of enemies and potential enemies, together with many innocent persons, by the old conspiratorial technique of espionage and terror."[58] Yet, a full confession of Stalin's heinous crimes neither exonerated him nor preserved all the promise of the system he built. Stalin, Cowley earlier stressed, represented socialism's great hope, part and parcel. He alone bore the primary responsibility for its disintegration. The belated efforts to separate Stalin from the Soviet Union and salvage the revolution's wreckage proved futile. *TNR* began to reexamine the world in another context. France and Great Britain were fighting for their lives against the totalitarian menace. While their fates hung in balance and the United States offered its help, the editors gradually gained a new appreciation for the meaning of true democracy.

Of all the editors, Cowley took the news the hardest. In 1940, he renounced all his communist sympathies and, in lockstep with many other liberals of his persuasion, withdrew from front organizations. From then on, he refrained from issuing any statements and signing any letterheads. Feeling "pretty much alone" at that moment, Cowley strained to make peace with a friend and himself in a long mea culpa he wrote to Edmund Wilson.[59] The letter ended with a stanza from a poem "addressed to the peoples of tomorrow":

Think back on us, the martyrs and the traitors,
Of cowards even, swept by the same flood
Of passion toward the morning that is yours:
O children born from, nourished with our blood.

The chastened radical reconciled himself to his tattered ideas with less difficulty than his bruised ego. "Getting involved in these feuds, and vendettas of the intelligentsia," he wrote, "is like being an unwilling participant in a Harlem orgy." The relentless volley of "character assassinations" and "symbolic murders" fueled personal malice and spite rather than substantial debate. Weary and confused, the editor longed to flee from political matters to the familiar sanctuary of literature and the arts.

Cowley might well have turned to his own magazine for relief and inspiration. Although he regarded social issues as within his proper domain, he never completely acquiesced to the communist-influenced popular front culture, in which art was sacrificed for the sake of politics. The "vast neutral area of literature," he believed, encompassed a wide gamut of "human emotions" and "values" outside the restricted bounds of ideology.[60] Indeed, throughout the late 1930s, in the back of the book and elsewhere, *TNR* continued to serve as a gallery for the most talented writers in the United States and the world. W. H. Auden, for example, composed a tender, eulogistic poem in memory of W. B. Yeats (who published a good deal of work in the magazine) upon the Irishman's death in 1939. The almost forgotten movie and jazz critic Otis Ferguson treated readers each week to acerbic, lively reviews. "The Civil War gets very civil," he noted in a summary of the plot of *Gone With the Wind*, "and there is a wonderful bonfire and there are young loves and balls and plantations and practically everything." No matter how politically sensitive the subject, a fine author kept his respect for the beauty of the language and rarely resorted to propaganda. Ignazio Silone contributed a stinging satire on Mussolini's racial prejudice. Thomas Wolfe's breathtaking narrative of a trainride he took through Germany in 1937 depicted the mistreatment of a Jewish passenger as a "tragedy of man's cruelty and his lust for pain." Thomas Mann rejoiced over his decision to emigrate to the United States, a "great country." Archibald MacLeish also waxed lyrical about his nation's abundant promises to humanity. In the face of human savagery unparalleled in history, the civilized tradition of poetry and prose still flourished in *TNR*.[61]

Around the world, democracy was under siege in 1940 and 1941, and *TNR* found itself in a race against time. Other than the popular front—an empty slogan—and international socialism—a lost cause—the editors had not given foreign policy much thought. In general, they recommended a combination of strict neutrality with domestic reforms for the purpose of achieving "internal strength."[62] The bitter experiences of World War I and Versailles underlay the editors' isolationism and general indifference to affairs in Europe. The United States should stay out of the conflict unless a fascist victory appeared imminent. France's fall in the spring and Hitler's inexorable march across the continent portended such a terrifying outcome. As Great Britain battled for its survival, the president was urged "to get tough" and adopt a stronger defense posture.[63] Bliven privately took exception to the "diehard pacifists," and Cowley seriously wondered whether the United States could afford not to intervene.[64] In autumn and March of the following year, *TNR* wholeheartedly backed Roosevelt's "lend-lease" policy, which supplied Britain with military equipment. On August 25, 1941, four months before the Japenese attacked Pearl Harbor, *TNR* called for a declaration of war against the axis powers.[65] Seldom in its history did it present a clearer choice between freedom and oppression than in the victory of the United States and defeat of the Nazis.

Unfortunately, the surge of patriotism and good intentions coincided with the sag of morale at *TNR*'s offices. Away from the political squabbles, the business side of the operation was seeing red of a different sort: the magazine continued to lose money at a record rate. The publisher so much as advertised the fact that it would "never be a profit-making enterprise" in an urgent plea on the back page to attract more subscribers.[66] At one point, Bliven briefly considered shoring up the circulation base, and thereby ending a sibling rivalry, by merging *TNR* with its cousin, *The Nation*. (For years his pet taunt was "he ought to be at *The Nation*.")[67] Disgruntled staffers talked behind the editors' backs. "Furtive whispering and impolite laughter could be heard from cubicle to cubicle," remembers Alfred Kazin, who did a brief stint at *TNR*.[68] Otis Ferguson, the office wag, derived a perverse pleasure from pointing out the "bearded similes" and "pious liberalisms" in "Buster" Bliven's work and compared the prose in his denser expositions to "making two bites out of a cherry."[69] Not surprisingly, he was excluded from editorial meetings. This was to everyone's detriment, for the individuals responsible for the magazine probably needed a little humor to leaven the seriousness with which they had approached their trying tasks. "People who work for The New Republic always think about The New Republic," Cowley once told Edmund Wilson.[70] In Croly's day, Francis Hackett left in a huff, Lippmann branched out in a different direction as a columnist, and middle-level editors came and went as they pleased. Afterwards, the triumvirate of Bliven, Soule, and Cowley worked together in relative harmony and spoke their official piece in unison for more than a decade, a remarkably long time considering the volatile subject matter in the journal of opinion. It was only natural for Cowley and the others with frayed nerves to suffer from "moral fatigue."[71]

The upheaval in the international sphere matched on a larger scale the tumult at *TNR*. Since their move to Britain in the mid-1920s, Dorothy and Leonard Elmhirst had continued to provide generous subsidies and largely left the editors to their own devices. In late 1940, however, the German air raids on London and the anxious wait for U.S. support led to their growing impatience with the editors' slow tilt toward intervention. On this very rare occasion, the owners did not hesitate to share their disagreements with their employees. Leonard traveled across the Atlantic and held a series of meetings with Bliven. Dorothy arranged the appointment of Michael Straight, the second son of Willard, as *TNR*'s Washington editor and supplied him with an office in the nation's capital.[72] (Three years before, as a student at Cambridge, Michael had defected from the Blount—Burgess—Philby communist spy-ring, as he confessed in his subsequent autobiography.) Michael recounted the story behind his first contribution on February 17, 1941:

> I telephoned Bruce Bliven and told him what I wanted to do. He knew that I would be a loose cannon, rolling around on the decks of *The New Republic*, but he welcomed me aboard. He asked when he might expect a short article from me. I said that I had already started to work on a thirty-thousand-word report on our defense program. Bruce swallowed hard and promised to publish it in a special supplement.[73]

The supplement's anonymity, and the absence of Straight's name in the masthead, kept *TNR*'s newest addition a secret from readers. His arrival probably commanded less attention than the departure of several familiar writers. For, in the meantime, Bliven decided to do a bit of housekeeping by firing his tormentor Otis Ferguson and two of Roosevelt's staunchest critics, the increasingly conservative author of the financial column "Other People's Money," John Flynn, and the reigning TRB, Jonathan Mitchel. Edmund Wilson, back for another engagement as coliterary editor, was given his walking papers after unsuccessfully conspiring to unseat Bliven, who was able to capitalize on his long-standing relationship with the owners. In the reshuffling of personnel, Cowley and Soule saw their editorial duties severely curtailed.[74] Both men protested what they viewed as the Elmhirsts' interference in the magazine and Bliven's autocratic handling of the affair. Cowley believed they were demoted because the Elmhirsts considered their politics "too radical," one of a few plausible theories.[75] Bliven, in nothing short of a miracle, emerged from the decade the least battle-worn of the editors. He managed to dabble in Soule's theories for planning and Cowley's Soviet sympathizing without letting either become an obsession and gave each individual, including the redoubtable Edmund Wilson, free rein and the chance to speak his piece. In the center of the ideological maelstrom, the former beat reporter did his yeomanly services and deftly put pieces of the "paper," as he usually referred to it, together every week while refereeing between various in-house and outside writers—virtually all of whom had their axes to grind. That he successfully kept the peace for so long testified to his perseverence and poise on this high plane of discourse. *TNR* was, by nature, a ticking time bomb.

Indeed, the magazine's overall performance during the red decade tested the value of its primary goal to stimulate public debate and social awareness. Judged by the magazine's own lofty standards, the editors, on balance, failed to enlighten their readers about one of the crucial issues of the time for liberals: the morality of communism. At the heart of their internecine quarrels, they exalted personal prejudices and pride over disinterested thought. The sham battles and paper politics, to use Soule's phrase, were largely motivated by self-interest. Because Cowley believed his detractors abused him and wanted his scalp, he felt as compelled to defend his honor and reputation as his opinions. The nature of Stalinism, in the process, became submerged. The literary editor might as well have returned to Paris to decipher a Dada poem, for all the guidance his essays on the Soviet trials provided liberals in their quest for a better world. At a moment in history when a disciple of the "lost generation" labored to rediscover himself and make his ideas count, he managed to remove himself further than ever from the mainstream of U.S. experience. In the 1920s, he at least could console himself with a clean conscience about the corrupted values of his culture. The unfortunate turn of events in 1939 and 1940 stripped him of any scrupulous claim to prescience and rendered his ideas irrelevant, a fatal ailment for a journalist of opinion.

TNR's decline into near oblivion resulted partly from intellectual vanity and conceit, but mostly from misguided moral zeal. The editors, in the company of countless other liberals, were too eager to leave their troubles behind in the idyllic universe they fabricated. With all its problems, the Soviet Union still represented humanity's shining hope. If only the United States could overcome reactionary resistance with such ease and make a longer march toward social progress. If only Roosevelt could emulate Stalin, the practical achiever and engineer, and really pledge a new deal. Overall, in fact, Stalin received fairer treatment during this period than did Roosevelt in *TNR*. The democratic–socialist wish list the editors filled out in their semi-mythical land exaggerated the extent of liberty that the Soviet Union's so-called democracy afforded and underestimated the extent of oppression under Stalinism. In a private letter to Leonard Elmhirst three years before his death, Herbert Croly roundly condemned the "highly centralized political tyranny" the Soviets had developed since the revolution.[76] Communism's "inability to supply human nature with many motives for cooperating with it" naturally precluded its application to pluralistic societies. Croly's healthy skepticism of utopian solutions required him to devise elastic solutions consistent with his democratic instincts and to keep wary of rigid dogma. The inevitability of class friction and complete subservience to the state violated his trust in individual freedom. In the 1930s, the New Deal's partial fulfillment of *TNR*'s aspirations for a social democracy in the United States led it to build its model elsewhere. Stalin appeared to have succeeded in archetypical collectivism where the magazine's own nation failed. The respect accorded Stalin and the cause he championed ended in the tears wept over his betrayal of the revolution, which, the editors finally realized, was a figment of their imagination. The side of *TNR* that turned its attention away from domestic reform and looked toward the New Jerusalem for salvation remained wedded to illusions about the future of liberalism and the United States.

. . . .

Conclusion

T NR HAD ALWAYS ENJOYED IMMENSE STAYING POWER
over the years. World War II hardly affected the smooth operation.
With the aid of Michael Straight, Bliven continued to direct the
magazine and, upon the U.S. entry into the war and the formation of
an alliance with the Soviet Union against the axis powers, did his
part in the enormous propaganda effort by presenting glowing accounts of "the people's revolution." While the Cold War ruptured
this expedient friendship, *TNR*'s abiding affection for the socialist
nation persisted a bit longer. A month before the 1948 presidential
election, the discovery of the Communist party's ties to the U.S. Progressive party ended Henry Wallace's short-lived reign as an editor
and the last chapter in the history of fellow traveling at *TNR*.

After retiring gradually from editorial duties, Bliven suffered a
heart attack in 1947 and left journalism entirely to write books until
his death in 1977. Soule also cut ties to the magazine in 1947 and
subsequently held a number of teaching posts in economics at col-
leges and universities, where he authored several additional books
on his favorite subject and further refined his proposals for national
planning. He died in 1970. Cowley left the magazine briefly to serve
in the Office of Facts and Figures, an agency (with an unfortunate
acronym, he confessed) staffed by writers and editors that was later
incorporated into the Office of War Information. His past association with radical organizations roused the ire of red-baiters on the
Dies Committee, eventually forcing him to resign. Cowley moved per-
manantly to Sherman, Connecticut, where he earned a living by writing reviews, working as a book editor, and lecturing. Two prestigious

academies of letters bestowed honors on him for his distinguished work as a literary critic. Today, the venerable octogenarian's contributions still grace the pages of such publications as *The New York Times Book Review* and *The Yale Review*. The Straights' reign at *TNR* drew to a close in 1953 when Dorothy decided to sell the paper to another wealthy philanthropist, by which time her investment had averaged 95,000 dollars per year or about 3.7 million dollars for her 38 years of support.[1]

The question remains what purpose such a magazine as *TNR* actually serves. For Bliven, the "freedom otherwise unavailable" to a journalist made the whole enterprise worthwhile.[2] Although dailies do fight crusades, he maintained, the profit motive, "even if only unconsciously," creates a "milieu of conformity" among their editors. Financial independence liberated *TNR* from such constraints. Moreover, by definition, the journal of opinion cannot fall back on the mere presentation of news. A critique of *TNR* appearing in a 1936 issue of *Saturday Review* inadvertently confirmed the magazine's value.[3] The writer (an editor of *Colliers*, another weekly magazine), who lodged a complaint against *TNR* for basing comments on "other people's facts," could not have been reading it very closely. The magazine did conduct and publish original investigation studies of economic imbalances in 1924, and reportage series in 1930 were every bit as fresh and important to an understanding of daily affairs, as the information in the average newspaper. More important, the issues the magazine chose to cover and the judgments formed about them effectively debunked the myth of "facts" in the press. Whose duty, after all, was it in the Fourth Estate to determine the veracity of something with any degree of certainty? A single sensationalist account of Roosevelt in a Hearst paper could probably lay the pretense of objectivity to rest, but in fact, no single source of news monopolizes the so-called truth. "The New Republic Idea," as enunciated by Croly, aimed to weigh the relative merits of a given side of a question and enable readers to decide for themselves. When it worked, the curious reader gained timely insights no other type of publication could rival.

The two skills of political philosophy and advocacy journalism, in principle, were to keep the editors out of ivory towers and on the main street of U.S. existence where, as Cowley once wrote, the only weapon they used was their typewriters. In the war of words, the editors rarely settled for a truce. Tasks required them to immerse themselves in the affairs around them to gain a sharper focus. Croly and his magazine had the foresight, just before the economic collapse in 1929, to lay up a reserve of programs for the next wave of reform. It was in keeping with Croly's avowed intentions that at the moment of the apparent liberal triumph through the New Deal, *TNR* should find so much to criticize and constantly demand bolder action.

The eventual cessation of reform activity meant lowering expectations about the final form of the welfare state. "Boy and man . . . we haven't yet discovered . . . a method of research checks . . . to test our social effectiveness," *TNR* mused in 1939.[4] One possible but unreliable method may have tested the correlation between their ideas on paper and in action. Whereas the editors' abstract notions for humanizing capitalism in 1914 had presaged the direction of U.S. government within the following 25 years, the Soviet paradigm during the popular front era bore little connection to either international or domestic reality. In the midst of the internal squabbles and mental cannibalism, the intellectuals at *TNR* sheltered themselves from the harsh truth of their cause and events in general. Mired in its own marginality, the magazine of that era came perilously close to becoming inconsequential.

The editors' earnest efforts to effect social change without sacrificing intellectual integrity often put them at a disadvantage. Written for the "superior" few, *TNR* implicitly rejected the premise of egalitarianism and favored, as Weyl argued, "the equalization of opportunities" rather than people. Although Croly deeply sympathized with the masses, he distrusted their instincts. The analogous difficulty literary people faced in accurately portraying the working class, which Alvin Johnson outlined, repeatedly nagged the editors. A guilty Weyl felt uncomfortable in the company of the downtrodden and relied on prefabricated notions to describe the character of the Jew. The sense of ethereality and distance in Edmund Wilson's reportage pieces showed less intimacy with his subject than his writing on literary matters. He, more than anyone else, resided exclusively in the world of ideas. Cowley's attempts to form a bond between brain workers and muscle workers in Harlan County foundered.

The multitudes, moreover, rarely acted in their own best interests. Their reluctance to protest their lot by supporting a third party frustrated *TNR*'s best-laid plans every four years. The editors wanted government for the people in spite of the people. Their disenchantment with the average citizen's political acumen resonated throughout Croly's proposal for an elite corps of engineers and Soule's supreme planning council. The "thin red line of experts" the latter trusted to protect the masses had to rescue them from their vices first. *TNR*'s frequent jousts with the tyranny of the majority shared its difficulty in reconciling individual interests with a public good.

This resistance to popular pressure and rectitude bred antipathy toward politics, a game *TNR* always played grudgingly. Nothing ever seemed to go according to plan. The electorate failed to see through the veneer of Coolidge prosperity and overwhelmingly endorsed the New Deal's partial solutions. The trouble was that much of *TNR*'s dispassionate and finely honed analyses treated politics as a purely logical discipline, not as a matter of perception. Most people like upbeat news and want to believe in their president. In disdain of the great man theory of history, *TNR*'s clinical strategies stressed the primacy of policy over politicians. After growing disenchanted with Theodore Roosevelt's dynamic leadership and Woodrow Wilson's honorable statesmanship, Croly had vowed never again to fall under the spell of a politician. LaFollette appeared incidental to the campaign and party in 1924. Perhaps Al Smith, in the following election, received the only fair and faithful appraisal of any candidate in the magazine through 1940. In sizing up Smith's vices—his suspect liberalism—and virtues—the inspiring rags-to-riches story—Croly managed to make the maximum amount of political hay out of the man. *TNR* took a different tack in the two subsequent campaigns. Against the frightening European Messiah principle, Bliven warned early in the Depression of the threat of demagogues. An innate aversion to the cult of personality prevented him from ever succumbing completely to FDR's legendary charm and mystique.

"The center holds" was another axiom lost on the editors whose narrow spectrum consisted almost exclusively of left-wing thought. They enjoyed the luxury of writing off right wingers as reactionaries or fascists and debating issues on their own terms. Outside this vacuum, however, conservatives possessed sufficient power to torpedo virtually every liberal proposal. Politicians of *TNR*'s persuasion had less room than met its eye. The bitter animosities that the New Deal raised among the wealthy, which so perplexed Bliven, strengthened the Republican's hand and, in turn, stifled Roosevelt. No matter how vehemently he inveighed against his class' "money-changers" and lurched toward the left, the combined forces of "GOP Bourbons" and southern Democrats pulled him back toward the middle. Roosevelt's skill at balancing competing interests against formidable odds was the stuff of his political genius and explains, in the view of a number of historians, the success of his presidency. Such a strength seemed alien to *TNR*; Bliven's belated appreciation for Roosevelt grew only after the New Deal's completion. Adopting a

Churchillian pose, the editor realized it was the worst form of government, except for all the others. Roosevelt's spirited bid for a third term engaged *TNR* in partisan politics for the first time since its founding, a sport in which it participated with surprising relish. The editors confronted the constant challenge of operating within the system while sacrificing as few of their principles as possible.

Bliven thereby preserved the magazine's objectivity—to a point. What this technique lacked, unfortunately, was a human dimension. The vast electorate, by nature, ordinarily casts its ballot on the basis of a candidate's intrinsic appeal, to the exclusion of his specific positions. The United States' abiding affection for Roosevelt granted him considerable leeway in laying out his programs. Because the president and the New Deal were inextricably linked, he emerged as liberalism's symbol and savior. *TNR* gradually recognized the necessity of finding heroes and championing its cause; people did not live by ideas alone.

Within *TNR*'s slender purview, in other words, there existed an ineluctable tension between theory and practice. The translation of an idea as potent as nationalism into action proved extremely dangerous. Croly's incessant calls for the centralization of power, in the end, strained his democratic convictions. The bitter experience of World War I and the hysteria surrounding the red scare crackdown highlighted the unforeseen perils of relying on the government to carry out one's agenda. Denied access to Washington for the next 12 years, liberals were temporarily relieved of the responsibilities of putting their ideas into practice. Hugh Johnson's stormy reign at the NRA evoked images of Mussolini and Hitler and spelled potential disaster for labor. Business's prominence in the first phase of the New Deal showed the incipient signs of a corporate oligarchy. Soule temporarily evacuated his orderly universe of a planned society to speculate on the imminent violence resulting from a revolution. The NRA's timely demise and the passage of a number of reforms to the editors' liking emboldened them to renew the drive for social democracy. But with the major components of the welfare state firmly set into place by 1938, the government had reached the limits of its size for the moment. *TNR* prudently accepted half a loaf with the intention of bargaining piecemeal for the rest—at least in the United States. The depiction of collectivization and five-year plans as a supercharged New Deal permitted liberals to continue their crusade by shifting the battlefield to another nation. Communism, by any other name, became the new progressivism; the Soviet Union, the city on the hill. Stalin's ultimate betrayal of the revolution slowly sensitized the editors to the horrors of the modern totalitarian state and the pitfalls of their ideological mischievousness. The United States' precious tradition of freedom, they gradually concluded, merited respect. Once again, they learned that a government entrusted with safeguarding liberty could just as easily turn into a tool of oppression. The Crolian dilemma—Jeffersonian democracy or Hamiltonian centrality—awaited a liberal resolution.

The transformation of society *TNR* envisaged failed to come about largely because the magazine underestimated the nation's stable character. Whenever, the society appeared under intense pressure, the editors habitually prepared for the collapse that did not occur. In 1919, Alvin Johnson proposed a domino theory of upheaval, and Weyl hid himself in his no man's land of Armageddon. Thirteen years later, Bliven hit the streets searching for restlessness but found a numb populace. In his travels, Cowley commented on the fear of change among the Depression's victims. The resiliency and static nature of U.S. institutions mystified the editors. To their perpetual frustration, the average citizens' craving for comfort and security made them wary of visionary schemes. Thus, workers' concern for the "solid, warm facts of kindliness, clothes [and] food" which Lippmann described in *Drift and Mastery* spurred them to organize unions in order to receive a fair share of the pie and join the vast ranks of the middle class.

While this goal propelled the editors to redress the imbalance between management and labor and incited one of the true revolutions in the U.S. context, it severely narrowed political and social horizons. The quadrennial campaigns to forge a farmer–labor party proved futile because unions—from Gompers on—preferred to stick to bread-and-butter issues and avoid taking chances. In England, the Labour Party Croly so revered successfully capitalized on a history of sharp class divisions to gain tangible power. On this side of the Atlantic, by contrast, workers whose imaginations were seized by hopes of upward mobility were afraid of rocking the boat. The General Electric advertisements in the magazine told the story of the American dream and the nation's primary and indigenous ideology: capitalism. To make any sort of impact, *TNR* had to tailor its philosophy to fit this orthodoxy.

For all the radical rhetoric, *TNR* basically and consistently pledged its allegiance to the system. "Reform as you would preserve," stated Macaulay's dictum—a prescription to keep the framework's best features intact. The editors' relentless attacks on the economy attested to their faith in its fundamental soundness and in their own ideas for ensuring that it reached its potential.

Lippmann's tirades against "stupidity, waste, and greed" and Soule's against anarchy and chaos preached a sober economic rationalism. No one on Wall Street would have taken exception to the latter's arguments for ending topsy-turvy business cycles. The correct adjustment of the valves turned the engine on full throttle and produced, to the benefit of all, Weyl's "social surplus" and Soule's "economy of abundance." A belief that continued growth would democratize prosperity—that a high tide would raise all ships—spared it the hard choices of massive redistributions of wealth or deep structural reforms. Soule's Keynesian combination of deficit financing and pump priming represented a fast, efficient, but painless means of increasing national income and purchasing power. Except for an occasional tax soaking and some verbal abuse, the rich were let off fairly easy. Under *TNR*'s tepid type of socialism, they were merely required to pay their dues, as were everyone else.

In the economic realm, *TNR*'s creed supplanted an outmoded and unjust order with a new society built on mutual obligation. It took 30 years, though, for private privilege and greed to surrender any ground to the higher ideal of a public interest. Weyl's notion of consumerism vested the people with the power to band together to pursue their common interests in achieving economic security. Soule's plan for the "socialization of wealth" was not to collectivism so much as collective responsibility. The rewards of U.S. abundance were channeled into socially productive and humane purposes. By insuring against unemployment, hunger, and old age, the guarantor state remembered the forgotten person's stake in the community at large. Liberals updated the meaning of "general welfare" in the Constitution's preamble to reflect the twentieth century's realities.

Had Croly lived to see many of his ideas come to fruition in the welfare state, he would have withheld his complete blessing. For in 1940, *TNR*'s reconstructed New Dealers forsook a vital element of the founding editor's legacy. Croly's organic concept of culture transcended the narrow pecuniary concerns of consumerism. His holistic vision of human brotherhood and social regeneration extolled the virtues of a nation of saints and heroes rather than mere materialists. Bliven and Soule's nostalgic evocation of their forebear's homiletic messages in the late 1930s, by contrast, adorned a practical but mundane collection of reforms. Hardened by a world war and the Great Depression, U.S. citizens braced themselves for an uncertain future (and another world war) by clinging to their stable positions in society and the renewed hope of better days to come. The temporary end of reform heralded liberalism's triumph as well as defeat. While the impulse for change and renewal momentarily withered, a tradition still thrived. In a world seemingly gone amok, the immortality of democratic institutions fulfilled, if not all, then at least a precious part of the U.S. promise.

Throughout the first half of its history, *TNR* lived up to its original billing. From its inception, it never stopped starting insurrections in readers' convictions and wielding influence out of proportion to its circulation. The "ripples in the pond" Croly vowed to start reached the furthest shores. As a sounding board for new and innovative ideas, *TNR* set unique standards for journalism. It functioned neither as a money-making enterprise nor as a conventional source of news. The honorable service the publication rendered to the nation was to enrich its intellectual life and leaven public opinion. Whether one agreed with it or not, *TNR* earned profound respect. On the occasion of *TNR*'s fiftieth anniversary, Walter Lippmann defined the editorial aims: "a journal of unopinionated opinion—one that would be informed, disinterested, compassionate, and brave . . . in the perspective of civility in our western society,"[5] Liberals of those years had few closer and trustworthier friends than this organ of reform. For such qualities entitled *TNR* to undertake the bold mission of fashioning a modern philosophy for the United States to meet the demands of the modern age.

. . . .

Notes

PREFACE

1. Herbert Croly, "The New Republic Idea," *TNR*, December 6, 1922.
2. Croly to Leonard Hand, January 5, 1914. Quoted in Charles Forcey, *The Crossroads of Liberalism* (New York: Oxford University Press, 1961), p. 124.
3. Alfred Kazin, *Starting Out In The Thirties* (Little, Brown, 1962), p. 10.

INTRODUCTION: RIPPLES IN A POND

1. Croly's parents are portrayed in Charles Forcey, *Crossroads of Liberalism* (New York: Oxford University Press, 1961), Chapter 1 and David Levy, *Herbert Croly and The New Republic* (Princeton, New Jersey: Princeton University Press, 1984), Chapters 1 and 2.
2. Croly's physical appearance is drawn from a memorial issue, *TNR*, July 16, 1930, and photographs in *TNR*'s historical collection. Levy, in *Croly and The New Republic*, "Preface" and "Conclusion," paints a vivid psychological portrait; Forcey, *Crossroads*, describes his personal work habits and daily routine, Chapter 1.
3. This section relies primarily on Henry F. May, *The End of American Innocence* (New York: Oxford University Press, 1961); Charles Madison, *Leaders and Liberals in the Twentieth Century* (New York: F. Ungar, 1961); George Mowry, *Theodore Roosevelt and the Progressive Movement* (New York: Hill & Wang, 1963).
4. Alvin Johnson, *Pioneer's Progress* (Lincoln, Nebraska: University of Nebraska, 1960), p. 124.
5. Johnson, *Pioneer's Progress* p. 125.
6. Forcey, *Crossroads*, p. 131.
7. Levy, *Croly and The New Republic*, pp. 138–39.
8. Herbert Croly, *The Promise of American Life* (New York: Harper & Row, 1963). Citations follow the order of quotations in the text; pp. 29, 72, 453.
9. Croly, *Promise*, pp. 22, 372, 391–393, 453.
10. Herbert Croly, *Progressive Democracy* (New York: Macmillan, 1914), pp. 38, 393, 363, 373.
11. Croly, *Progressive Democracy*, pp. 363, 373.
12. Walter Weyl, *The New Democracy* (New York: Mitchell Kennerly, 1914), pp. 403, 31, 207.
13. Weyl, *New Democracy*, pp. 347, 148, 278, 329, 261.
14. Walter Lippmann, *A Preface to Politics* (New York: Mitchell Kennerly, 1914), pp. 44, 317, 36.

15. Walter Lippmann, *Drift and Mastery* (New York: Mitchell Kennerly, 1914), pp. 196, 183, 188, 91, 255, 116, 50.

16. Lippmann, *Drift and Mastery*, pp. 255, 116, 50.

17. *Walter Weyl, An Appreciation* (New York: privately printed by a group of friends, 1922), p. 56.

18. Levy, *Croly and The New Republic*, p. 186; and Forcey, *Crossroads*, p. 170.

19. Johnson, *Pioneer*, p. 233.

20. Croly to Straight, March 12, 1914.

21. Herbert Croly, *Willard Straight* (New York: Macmillan, 1924), p. 474.

22. Croly, *Straight*, p. 472.

23. Michael Straight, *After a Long Silence* (New York: Norton, 1983), p. 22.

24. Quoted in Forcey, *Crossroads*, p. 12.

25. Croly to Straight, September 30, 1913.

26. W. A. Swanberg. *Whitney Father, Whitney Heiress* (New York: Scribners, 1980), p. 227.

27. Forcey, *Crossroads*, p. 124; and Croly to Straight, September 30, 1914 (enclosure).

28. Croly to Straight, September 30, 1914 (enclosure).

29. Philip Littell, "As a Friend," *TNR Croly Memorial Issue*, July 16, 1930, pp. 243–44.

30. Croly to Straight, September 30, 1914 (enclosure).

31. Croly to Frankfurter, undated, 1913.

32. Straight to Croly, October 6, 1913; and Straight to Croly, undated, September 13, 1913.

33. Croly to Straight, September 30, 1914.

34. Straight to Croly, October 6, 1913.

35. Straight to Croly, October 15, 1913.

36. Croly to Straight, October 8, 1913.

37. Croly to Straight, October 6, 1913.

38. Walter Lippmann, "Remarks on the Occasion of This Journal's 50th Year," *TNR*, March 21, 1964, p. 14; and Straight to Croly, July 24, 1914.

39. Walter Lippmann, "Notes for a Biography," *TNR Herbert Croly Memorial Issue*, July 16, 1930, pp. 250–52. Forcey and Steel base their secondary accounts of Croly's aversion to Platonism on this piece. According to Straight's direct correspondence, he actually favored the notion.

40. Ronald Steel, *Walter Lippmann and the American Century* (Boston: Little, Brown, 1980), p. 68.

41. Straight to Croly, January 29, 1914; Croly to Straight, October 15, 1913.

42. Forcey, *Crossroads*, pp. 174, 181.

43. Croly to Straight, September 22, 1913.

44. Straight to Croly, February 13, 1914; *The National Encyclopedia of American Biography*, Vol. 32 (New York: James T. White, 1945), p. 375.

45. Straight to Croly, December 2, 1914.

46. Straight to William Barnes (Chairman of the Republican Committee of New York), April 21, 1914.

47. Forcey, *Crossroads*, p. 175.

48. Straight to Croly, March 1, 1915.

49. Straight to Croly, October 6, 1913.

50. Straight to Croly, October 8, 1913.

51. Quoted in Levy, *Croly and The New Republic*, p. 216.

52. Straight to Croly, October 15, 1913. (guestlist); and framed menu hung at *TNR*'s offices.

53. Forcey, *Crossroads*, p. 178; and Weyl to T. Roosevelt, August 4, 1914.

54. T. Roosevelt to Weyl, August 6, 1914.

55. Steel, *Lippmann*, p. 76.

56. Croly to Straight, January 29, 1914.

57. Straight to Croly, October 16, 1913.

┆THE BUSINESS OF LIVING: 1914–16

1. Dorothy's youth and courtship are detailed in W. A. Swanberg, *Whitney Father, Whitney Heiress* (New York: Viking, 1980), pp. 236 and 289–96. "The power of the paper is extraordinary," D. Straight to W. D. Straight, February 21, 1913. Quoted in Swanberg, *Whitney Father*, p. 385.

2. For Straight's background and education, see Swanberg *Whitney Father*, pp. 253–54, 255–57, 303–10; and Charles Forcey, *The Crossroads of Liberalism* (New York: Oxford University Press, 1961), pp. 170–77. The Whitney opposition to the marriage is described in Swanberg *Whitney Father*, p. 301. Kipling is quoted in Swanberg *Whitney Father*, p. 287.

3. *TNR*, November 7, 1914, p. 1.

4. *TNR*, December 26, 1914, p. 1.

5. Hallowell to Straight, November 23, 1914,

6. Malcolm Cowley, *The Dream of the Golden Mountains* (New York: Penguin, 1964), p. 10.

7. *TNR*, December 16, 1916, p. 193.

8. *TNR*, June 26, 1915, V.

9. *TNR*, April 17, 1915, p. 31.

10. *TNR*, November 6, 1915, pp. 2–3; source of subscriptions from Hallowell to Straight, February 17, 1914 (business enclosure).

11. D. Straight to Croly, November 4, 1914.

12. Privately issued direct mailer, July 16, 1915 (*TNR* Historical Files).

13. Eric Goldman, *Rendezvous With Destiny* (New York: Vintage, 1962), p. 223.

14. Offices are described in Bruce Bliven, *Five Million Words Later* (New York: John Day, 1970), p. 165; and Cowley, *Golden Mountains*, pp. 1–3.

15. Editorial procedure confirmed in all of the editors' work, including Herbert Croly, *Willard Straight* (New York; Macmillian, 1924), p. 373; Croly to Bourne, October 5, 1914.

16. Alvin Johnson, *Pioneer's Progress* (Lincoln, Nebraska: University of Nebraska, 1960), p. 233.

17. Lippmann's comment in *Walter Weyl, An Appreciation*, pp. 184–85.

18. Hallowell to Straight, November 14, 1915.

19. Straight to Croly, April 21, 1915.

20. Straight to Croly, March 1, 1915.

21. Swanberg, *Whitney Father*, pp. 370–71.

22. Croly, *Straight*, p. 373.

23. Straight to Croly, November 17, 1914.

24. Straight to Lippmann, February 23, 1915.

25. Straight to Croly, May 7, 1915.

26. Straight to Lippmann, May 7, 1915.

27. The "tell Herbert letters" are quoted in Swanberg, *Whitney Father*, pp. 404–08.

28. Croly to Straight, March 2, 1916.

29. *TNR*, March 11, 1916, p. 139.

30. *TNR*, May 6, 1915, p. 48.

31. Easley to Gordon, May 8, 1915.

32. Easley to Davison, May 21, 1915.

33. Marc Karson, *Organized Labor in the Progressive Era* (Minneapolis: University of Minnesota Press, 1960), p. 127.

34. Croly to Straight, December 3, 1915.

35. Ronald Steel, *Walter Lippmann and the American Century* (Boston: Little, Brown, 1980), p. 76.

36. Croly to T. Roosevelt, January 30, 1915.

37. Reviews are discussed in Frank L. Mott, *A History of American Magazines*, Vol. 3 (Cambridge, Massachusetts: Harvard University Press, 1938), pp. 22–23.

38. Straight to Croly, March 25, 1915.

39. *TNR*, December 5, 1914, p. 4.

40. "The Paradox and Human Factor," *TNR*, January 2, 1915, p. 28.

41. "Women and Labor—Objects of Charity," *TNR*, January 23, 1915, p. 10.

42. "The Dangerous Class," *TNR*, May 8, 1914, pp. 7–8.

43. *TNR*, February 20, 1915, p. 27; and January 30, 1915, p. 12.

44. Steel, *Lippmann*, pp. 23–24.

45. Walter Lippmann, "Life is Cheap," *TNR*, December 12, 1914, pp. 12–14.

46. Walter Lippmann, "The Campaign Against Sweating," *TNR*, March 27, 1915, p. 2.

47. Quoted in Daniel Aaron, *Writers on the Left* (New York: Harcourt, Brace & World, 1961), pp. 205–06.

48. Alvin Johnson, "The American Workingman," *TNR*, September 29, 1917, pp. 249–50.

49. *Weyl*, p. 43.

50. Walter Weyl, "Equality," *TNR*, January 23, 1915, pp. 13–14.

51. Walter Weyl, "Industrial Apostasy," *TNR*, May 20, 1916, pp. 54–56.

52. "Money Wanted," *TNR*, June 24, 1916 and July 29, 1916, pp. 315–16.

53. For a detailed account of this dispute, see Philip Taft, *Organized Labor in American History* (New York: Harper & Row, 1964), pp. 334–37.

54. *TNR*, May 8, 1915, pp. 2–3.

55. "The Closed Mind," *TNR*, May 1, 1915, pp. 316–17.

56. Walter Lippmann, "Mr. Rockefeller on the Stand," *TNR*, January 30, 1915, pp. 12–13. Identified in Arthur Schlesinger, Jr., ed., *Early Writings of Walter Lippmann* (New York: Liveright, 1970), pp. 262–66. Also "The Rockefeller Plan in Colorado," *TNR*, October 9, 1915, pp. 249–50.

57. "Railroad Strike," *TNR*, August 9, 1916, pp. 54–55.

58. Lippmann's letter is cited in Wilson to Norman Hapgood, September 25, 1916.

59. Walter Lippmann, "The Railroad Crisis and After," *TNR*, August 26, 1916, pp. 80–82; Lippmann, "An Ineffective Remedy," *TNR*, November 25, 1916, pp. 83–84; "The Averted Railway Strike," *TNR*, September 9, 1916, pp. 130–31. (Three articles are identified in Schlesinger, *Early Writings*, pp. 216–24.)

60. "Unionism vs. Anti-Unionism," *TNR*, September 23, 1916, pp. 178–80.

61. "So-Called Industrial Peace," *TNR*, January 30, 1915, pp. 6–7.

62. "Newspaper Incitement to Violence," *TNR*, October 21, 1916, pp. 283–85.

63. Karson, *Organized Labor*, p. 124.

64. "Industrial Conflict," *TNR*, August 28, 1915, pp. 89–94.

65. "Labor as a National Commodity," *TNR*, December 2, 1916, pp. 112–14.

66. *TNR*, January 22, 1916, pp. 287–90.

67. "Hours of Work Must Be Limited," *TNR*, April 22, 1916, pp. 306–08; and "Eight Hours for Work," *TNR*, September 8, 1915, pp. 170–71.

68. "Before the Court," *TNR*, December 5, 1914, pp. 10–11.

69. Walter Lippmann, *TNR*, November 7, 1914, pp. 5–6. (Identified in Schlesinger, *Early Writings*, pp. 201–03.)

70. *TNR*, June 5, 1914, p. 4.

71. "What Uncle Sam Does Not Do for Women in Industry," *TNR*, July 29, 1916, pp. 324–26.

72. "Industrial Conflict," *TNR*, August 28, 1915, pp. 89–94.

73. *TNR*, May 6, 1916, pp. 5–6.

74. "A Government Plan for Health Insurance," *TNR*, May 20, 1916, pp. 55–56.

75. "Federal Use of the Unemployed," *TNR*, April 10, 1915, pp. 250–51.

76. *TNR*, January 1, 1916, p. 208.

77. "Education and Work," *TNR*, March 11, 1916, pp. 145–46.

78. "The Model of Scientific Investigation," *TNR*, December 4, 1915, pp. 126–27.

79. *TNR*, January 2, 1915, p. 5.

80. "Democratic Control of Scientific Management," *TNR*, December 23, 1916, pp. 204–05.

81. "Salvaging the Unemployable," *TNR*, October 2, 1915, pp. 221–22.

82. *TNR*, March 27, 1915, pp. 2-3.

83. "Wanted—An Immigration Policy," *TNR*, December 26, 1914, pp. 10–11.

84. Forcey, *Crossroads*, pp. 57–58.

85. Walter Weyl, "Industrial Apostasy," *TNR*, May 20, 1916, pp. 64–66.

86. Steel, *Lippmann*, pp. 189–92.

87. David Phillips, "Jews Are Not Aliens," *TNR*, November 30, 1918, p. 104.

88. Richard Hofstadter, *The Age of Reform* (New York: Vintage, 1955), pp. 135–66.

89. Johnson, *Pioneer's Progress*, p. 234.

90. Francis Hackett, *I Chose Denmark* (New York: Doubleday & Doran, 1940), p. 63.

91. Steel, *Lippmann*, pp. 177–78.

92. Holmes to Laski, January 4, 1920. In Mark De Wolfe, ed. *Holmes–Laski Letters* (Cambridge, Massachusetts: Harvard University Press, 1953), p. 231.

93. Bliven, p. 156.

94. "The Future of the Socialist Party," *TNR*, January 16, 1915, pp. 10–12.

95. *TNR*, June 24, 1916, p. 182.

96. "How Can the Socialist Party Live?" *TNR*, December 2, 1916, pp. 110–12.

97. Herbert Croly, "The Two Parties in 1916," *TNR*, October 21, 1916, pp. 286–96.

98. "Homeless Radicals," *TNR*, July 11, 1916, pp. 211–12.

99. W. J. Ghent, "Socialist Degeneration," *TNR*, January 9, 1915, pp. 23–24; and "The Glorious Opportunity," *TNR*, January 16, 1915, p. 24.

100. Granville Hicks, *John Reed: The Making of a Revolutionary* (New York: Macmillan, 1936), p. 172,

101. "Presidential Competence," *TNR*, November 21, 1914, p. 7.

102. "Unregenerated Democracy," *TNR*, February 5, 1916, pp. 17–19.

103. Arthur Link, *Woodrow Wilson and the Progressive Era* (New York: Harper & Row, 1954), pp. 55–56.

104. Herbert Croly, "The Two Parties in 1916," *TNR*, October 21, 1916, pp. 286–96.

105. Croly to Straight, March 18, 1916.

106. Croly to Straight, March 24, 1916.

107. Croly to Straight, March 18, 1916.

108. Steel, *Lippmann*, p. 107.

109. Hapgood to Wilson, September 28, 1916. Arthur S. Link, ed. *The Papers of Woodrow Wilson* (Princeton, New Jersey: Princeton University Press, 1982), pp. 86–88; and Lippmann to Wilson, August 21, 1916, pp. 62–63.

110. Straight to Lippmann, May 7, 1915.

111. Lippmann to Straight, April 6, 1916.

112. Croly, *Straight*, p. 454.

113. Croly to Straight, October 7, 1916 (and enclosure of rough draft of Straight's letter).
114. Willard Straight, "A Letter from Mr. Straight," *TNR*, October 28, 1916, pp. 313–14.

¦A BATTALION OF DEATH: 1917–19

1. For excellent biographical material on Lippmann, see Ronald Steel, *Walter Lippmann and the American Century* (Boston: Little, Brown, 1980); and Charles Forcey, *The Crossroads of Liberalism* (New York: Oxford University Press, 1961), pp. 88–121.
2. Weyl's early years are traced in Forcey, *Crossroads*, New York. *Walter Weyl, An Appreciation* (New York: privately printed by a group of friends, 1922) pp. 52–58; and Alvin Johnson, *Pioneer's Progress* (Lincoln, Nebraska: University of Nebraska, 1960).
3. Lippmann to Wilson, February 6, 1917.
4. Steel, *Lippmann*, p. 109.
5. Bruce Bliven, "The First Forty Years," *TNR Fortieth Anniversary Issue*, November 1954, pp. 6–10.
6. Forcey, *Crossroads*, p. 225.
7. C. W. Swanberg, *Whitney Father, Whitney Heiress* (New York: Viking, 1980), p. 404.
8. Croly to Straight, April 11, 1917.
9. "American Labor Policy," *TNR*, June 29, 1918, pp. 250–51.
10. Marc Karson, *Organized Labor in the Progressive Era* (Minneapolis: University of Minnesota Press, 1960), p. 255.
11. Philip Taft, *Organized Labor in American History* (New York: Harper & Row, 1964), p. 248.
12. *TNR*, August 31, 1918, pp. 121–22.
13. "Breaking the Labor Truce," *TNR*, December 22, 1917, pp. 197–98.
14. "The Winning of Labor," *TNR*, December 22, 1917, pp. 49–50.
15. "Recognition for Labor," *TNR*, November 24, 1917, pp. 84–86.
16. "The Socialist Program," *TNR*, September 14, 1918, pp. 182–83.
17. "Labor and the New Social Order," *TNR*, February 16, 1918, p. 2.
18. "Women in Industry," *TNR*, October 26, 1918, pp. 365–66.
19. "Industrial Citizenship for Women," *TNR*, July 13, 1918, pp. 304–05.
20. "Industrial Citizenship for Women," *TNR*, July 13, 1918, pp. 304–05.
21. *TNR*, December 26, 1914, p. 5.
22. Randolph Bourne, *War and the Intellectuals* (New York: Harper & Row, 1964), p. 12.
23. Forcey, *Crossroads*, p. 238.
24. W. Straight to D. Straight, May 12, 1918. Quoted in Swanberg, *Whitney Father*, p. 408.
25. Herbert Croly, *Willard Straight* (New York: Macmillan, 1924), p. 481.

26. Steel, *Lippmann*, pp. 334–35.

27. *TNR Herbert Croly Memorial Issue*, July 16, 1930, pp. 250–52.

28. David M. Kennedy, *Over Here* (New York: Oxford University Press, 1980), pp. 262–65; Karson, *Organized Labor*, pp. 204–05; Taft, *Labor in American History*, p. 248.

29. "Organization or Anarchy," *TNR*, July 21, 1917, pp. 320–28.

30. Croly to Thomas D. Eliot, August 17, 1917.

31. "The Issue in Butte," *TNR*, September 22, 1917, pp. 215–17.

32. *TNR*, December 15, 1917, pp. 160–61.

33. "Tying Up Western Lumber," *TNR*, September 29, 1917, pp. 242–44; and "Common Sense and the IWW," *TNR*, April 27, 1918, pp. 375–76.

34. "From the Associated Press," *TNR*, October 6, 1917, p. 275; and "Associated Press and the IWW," *TNR*, December 1, 1917, pp. 126–27.

35. *TNR*, August 24, 1918, pp. 88–89.

36. "From an IWW in Jail," *TNR*, May 23, 1918, p. 234; and "Never Mind What You Think About the IWW," *TNR*, June 22, 1918, p. iii.

37. *TNR*, May 4, 1918, p. 3.

38. *TNR*, February 13, 1918, p. 93.

39. *TNR*, September 28, 1918, p. 240.

40. *TNR*, September 21, 1918, p. 210.

41. Kennedy, *Over Here*, p. 78.

42. Roosevelt to Straight, June 1, 1917.

43. Straight to Roosevelt, June 9, 1917.

44. Easley to Straight, September 25, 1917.

45. Straight to Easley, September 29, 1917.

46. Walter Lippmann, "Notes For a Biography," *TNR Herbert Croly Memorial Issue*, July 16, 1930, pp. 250–52.

47. "Freedom of Speech: Whose Concern," *TNR*, February 22, 1919, pp. 102–03.

48. Kennedy, *Over Here*, p. 283.

49. "Woman's Work After the War," *TNR*, January 25, 1917, pp. 358–59.

50. "A New Alien and Sedition Law," *TNR*, November 26, 1919, p. 366.

51. "The Labor Situation," *TNR*, February 22, 1919, pp. 185–86.

52. Croly to Wilson, October 19, 1917.

53. Croly, "The Mob in High Places," *TNR*, December 17, 1918. Identified in folder at *TNR* filled with original Croly manuscripts (most deal with foreign policy).

54. Walter Lippmann "Notes for a Biography" *TNR Herbert Croly, Memorial Issue*, July 16, 1930, pp. 250–52.

55. Walter Lippmann, "Unrest," *TNR*, November 12, 1919, pp. 315–22.

56. Alvin Johnson, "Is Revolution Possible," *TNR*, November 26, 1919, pp. 367–73.

57. Walter Weyl, *Tired Radicals and Other Essays* (New York: Heubsch, 1922), pp. 15–20.

0

THE LOST AND FOUND GENERATION: 1920–24

1. Lunches and editorial conferences are described in Bruce Bliven, *Five Million Words Later* (New York: John Day, 1963) pp. 164–66, 203; T. S. Mathews, *Name and Address* (New York: Simon & Schuster, 1960), pp. 186–87; Malcolm Cowley, *The Dream of the Golden Mountains* (New York: Penguin, 1980), pp. 1–2; Interview with Mrs. D. F. Updike, editorial secretary at *TNR* in the late 1920s, conducted on March 27, 1983.

2. Alfred Kazin, *New York Jew* (New York: Knopf, 1978), p. 128.

3. Wilson to Stanley Dell, March 4, 1921. In Elena Wilson, ed., *Letters on Literature and Politics—1912-1972* (New York: Farrar, Straus & Giroux, 1977), pp. 66.

4. Bliven, *Five Million*, p. 203.

5. C.W. Swanberg, *Whitney Father, Whitney Heiress* (New York: Viking, 1980), p. 482.

6. Frank L. Mott, *A History of American Magazines*, Vol. 3 (Cambridge, Massachusetts: Harvard University Press, 1960), p. 211.

7. *N.W. Ayer & Son's Annual Directory of Newspapers and Periodicals* (Philadelphia: Ayer, 1918–25).

8. Arthur Link, "What Happened to the Progressive Movement in the 1920's," in *Twentieth Century America: Recent Interpretations*, edited by Barton J. Bernstein and Allen J. Matusow (New York: Harcourt, Brace, Jovanovich, 1972), p. 120.

9. Malcolm Cowley, *Exile's Return* (New York: Penguin, 1979), p. 63.

10. Walter Lippmann, "Can the Strike be Abandoned?" *TNR*, January 21, 1920, pp. 214–17.

11. Ronald Steel, *Walter Lippmann and the American Century* (Boston: Little, Brown, 1980), pp. 181–83.

12. Walter Weyl, *Tired Radicals and Other Essays* (New York: Heubsch, 1922), pp. 14–21.

13. Charles Forcey, *The Crossroads* of Liberalism (New York: Oxford University Press, 1961), pp. 296–97.

14. "Hoover and the Issues," *TNR*, February 4, 1920, pp. 281–83.

15. Robert M. Lovett, *All Our Years* (New York: Viking Press, 1948), p. 176.

16. Lippmann to Frankfurter, April 7, 1920. Quoted in Steel, *Lippmann*, p. 168.

17. Lippmann, "Hoover and the Issues," *TNR*, February 4, 1920, pp. 282–83. Identified in Steel, *Lippmann*, p. 612.

18. Charles Merz, "Mr. Hoover and *The New Republic*," *TNR*, March 30, 1920, p. 3.

19. Lovett, *All Our Years*, pp. 176–77.

20. George Soule, "HC's Liberalism: 1920–28," *TNR Herbert Croly Memorial Issue*, July 16, 1930, pp. 253–57.

21. Walter Lippmann, "Chicago, 1920," *TNR*, July 23, 1920, pp. 108–10. Identified in Schlesinger, *Early Writings*, pp. 186–94.

22. "Harding," *TNR*, June 23, 1920, p. 100.

23. Lippmann, "Is Harding a Republican," *TNR*, July 21, 1920, pp. 219–20.

24. "The Democratic Party and the Liberal Vote," *TNR*, September 22, 1920, pp. 82–83.

25. Walter Johnson, *William Allen White's America* (New York: Henry Holt, 1947), p. 181.

26. "Throwing One's Vote Away," *TNR*, October 6, 1920, pp. 134–35.

27. "The Use of a Protest Vote," *TNR*, October 27, 1920, pp. 204–05.

28. "The Prospect of Harding," *TNR*, January 29, 1920, pp. 108–10.

29. Herbert Croly, "The Eclipse of Progressivism," *TNR*, October 27, 1920, pp. 210–16.

30. Croly, "Eclipse," pp. 210–16.

31. "Sickness of Politics," *TNR*, June 7, 1922, pp. 32–34.

32. "A Nation Stalled," *TNR*, November 8, 1922, pp. 264–66.

33. "Republicans in the Sargasso Sea," *TNR*, July 5, 1922, pp. 147–48.

34. "Sickness of Politics," *TNR*, June 7, 1922, pp. 32–34.

35. "Progressivism Reborn," *TNR*, December 13, 1922, pp. 56–57.

36. "Sickness of Politics," *TNR*, June 7, 1922, pp. 32–34.

37. "Carry On," *TNR*, October 4, 1922, p. v.

38. *TNR*, November 8, 1922, p. iv.

39. Herbert Croly, "The New Republic Idea," *TNR*, December 6, 1922.

40. "Problem of the Smith Candidacy," *TNR*, March 19, 1924, pp. 87–88.

41. *TNR*, May 28, 1924, pp. 4–5.

42. Richard Hofstadter, *The Age of Reform* (New York: Vintage, 1955), p. 166.

43. Bruce Bliven, "The Democracy Fumbles," *TNR*, July 9, 1924, p. 194.

44. Felix Frankfurter, "Why Mr. Davis Shouldn't Run," *TNR*, April 16, 1924, pp. 193–95. Identified in Bruce Allen Murphy, *The Brandeis and Frankfurter Connection* (New York: Doubleday, 1983), p. 90. Also Frankfurter to Bliven, July 6, 1923; Bliven to Frankfurter, July 6, 1923; and Croly to Frankfurter, January 7, 1925, for further details on Frankfurter's relationship to the magazine.

45. *TNR*, August 6, 1924, pp. 285–87.

46. *TNR*, June 25, 1924, pp. 113–15.

47. Bruce Bliven, "Hail to the Accidental Chief," *TNR*, June 18, 1924, pp. 92–93.

48. "Republican Economics," *TNR*, June 25, 1924, pp. 113–15.

49. "The Greatness of Andrew Mellon," *TNR*, April 16, 1924, p. 106.

50. Herbert Croly, "Why I Shall Vote for La Follette," *TNR*, October 24, 1924, pp. 170–74.

51. *TNR*, September 24, 1924, p. iv.

52. *TNR*, September 3, 1924, p. 3.

53. *TNR*, March 25, 1920, p. 370.

54. *TNR*, January 25, 1922, p. 23.

55. *TNR*, May 21, 1924, p. 322.

56. *TNR*, January 25, 1922, p. 23.

57. "The Economic Position of the Farmer," *TNR*, December 27, 1922, pp. 106–08; *TNR*, October 17, 1923, pp. 194–97; "What the Farmers Can Really Do," *TNR*, December 27, 1922, pp. 296–98.

58. Bruce Bliven, "Why the Farmer Sees Red," *TNR*, November 7, 1923, pp. 273–75.

59. "The Newest Agrarianism," *TNR*, April 9, 1924, pp. 167–68.

60. "The Farmer–Capitalist Myth," *TNR*, July 30, 1924, pp. 263–65.

61. Bruce Bliven, "Do Workingmen Deserve Homes?" March 5, 1924, pp. 39–41.

62. "The Wooing of Labor," *TNR*, September 24, 1924, pp. 39–41.

63. "Dr. Butler's Buncome," *TNR*, September 10, 1924, p. 7.

64. "The LF Platform," *TNR*, June 18, 1924, pp. 3–6.

65. Lippmann, "Why I Shall Vote for Davis," *TNR*, October 29, 1924, pp. 218–19.

66. Steel, *Lippmann*, p. 223.

67. David Kennedy, *Over Here* (New York: Oxford University Press, 1980), p. 286.

68. *TNR*, November 5, 1924, p. 230.

69. "Barriers to Progressivism," *TNR*, November 5, 1924, pp. 24–42.

70. Lovett, *All Our Years*, p. 182.

71. Kenneth MacKay, *The Progressive Movement of 1924* (New York: Octagon Books, 1966), p. 221.

72. "The Progressive Attack on Monopoly," *TNR*, October 29, 1924, pp. 211–13.

73. "Progressives and Monopoly," *TNR*, July 23, 1924, pp. 226–27.

74. "The Meaning of the LF Candidacy," *TNR*, July 16, 1924, pp. 196–97; and "Why I Shall Vote for LF," *TNR*, October 19, 1924, pp. 217–19.

75. "Programs and Periodicals," *TNR*, October 22, 1924, pp. 216–17; and *TNR*, October 13, 1914, pp. 157–58.

76. Advertising piece, ca. 1924.

77. *TNR*, October 13, 1924, pp. 157–58; and "The Use of an Election Deadlock," *TNR*, August 13, 1924, pp. 314–15.

78. Eric Goldman, *Rendezvous With Destiny* (New York: Vintage, 1954), p. 227.

79. "The AFL Stays in Politics," *TNR*, August 20, 1924, pp. 7–9; and MacKay, *The Progressive Movement*, p. 205.

80. *TNR*, November 5, 1924, pp. 261–62.

81. MacKay, *The Progressive Movement*, p. 211.

82. "The Possible Consolation," *TNR*, November 19, 1924, pp. 285–87.

83. "Can There Be a New Party?" *TNR*, November 26, 1924, pp. 3–5.

84. *TNR*, November 19, 1924, p. 280.

85. "The Outlook of Progressivism," *TNR*, December 10, 1924, pp. 60–64.

86. *TNR*, December 31, 1924, p. 29.

87. "Child, Labor, The Home, and Liberty," *TNR*, December 2, 1924, p. 32.

88. *TNR*, December 31, 1924, pp. 134–35.

89. *TNR*, December 17, 1924, pp. 83–84.
90. *TNR*, December 31, 1924, pp. 134–35.
91. *TNR*, December 17, 1924, pp. 77–78.

⁝ TWO DEAD MEN: 1925–28

1. C. W. Swanberg, *Whitney Father, Whitney Heiress* (New York: Viking, 1980); pp. 351–52; and David Levy, *Herbert Croly of The New Republic* (Princeton, New Jersey: Princeton University Press, 1985), p. 276.
2. Croly to D. Straight, June 23, 1925.
3. Herbert Croly, "Christianity as a Way of Life," *TNR*, July 23, 1924, pp. 232–34; and "Christians, Beware!" *TNR*, November 25, 1925, pp. 12–14.
4. Bruce Bliven, *Five Million Words Later* (New York: John Day, 1963), p. 203.
5. Frankfurter to Croly, July 6, 1925.
6. Croly to Frankfurter, January 7, 1925.
7. Croly to D. Elmhirst, September 14, 1926.
8. Malcolm Cowley, *The Dream of the Golden Mountains* (New York: Penguin, 1980), p. 9.
9. Croly to D. Elmhirst, December 24, 1926; *N. W. Ayer & Son's Annual Directory of Newspapers and Periodicals* (Philadphia: N. W. Ayer, 1920–1930), for circulation figures; and Levy, *Croly*, p. 272.
10. Wilson to Stanley Dell, February 19, 1921. Quoted in Elena Wilson, ed., *Edmund Wilson: Letters on Literature and Politics* (New York: Farrar, Straus & Giroux, 1977), pp. 35–36.
11. Levy, *Croly*, p. 272.
12. Croly to D. Elmhirst, June 23, 1925.
13. For the magazine's finances and reorganization, see Memorandum, October 25, 1924, Mebane to Kincaid, November 13, 1924, and Baldwin to Gorton, November 20, 1924, Willard Straight papers, Cornell University Library, Ithaca, New York; and Levy, *Croly*, p. 272.
14. Bruce Bliven, "The First Forty Years," *TNR Fortieth Anniversary Issue*, November 1954, pp. 6–10.
15. Conversation with John Midgely, former Washington correspondent for *The Economist*, upon the retirement of the longest-reigning TRB, Richard Strout, in 1983.
16. *TNR*, March 10, 1926, p. iv.
17. Frank L. Mott, *A History of American Magazines*, Vol. 3 (Cambridge, Massachusetts: Harvard University Press, 1960), pp. 208–09.
18. *TNR*, September 28, 1927; December 5, 1927; May 16, 1928; September 12, 1928; and other issues.
19. "Building Coming Down," *TNR*, July 18, 1928, p. iii.
20. Alvin Johnson, *Pioneer's Progress* (Lincoln, Nebraska: University of Nebraska, 1960), pp. 271–88; Levy, *Croly*, pp. 269–71.
21. Bruce Bliven, "Boston's Civil War," *TNR*, June 29, 1927, pp. 142–43.
22. "The Lesson of It for Liberals," *TNR*, September 28, 1927, pp. 136–37.

23. "Why Boston Wishes to Hang Sacco & Vanzetti," *TNR*, May 25, 1927, pp. 4–6.

24. Quoted in William E. Leuchtenburg, *The Perils of Prosperity: 1914–1932* (Chicago: The University of Chicago Press, 1958), p. 72.

25. Levy, *Croly*, p. 286.

26. "To NR Readers," September 31, 1927, p. ii; and Croly to L. Elmhirst, October 6, 1927.

27. Bruce Bliven, "The Dedham Jail: A Visit to Sacco and Vanzetti," *TNR*, June 22, 1927, pp. 120–23.

28. Herbert Croly, "Dictating To the Future," *TNR*, October 26, 1927, pp. 247–49. Identified in *TNR* Historical Files, Washington, D.C.

29. Bruce Bliven, "The First Forty Years" *TNR Fortieth Anniversary Issue*, pp. 6–10; and Malcolm Cowley, *Exile's Return* (New York: Penguin, 1976), p. 221.

30. "A Catholic President?" *TNR*, March 23, 1927, pp. 128–31.

31. "More About Catholicism and the Presidency," *TNR*, May 11, 1927, pp. 315–17.

32. "A Catholic President?" *TNR*, March 23, 1927, pp. 128–31; "A Good American and a Good Catholic," *TNR*, April 27, 1927, pp. 260–62; "Al Smith's Dilemma," *TNR*, May 18, 1927, pp. 341–43.

33. "The Progressive Voter: He Wants to Know," *TNR*; July 25, 1928, pp. 242–47.

34. "Agitation Through Action," *TNR*, September 12, 1928, pp. 84–86.

35. Herbert Croly, "How is Hoover?" *TNR*, June 27, 1928, pp. 138–40.

36. John D. Hicks, *Republican Ascendancy* (New York: Harper Torchbooks, 1960), p. 202.

37. "Herbert Hoover's Great Illusion," *TNR*, August 22, 1928, p. 35.

38. Croly to D. Elmhirst, December 1, 1927.

39. "Governor Smith and the Progressives," *TNR*, February 1, 1928, pp. 284–86.

40. "The Reality of Unemployment," *TNR*, February 15, 1928, pp. 337–39.

41. "The Quality of Al Smith," *TNR*, August 9, 1928, pp. 31–33.

42. Croly to D. Elmhirst, December 1, 1927.

43. "Behold: The Bridegroom," *TNR*, July 11, 1928, pp. 186–87; Croly to L. Elmhirst, July 27, 1928. According to this letter, Croly wrote "practically all the articles" on Smith and the campaign.

44. "Al Smith and Tammany Hall," *TNR*, October 10, 1928, pp. 188–91.

45. Herbert Croly, "Smith of New York," *TNR*, February 22, 1928, pp. 9–14.

46. Croly to D. Elmhirst, July 23, 1928.

47. "Why Progressives Should Vote for Smith," *TNR*, September 5, 1928, pp. 58–60.

48. Paul Douglas, "Why I Am for Thomas," *TNR*, October 24, 1928, pp. 268–70.

49. Norman Thomas, "Norman Thomas on Al Smith," *TNR*, January 5, 1928, pp. 75–76.

50. "The Presidential Campaign—Observation and Guesses," *TNR*, February 15, 1928, pp. 335–37; and "Why Progressives Should Vote for Smith," *TNR*, September 5, 1928, pp. 58–60.

51. Croly to L. Elmhirst, July 27, 1928.

52. Bliven, *Five Million Words*, p. 177; Croly to D. Elmhirst, October 7, 1928; Croly to Frankfurter, October 7, 1928.

53. Barton J. Bernstein, "The Worker in an Unbalanced Society," In *Twentieth Century America: Recent Interpretations*, edited by Barton J. Bernstein and Allen J. Matusow (New York: Harcourt, Brace, Jovanovich, 1972), p. 176.

PAPER POLITICS: 1929–32

1. Mathews and Huling are quoted in Alfred Kazin, *New York Jew* (New York: Knopf, 1978), pp. 242–43; biographical material on Wilson is also extensive in Malcolm Cowley, *The Dream of the Golden Mountains* (New York: Penguin, 1980); Alden Whitman, "Edmund Wilson Dies," *New York Times*, June 13, 1972, p. 1; and David Aaron, Introduction to *Letters of Edmund Wilson 1912–1972*. Elena Wilson, ed., *Letters on Literature and Politics*. (New York: Farrar, Straus and Giroux, 1973).

2. For Soule's background, see R. Alan Lawson, *The Failure of Independent Liberalism: 1930–1941* (New York: G. P. Putnam's Sons, 1971), pp. 67–70; "George H. Soule Jr. Dies at 82, Ex-Editor of The New Republic," *New York Times*, April 15, 1970, p. 52, Cowley, *Golden Mountains*; some of the correspondence of his wife, Isabel, at the University of Oregon, also provides a brief glimpse of his character.

3. See Cowley, *Golden Mountains*, pp. 6–7.

4. Richard H. Pells, *Radical Visions and American Dreams* (Boston: Houghton, Mifflin, 1969), p. 35.

5. Edmund Wilson, "Lawrence Mass.," *TNR*, November 25, 1931, pp. 36–39.

6. Edmund Wilson, "Detroit Motors," *TNR*, March 25, 1931, pp. 145–50.

7. Edmund Wilson, "The Jumping-Off Place," *TNR*, December 23, 1931, pp. 156–58; and Carey McWilliams, *The Education of Carey McWilliams* (New York: Simon & Schuster, 1978), p. 69.

8. Edmund Wilson, "Hull House—1932," (three-part series), *TNR*, January 18, 1932, pp. 260–72; January 25, 1932, pp. 287–90; February 2, 1932, pp. 317–22.

9. Wilson to Perkins, July 1, 1931.

10. Edmund Wilson, "The Enchanted Forest," *TNR*, October 28, 1931, pp. 290–94.

11. Bruce Bliven, "On the Bowery," *TNR*, March 19, 1930, pp. 120–22.

12. George Soule, "Class War in Rhode Island," *TNR*, August 5, 1931, pp. 308–12.

13. Malcolm Cowley, "Red Day in Washington," *TNR*, December 21, 1932, pp. 153–55; and Cowley, *Golden Mountains*, Chapters 9 and 12.

14. Cowley, *Golden Mountains*, Chapters 7 and 11; Wilson to Dreiser, May 12, 1932, In Elena Wilson, ed., *Edmund Wilson: Letters on Literature and Politics* (New York: Farrar, Straus, & Giroux, 1977), pp. 222–23; and Wilson to Frank, June 17, 1932, In Wilson, *Letters*, pp. 223–24.

15. Quoted in Arthur A. Ekirch, *Ideologies and Utopias* (Chicago: Quadrangle Books, 1969), p. 55.

16. Quoted in Arthur M. Schlesinger, Jr., *The Crisis of the Old Order: 1919–1933* (Boston: Houghton, Mifflin, 1957), p. 202.

17. George Soule, *A Planned Society* (New York: Macmillan, 1932), p. 121.

18. Soule, *Planned Society*. Citations follow order of quotations in the text: pp. 266–68, 153, 270.

19. Frankfurter to Bliven, June 13, 1931.

20. Dos Passos to Wilson, January 14, 1931, In Townsend Ludington, ed. *The Fourteenth Chronicle: Letters and Diaries of John Dos Passos* (Boston: Gambit, 1973), pp. 376–98.

21. Hallowell, "The Position of the Progressive," *TNR*, February 4, 1931, pp. 324–26.

22. George Wilson, "An Appeal to Progressives," *TNR*, January 14, 1931, pp. 234–38.

23. Wilson to Christian Gaus, July 31, 1931, In Wilson, *Letters*, pp. 210–11.

24. Wilson to Paul Elmer More, April 22, 1933, In Wilson, *Letters*, pp. 229–30.

25. George Wilson, "What Do the Liberals Hope For?," *TNR*, February 10, 1932. pp. 345–48.

26. Wilson's role in the Wilder controversy was described by Cowley in an interview with the author, August 25, 1984; Michael Gold, "Wilder: Prophet of the Genteel Christ," *TNR*, October 22, 1930, pp. 266–67.

27. Edmund Wilson, "Economic Interpretation of Wilder," *TNR*, November 26, 1930, pp. 31–32; his authorship is identified in Edmund Wilson, "The Literary Class War: I," *TNR*, May 4, 1932, pp. 319–23; Edmund Wilson, "The Literary Class War: II," *TNR*, May 11, 1932, pp. 319–23.

28. Cowley, *Golden Mountains*, pp. 75–76.

29. Wilson to Frank, June 17, 1932, In Wilson, *Letters*, pp. 223–24.

30. Hallowell, "The Position of the Progressive," *TNR*, February 4, 1931, pp. 324–26.

31. Stuart Chase, "Mr. Chase Replies," *TNR*, February 10, 1932, pp. 347–49.

32. Norman Thomas, "The Position of the Progressive," *TNR*, February 11, 1931, pp. 354–55.

33. Upton Sinclair, "The Position of the Progressive," *TNR*, February 1, 1931, pp. 354–55.

34. George Soule, "Hard-Boiled Radicals," *TNR*, January 21, 1931, pp. 261–65.

35. "Humpty Dumpty Hoover," *TNR*, June 23, 1930, pp. 137–39.

36. Bliven to Frankfurter, June 17, 1931; and Frankfurter to Bliven, June 19, 1932.

37. "The Hoover Fairy Tale," *TNR*, August 24, 1932, pp. 30–31; and "Republicans and Prohibition," *TNR*, June 22, 1932, p. 141.

38. Stuart Chase, "A New Deal for America," *TNR*, June 29, 1932, pp. 169–71. In all likelihood, Raymond Moley, a top Roosevelt adviser, lifted the phrase from the magazine, Arthur Schlesinger argues in Schlesinger, *Crisis*, pp. 532–33. But, it probably was not very original. The historian traces its usage to Henry James, Mark Twain, and Brooks Adams. Still if *TNR* indeed popularized the term, it proves that the magazine was being read and noticed.

39. "Is Roosevelt a Hero?" *TNR*, April 1, 1931, pp. 165–67; and "Roosevelt's Resolution," *TNR*, November 9, 1932, pp. 340–41.

40. "The Democratic Bid," *TNR*, July 13, 1932, pp. 219–20.

41. Edmund Wilson, "The Hudson River Progressive," *TNR*, April 5, 1933, pp. 219–20.

42. Bruce Bliven, "Franklin D. Roosevelt: The Patron of Politics," *TNR*, June 1, 1932, pp. 62–64.

43. Quoted in Otis Graham, *Toward a Planned Society* (New York: John Wiley & Sons, 1968), p. 14; and "How Shall We Vote?" *TNR*, August 17, 1932, pp. 4–6.

44. George Wilson, "The Hudson River Progressive," *TNR*, April 15, 1953, pp. 219–20.

45. Bruce Bliven, "Franklin D. Roosevelt: The Patron of Politics," *TNR*, June 1, 1932, pp. 62–64.

46. "Norman Thomas for President," *TNR*, July 20, 1932, p. 245. For details of campaign, see Schlesinger, *Crisis*, pp. 198–200.

47. "How We Shall Vote," *TNR*, August 7, 1932, pp. 4–6.

48. "Progressives at Cleveland," *TNR*, July 30, 1932, pp. 258–59.

49. Bruce Bliven, "Waiting for 1936," *TNR*, October 19, 1932, pp 252–53.

50. Cowley, *Golden Mountains*, p. 112.

51. George Soule, "William Z. Foster: Henry Ford of the Labor Movement," *TNR*, October 5, 1932, pp. 196–99.

52. Cowley, *Golden Mountains*, Chapter 11; and Daniel Aaron, *Writers On the Left* (New York: Harcourt, Brace, & World, 1961), pp. 197–98.

53. Mumford to Wilson and Cowley, August 17, 1932. Quoted in Aaron, *Writers On the Left*, p. 258.

54. Cowley, *Golden Mountains*, pp. 113–15.

55. "Results of the '32 Election," *TNR*, November 30, 1932, p. 56.

56. "Stealing Votes from the Reds," *TNR*, February 1, 1933, p. 312.

57. David Shannon, *The Socialist Party of America* (New York: Macmillan, 1955), p. 225.

58. Bruce Bliven, "New England is Waiting," *TNR*, December 20, 1933, pp. 137–39.

59. Malcolm Cowley, "The Flight of the Bonus Army," *TNR*, August 17, 1932, pp. 13–15.

60. George Soule, "Hard-Boiled Radicals," *TNR*, January 21, 1931, pp. 261–65.

61. Soule, *Planned Society*, p. 275.

62. Cowley, *Golden Mountains*, p. 12.

A GOOD RADIO VOICE: 1933–36

1. Bliven's autobiography, *Five Million Words Later* (New York: John Day, 1963), provides a wealth of detail on his lengthy career at *TNR*. See also Alden Whitman, "New Republic Editor Dies," *New York Times*, May 29, 1977, p. 28; Croly's observations of Bliven in Croly to D. Elmhirst, December 4, 1926; Bliven and Soule's rate of productivity was calculated in Bliven, *Five Million Words*, p. 210.

2. Circulation figures from *N. W. Ayer & Son's Annual Directory of Newspapers and Periodicals* (New York: Ayer, 1937–1940).; deficit estimated in Bliven, *Five Million Words*, p. 208; see also Cowley to Wilson, June 27, 1936.

3. Bliven to Cowley, August 1, 1939.

4. Thurber, "The Wizard of Chitenango," *TNR*, p. 141; Cowley to Wilson, August 10, 1934; Malcolm Cowley, *The Dream of the Golden Mountains* (New York: Penguin, 1980), pp. 264–65.

5. Cowley, *Golden Mountains*, pp. 260–61.

6. Carl N. Deglar, *Out of Our Past* (New York: Harper & Row, 1959), pp. 379–417; James MacGregor Burns *The Lion and the Fox* (New York: Harcourt, Brace, & World, 1956), pp. 139, 143–44, 148, 219–22, 224–26; Quoted in William E. Leuchtenburg, *Franklin D. Roosevelt and the New Deal* (New York: Harper Torchbooks, 1963), p. 43.

7. Leuchtenburg, *Roosevelt and the New Deal*, p. 338; and Schlesinger, *The Politics of Upheaval* (Boston: Houghton, Mifflin, 1960), p. 648.

8. "Mr. Roosevelt's Task," *TNR*, March 8, 1933, pp. 88–90.

9. Bruce Bliven, "Washington Kaleidoscope," *TNR*, August 16, 1933, pp. 8–11.

10. "Roosevelt's Plan for Security," *TNR*, June 20, 1934, p. 141.

11. "Mr. Roosevelt's Intention," *TNR*, August 22, 1934, p. 34.

12. "The New Deal in Practice," *TNR*, July 5, 1933, pp. 197–99.

13. George Soule, "Roosevelt Confronts Capitalism," *TNR*, October, 18, 1933, pp. 269–70.

14. Bruce Bliven, "Washington Kaleidoscope," *TNR*, August 16, 1933, pp. 8–11.

15. Bruce Bliven, "Washington Kaleidoscope," *TNR*, August 16, 1933, pp. 8–11.

16. "General Johnson Goes Fascist," *TNR*, October 25, 1933, pp. 294–95; "Crack Down on the General," *TNR*, August 1, 1934, pp. 304–05; "The Roosevelt Truce," *TNR*, October 10, 1934, pp. 228–29.

17. "The New Deal in Practice," *TNR*, July 5, 1933, pp. 197–99.

18. "Social Control vs the Constitution," *TNR*, June 12, 1935, pp. 16–18.

19. "The Unemployed People," *TNR*, November 28, 1934, pp. 61–62.

20. Bruce Bliven, "New England Is Waiting," *TNR*, December 20, 1933, pp. 157–59.

21. Leuchtenburg, *Roosevelt and the New Deal*, p. 122.

22. "Muddling Through the Unemployed," *TNR*, April 4, 1934, pp. 201–02.

23. "The New Deal Begins," *TNR*, March 15, 1933, p. 118; and "The Big, Bad Budget," *TNR*, January 17, 1934, pp. 266–67.

24. "Washington Notes," *TNR*, June 27, 1934, pp. 180–81.

25. "Mr. Roosevelt's First Year," *TNR*, March 14, 1934, pp. 116–17.

26. "Roosevelt Calms Capital," *TNR*, October 24, 1934, pp. 296–98; and "Mr. Roosevelt's First Year," *TNR*, March 14, 1934, pp. 116–17.

27. "Left, Right, Left," *TNR*, November 28, 1934, pp. 60–61.

28. "Roosevelt Drifts Right," *TNR*, April 18, 1934, pp. 256–58.

29. George Soule, *The Coming American Revolution* (New York: Macmillan, 1934). Citations follow order of quotations in the text: pp. 304, 294, 283, 282, 304.

30. Bliven's introduction to Groff Conklin, ed., *A New Republic Anthology: 1914–1935* (New York: Dodge Publishers 1936).

31. "Liberalism Twenty Years After," *TNR*, January 23, 1935, pp. 290–92.

32. Bruce Bliven, "The New Deal's Right Hand Man," *TNR*, November 21, 1934, p. 52.

33. "Mr. Roosevelt's New Order," *TNR*, January 16, 1935, pp. 262–63.

34. Quoted in Arthur Schlesinger, *The Coming of the New Deal* (Boston: Houghton, Mifflin, 1960), p. 268; and Carl N. Deglar, *Out of Our Past* (New York: Harper & Row, 1959), p. 389.

35. "Liquidate the WPA," *TNR*, January 1, 1936, pp. 211–12; "The Scandalous WPA," *TNR*, February 26, 1936, pp. 61–62; Bruce Bliven, "Washington Revisited," *TNR*, March 13, 1935, pp. 126–28.

36. "Still the Unemployed," *TNR*, April 18, 1936, pp. 236–37.

37. Leuchtenburg, *Roosevelt and the New Deal*, p. 130.

38. Quoted in Leuchtenburg, *Roosevelt and the New Deal*, p. 193.

39. "Roosevelt's Plan for Security," *TNR*, June 20, 1934, p. 141; "Inching Toward Social Security," *TNR*, May 1, 1935; George Soule, "Security for Americans," *TNR*, January 6, 1935, pp. 266–69. The social security system's shortcomings are discussed in Schlesinger, *The Coming of the New Deal* (Boston: Houghton, Mifflin, 1960), pp. 313–15; Paul Conklin, *The New Deal* (New York: Thomas Y. Crowell, 1967), pp. 60–62.

40. Cowley, *Golden Mountains*, p. 285.

41. "Is Britain Recovering?" *TNR*, July 11, 1934, pp. 226–28.

42. George Soule, "Security for Americans," *TNR*, January 6, 1935, pp. 266–69.

43. "It's Up to Labor," *TNR*, January 3, 1934, pp. 211–12.

44. "The New Deal as Education," *TNR*, November 29, 1933, p. 76.

45. "What Is Behind Toledo," *TNR*, June 6, 1934, pp. 86–88. For especially good reports of strikes, see Schlesinger, *Coming of New Deal*, pp. 394–96; Irving Bernstein, *Turbulent Years: A History of American Workers, 1933–1941* (Boston: Houghton, Mifflin, 1970), pp. 227–29; Broadus Mitchell, *Depression Decade* (New York: Harper Torchbook, 1969), pp. 275–77.

46. "Employers Throw Down the Gauntlet," *TNR*, March 28, 1934, pp. 172–73.

47. "1936—The Real Issue," *TNR*, July 15, 1936, pp. 282–83.

48. "The Editors' Choice," *TNR*, September 23, 1936 pp. 207–08.

49. "1936-The Real Issue," *TNR*, July 15, 1936, pp. 282–83.

50. "Father Coughlin's Program," *TNR*, April 24, 1935, pp. 298–99.

51. "Huey Proposes," *TNR*, March 20, 1935, pp. 146–47; and "Huey Long," *TNR*, September 18, 1935, pp. 146–47.

52. "Huey Proposes," *TNR*, March 20, 1935, pp. 146–47.

53. Bruce Bliven, "Upper-Class Muckerism," *TNR*, October 21, 1936, pp. 306–07.

54. "The Press and the Campaign," *TNR*, July 22, 1936, pp. 311–12.

55. Bruce Bliven, "Dear William Randolph," *TNR*, December 2, 1936, pp. 141–42.

56. "Fascism in the Funnies," *TNR*, September 18, 1935, p. 147.

57. "Thunder on the Right" Noverber 29, 1933, pp. 39–40.

58. Schlesinger, *Coming of New Deal*, p. 518.

59. George Soule, "Liberty League," *TNR*, August 26, 1936, pp. 63–67.

60. "Mr. Roosevelt and the Liberals," *TNR*, October 16, 1935, pp. 257–58; and Bruce Bliven, "Mr. Lippmann and a National Government," *TNR*, September 23, 1936, pp. 180–81.

61. "The Editors' Choice," *TNR*, September 23, 1936, pp. 287–88.

62. "Is Mr. Roosevelt Slipping?" *TNR*, August 14, 1935, pp. 5–6.

63. Bliven, *Five Million Words*, p. 221.

64. "Toward a New Party," *TNR*, May 23, 1935, pp. 33–34.

65. "A New Party—The Progress," *TNR*, May 29, 1935, pp. 60–61.

66. "Toward a New Party," *TNR*, May 23, 1935, pp. 33–34; and "A New Party and the Unions," *TNR*, July 10, 1935, pp. 236–37.

67. "New-Party Prospects," *TNR*, April 1, 1936 pp. 208–09.

68. Bruce Bliven, *TNR Fortieth Anniversary Issue*, pp. 8–11.

69. Rexford G. Tugwell, *To the Lesser Heights of Morningside: A Memoir* (Philadelphia: University of Pennsylvania Press, 1982), p. 214.

70. Quoted in "The New Republic Idea" (an advertising booklet aimed at corporate advertisers, 1941), pp. 5 and 12. See also Harold L. Ickes, *The Secret Diary of Harold L. Ickes: 1936–1939*, Vol. 2 (New York: Simon & Schuster, 1954), pp. 230, 267, 362, 428.

71. Rexford G. Tugwell, "The Meaning of the Greenbelt Towns," *TNR*, February 17, 1937, pp. 42–43.

72. Rexford G. Tugwell, "The Future of National Planning," *TNR*, December 9, 1936, pp. 162–64.

73. Harold L. Ickes, "Housing Under the P.W.A.," *TNR*, September 19, 1934, p. 161; and Harold L. Ickes, "The Federal Housing Program," *TNR*, December 1, 1934, pp. 155–57.

74. "FDR Reads TNR," *TNR*, May 1, 1935 (advertisement), p. iii.

75. R. Alan Lawson, *The Failure of Independent Liberalism: 1930–1941* (New York: G.P. Putnam's Sons, 1971), p. 70.

76. "The Brains Trust," *TNR*, June 7, 1938, pp. 84–85.

77. Bliven, *Five Million Words*, p. 220; and Cowley, interview July 1984.
78. Ickes to Broun, April 14, 1938.
79. "Balance Sheet of the New Deal," *TNR*, June 10, 1936, p. ii.
80. "The Editors' Choice," *TNR*, September 23, 1936, pp. 287–88; and "Voters' Handbook," *TNR*, September 23, 1936, p. ii.
81. James MacGregor Burns, *Roosevelt: The Lion and the Fox* (Harcourt, Brace & World, 1956), p. 334.
82. Conklin, *New Deal*, p. 14.
83. Bruce Bliven, "In the Land of the Cotton," *TNR*, March 21, 1933, pp. 152–56.
84. Bliven, *Five Million Words*, p. 220.
85. Leuchtenburg, *Roosevelt and the New Deal*, p. 164.
86. Cowley, *Golden Mountains*, pp. 18 and 184.
87. Bernstein, *American Workers*, pp. 170–71.
88. "Mr. Roosevelt's Blank Check," *TNR*, November 11, 1931, pp. 31–32.

HALF A LOAF: 1937–40

1. Malcolm Cowley, The Dream of the Golden Mountains (New York: Penguin, 1980), Chapter 22; "The New Republic Moves Uptown," pp. 260–69; and, for further description of the magazine's new offices, Alfred Kazin, *New York Jew* (New York: Knopf, 1978) pp. 21–23.
2. George Soule, "The Next Four Years," *TNR*, March 10, 1937, pp. 129–31.
3. "The President's Fighting Speech," *TNR*, September 29, 1937, pp. 701–02.
4. Bruce Bliven, "The Cassandra Racket," *TNR*, July 14, 1937, pp. 273–74.
5. This section is based on the second part, "The Press and the Public," *TNR*, March 17, 1937.
6. "Roosevelt's Strategic Retreat," *TNR*, August 4, 1937, pp. 347–48; and "Congress Adjourns," *TNR*, June 29, 1938, p. 200.
7. "After the 'Purge' at Home," *TNR*, October, 19, 1938, pp. 292–93; and "The President Reports," *TNR*, July 6, 1938, pp. 237–38.
8. "The President Takes the Stump," *TNR*, July 20, 1938.
9. John L. Lewis, "The Next Four Years," *TNR*, December 23, 1936, pp. 234–36.
10. Irving Bernstein, *Turbulent Years: A History of American Workers 1930–1941* (Boston: Houghton, Mifflin, 1970), p. 40; "The Editors' Choice," *TNR*, September 23, 1936, pp. 207–08.
11. Bruce Bliven, "Birthday Balance Sheet," *TNR*, August 4, 1937, pp.359–60.
12. Bruce Bliven, "Sitting Down in Flint," *TNR*, January 27, 1937, pp. 377–78; "Employer Trouble in Autos," *TNR*, January 13, 1937, pp. 314–15; Bernstein, *Turbulent Years*, pp. 480–97.

13. George Soule, "Labor's Decisive Victory," *TNR*, March 17, 1937, pp. 155–56.

14. "Girdler's Counter-Revolution," *TNR*, pp. 236–37; and Bernstein, *Turbulent Years*, pp. 480–98.

15. George Soule, "Panic Over Labor," *TNR*, June 23, 1937, pp. 175–76; "Labor Wins in Court," *TNR*, April 21, 1937, pp. 307–08; and Philip Taft, *Organized Labor in American History* (New York: Harper & Row, 1964), p. 521.

16. "Girdler's Counter-Revolution," *TNR*, July 7, 1937, pp. 236–37; George Soule, "The Next Four Years," *TNR*, March 10, 1937, pp. 129–31; George Soule, "Labor's Decisive Victory," *TNR*, March 13, 1937, pp. 153–56.

17. David Levy, *Herbert Croly of the New Republic* (Princeton, New Jersey: Princeton University Press, 1985), p. 236.

18. Bruce Bliven, *Five Million Words Later* (New York: John Day, 1963), pp. 201 and 250; and Bliven to D. and L. Elmhirst, May 19, 1942.

19. "The Depression Marches On," *TNR*, February 23, 1938, p. 58.

20. Bruce Bliven, "Confidential: To the President," *TNR*, April 20, 1938, pp. 317–18.

21. "The Depression," *TNR*, February 2, 1938, Part 2.

22. Bruce Bliven, "Confidential: To the President," *TNR*, April 20, 1938, pp. 317–18.

23. "Is This Recovery?" *TNR*, July 6, 1938, pp. 236–37.

24. Leuchtenburg, *Roosevelt and the New Deal*, p. 247.

25. James MacGregor Burns, *Roosevelt: The Lion and the Fox* (New York: Harcourt, Brace & World, 1956), p. 322.

26. "Is This Recovery?" *TNR*, July 6, 1938, pp. 236–37.

27. "What Uncle Sam Got for His Money," *TNR*, March 2, 1938, p. 86.

28. "Hope for Public Spending," *TNR*, April 13, 1938, p. 288.

29. George Soule, "After the New Deal II: The Legacy of the New Deal," *TNR*, May 24, 1939, pp. 68–71.

30. "Has Pump-Priming Failed," *TNR*, May 18, 1938, p. 333; "The Job for Congress," *TNR*, January 4, 1939, pp. 244–45; "If the WPA is Cut," *TNR*, February 1, 1939, p. 388.

31. "The WPA Appropriations," *TNR*, January 25, 1939, p. 330; "What Happens," October 19, 1938, p. 293.

32. William E. Leuchtenburg, *Franklin D. Roosevelt and the New Deal* (New York: Harper & Row, 1963), p. 274.

33. "Government Vandalism," *TNR*, July 14, 1937, pp. 265–66; "Killing the Writers' Project," *TNR*, August 23, 1939, p. 621.

34. "A Telegram About the WPA," *TNR*, June 28, 1939, pp. 199–201.

35. "The New Deal in Review," *TNR*, May 20, 1940, pp. 687–708; and "Where Housing Stands Today," *TNR*, December 28, 1938, pp. 216–17.

36. "The Slums Begin to Fall," *TNR*, June 7, 1939, p. 117.

37. Barton J. Bernstein, "The New Deal: The Conservative Achievements of Liberal Reform," In *Twentieth-Century America: Recent Interpretations*, edited by Barton J. Bernstein and Allen J. Matusow (New York: Harcourt, Brace, Jovanovich, 1977), p. 260.

38. Leuchtenburg, *Roosevelt and the New Deal*, p. 165.

39. "Where Housing Stands Today," *TNR*, December 28, 1938, pp. 216–17.

40. Bruce Bliven, "The Corn Belt Cracks Down," *TNR*, November 22, 1933, pp. 36–38; and "Home Thoughts from Afar," *TNR*, August, 31, 1933, p. 68.

41. Malcolm Cowley, "An American Tragedy," *TNR*, May 3, 1939, pp. 382–83.

42. "Alterations to the A.A.A.," *TNR*, January 22, 1936, pp. 276–78.

43. "New Deal in Review," *TNR*, May 20, 1940, pp. 687–708.

44. "New Deal in Review," *TNR*, May 20, 1940, pp. 687–708.

45. "Shoring Up Security," *TNR*, December 28, 1938; and "New Deal in Review," *TNR*, May 20, 1940, pp. 217–18.

46. George Soule, "Government Fights for Health," *TNR*, August 3, 1938, pp. 350–52.

47. "Voter's Handbook," *TNR*, October 7, 1940, Part 2.

48. "Reelect Roosevelt," *TNR*, July 22, 1940, pp. 102–03.

49. "The Campaign of Essence," *TNR*, November 4, 1940, pp. 613–64.

50. "A Third Party in 1940," *TNR*, May 4, 1938, pp. 382–83.

51. "Voter's Handbook," *TNR*, October 7, 1940, Part 2.

52. "This Man Willkie," *TNR*, September 2, 1940, Part II (figures for press run drawn from advertisement to supplement).

53. "Willkie and Wealth," *TNR*, September 9, 1940, pp. 538–39; "Willkie is Slipping," *TNR*, September 16, 1940, p. 372; "Mr. Willkie Pleads Guilty," *TNR*, September 16, 1940, pp. 373–76; "Mr. Willkie is Wrong," *TNR*, September 23, 1940, pp. 403–04.

54. "Voter's Handbook," *TNR*, October 7, 1940, Part 2; and "New Deal in Review," *TNR*, May 20, 1940, pp. 687–708.

55. George Soule, "After the New Deal: The Political Landscape," *TNR*, May 17, 1939, pp. 35–38; George Soule, "Toward a Planned Society," *TNR*, November 8, 1939 (25th anniversary issue), pp. 29–33; George Soule, "After the New Deal: The Legacy of the New Deal," *TNR*, May 24, 1939, pp. 68–71.

56. Bruce Bliven, "Looking at 1940," *TNR*, June 21, 1939, pp. 188–90.

57. Bruce Bliven, "Notes on the American Character," *TNR*, November 8, 1939 (25th anniversary issue), pp. 66–68.

58. Malcolm Cowley, "A Farewell to the 1930's," *TNR*, November 8, 1939 (25th anniversary issue), pp. 42–44.

59. "But, Grandpa," *TNR*, July 26, 1939 (advertisement) II; "Why Dad! Do You Question the Future?" *TNR*, March 8, 1939 (advertisement) II; "Oh, If Frank Ever Sees These," *TNR*, August 13, 1939 (advertisement), II; "Why Can This Man Have More and Work Less?" *TNR*, May 4, 1938 (advertisement) I.

HOPING FOR UTOPIA: 1932–40

1. Biographical material for Cowley is drawn primarily from Malcolm Cowley, *Exile's Return* (New York: Penguin, 1976); and Malcolm Cowley, *The*

Dream of the Golden Mountains (New York: Penguin, 1980). See also John W. Aldridge, *After the Lost Generation* (New York: McGraw-Hill, 1951); Alfred Kazin, *Starting Out in the Thirties* (Boston: Little, Brown, 1962), pp. 140–41. The "sins of silence" quotation is from Malcolm Cowley, *And I Worked at the Writer's Trade* (New York: Viking Press, 1978), p. 139.

2. Cowley, *Writer's Trade*, p. 156.

3. Malcolm Cowley, "Fellow Traveler," *TNR*, May 1, 1935, pp. 345–48.

4. Bruce Bliven, "Russia in Hope," *TNR*, December 2, 1931, pp. 60–62.

5. George Soule, "Does Socialism Work?" *TNR*, February 5, 1936, pp. 356–59.

6. Edmund Wilson, "Stalin as Icon," *TNR*, April 15, 1936, pp. 271–73; and "Russian Paradoxes," *TNR*, May 13, 1936, pp. 11–13.

7. Bruce Bliven, *Five Million Words Later* (New York: John Day, 1963), p. 232.

8. Cowley, *Writer's Trade*, p. 151.

9. Quoted in Frank Warren, *Liberals and Communism: The Red Decade* (Bloomington, Indiana: Indiana University Press, 1966) p. 68.

10. Cowley to Wilson, (undated, 1935 or 1936).

11. "A People's Front in America," *TNR*, January 8, 1936, pp. 240–42.

12. "The New Communist Line," *TNR*, June 14, 1938, pp. 144–45.

13. "Mr. Eastman as Oracle" (letter and reply), *TNR*, December 2, 1937, pp. 201–02.

14. "See Russia on May 1" (advertisement), *TNR*, March 12, 1930, p. ii; "Intertourist Inc." (advertisement), *TNR*, March 6, 1935, p. 109; "Red Indian Dance" (advertisement), *TNR*, December 28, 1938, p. 239; "Confessions of a Nazi Spy" (advertisement), *TNR*, June 14, 1939, p. 167.

15. "Public Opinion," *Time*, November 13, 1939, pp. 21–22.

16. Bliven, *Five Million Words*, p. 220; "Free Speech Again," *TNR*, August 3, 1938, pp. 347–48; Elizabeth Dilling, *The Red Network* (Kenilworth, Illinois: Published by author, 1934), pp. 48–51, 208, 266, 273, 317, 322–323.

17. "Un-American Lies," *TNR*, December 7, 1938, p. 112; "Case History of Red Hunt," *TNR*, December 6, 1939, pp. 185–89; Bliven to Cowley, July 18, 1939; "NR Protests to Dies," *New York Times*, October 27, 1938, p. 18; *New York Times*, November 12, 1939, p. 17.

18. Bliven, *Five Million Words*, p. 220.

19. Cowley, *Writer's Trade*, p. 134.

20. Malcolm Cowley, "Echoes from Moscow: 1937–1938," *Southern Review* Volume 20 (Winter 1984): 1–12; Malcolm Cowley, "The Record of a Trial," *TNR*, April 7, 1937, pp. 267–70; Malcolm Cowley, "Moscow Trial," *TNR*, May 18, 1938, pp. 50–51.

21. Cowley to Wilson, May 14, 1937.

22. Cowley to Wilson, October 31, 1938; and Warren, *Liberals and Communism*, pp. 170–71.

23. Bliven to Cowley, February 7, 1937.

24. "Soviet Chills and Fever," *TNR*, June 23, 1937, p. 174.

25. Malcolm Cowley, "Moscow Trial: 1938," *TNR*, May 18, 1938, pp. 50–51; and Malcolm Cowley, "The Purge Goes On," *TNR*, January 5, 1938, pp. 240–41.

26. "Another Russian Trial," *TNR*, February 3, 1937, pp. 399–402; and "Moscow Loses Caste," *TNR*, March 16, 1938, pp. 151–52.

27. Malcolm Cowley, "Record of a Trial," *TNR*, April 7, 1937, pp. 267–70.

28. Cowley to Wilson, October 31, 1938.

29. Malcolm Cowley, "Record of a Trial," *TNR*, April 7, 1937, pp. 267–70.

30. Bliven, "A Letter to Stalin," *TNR*, March 30, 1938, pp. 216–17.

31. Phone interview with Alfred Kazin, August 1984.

32. "Trotsky and the Russian Trials," *TNR*, May 19, 1937, pp. 49–50.

33. Malcolm Cowley, "Partisan Review," *TNR*, October 19, 1938, pp. 311–12.

34. Letters from the editors, "Partisan Review," *TNR*, November 9, 1938, pp. 19–20.

35. "Liberty and Common Sense," *TNR*, May 1, 1939, pp. 89–90.

36. Ferdinand Lundberg (secretary), "Committee for Cultural Freedom," *TNR*, June 28, 1939, pp. 216–18.

37. "In Reply to Mr. Lundberg," *TNR*, June 28, 1939, p. 202.

38. Cowley to Wilson, October 31, 1938.

39. Paul Hollander, *The Political Pilgrims* (New York: Oxford University Press, 1981), p. 55.

40. Lundberg, "Committee for Cultural Freedom," *TNR*, June 28, 1939, pp. 216–18.

41. Cowley, *Writer's Trade*, pp. 149–50.

42. Vincent Sheehan, "Brumaire: The Soviet Union as a Fascist State," *TNR*, November 9, 1939, pp. 7–9; and "Brumaire: II," *TNR*, November 15, 1939, pp. 104–06.

43. Wilson, "Complaints: The Literary Left," *TNR*, January 20, 1937, pp. 345–48.

44. Wilson to Cowley, April 15, 1937.

45. Edmund Wilson, *To the Finland Station* (Doubleday: New York, 1940), pp. 483–84.

46. Cowley, *Writer's Trade*, pp. 1–12, 133–53.

47. Cowley, *Writer's Trade*, pp. 1–12.

48. Dos Passos to Cowley, May 28, 1935, and Cowley to Dos Passos. In Townsend Ludington, ed. *The Fourteenth Chronicle: Letters and Diaries of John Dos Passos* (Boston: Gambit, 1973), pp. 346–347.

49. Bliven, *Five Million Words*, p. 194.

50. John P. Diggins, *Up From Communism* (New York: Harper & Row, 1975), pp. 90–91.

51. Cowley, "Disillusionment," *TNR*, June 14, 1939, p. 103.

52. Dos Passos, "The Death of Jose Robles," *TNR*, July 19, 1939, pp. 308–09; and Dos Passos to MacDonald, July 1939, In *Fourteenth Chronicle*, p. 529.

53. "In Reply to the Committee," *TNR*, August 23, 1939, p. 63.

54. "Picking Up the Pieces," *TNR*, October 8, 1939, pp. 294–97.

55. "Why Did Russia Do It?" *TNR*, September 6, 1939, pp. 18–19.

56. "Communist Imperialism," *TNR*, October 11, 1939, pp. 237–38; and "Russia Shakes the World," *TNR*, September 27, 1939, pp. 200–01.

57. "Stalin Spreads the War," *TNR*, December 13, 1939, pp. 218–20; and "How Not to Save Democracy," *TNR*, October 18, 1939, p. 286.

58. "Common Sense About Russia," *TNR*, November 5, 1939, pp. 98–100.

59. Cowley to Wilson, February 2, 1940.

60. "A Note on Marxian Criticism," *TNR*, January 30, 1935, p. 337.

61. W. H. Auden, "In Memory of W. B. Yeats," *TNR*, March 8, 1939, p. 123; Otis Ferguson, "Where was Moses," *TNR*, April 22, 1940 p. 336; Ignazio Silone, "Italian Anti-Semitism," *TNR*, November 23, 1938, pp. 67–69; Thomas Wolfe, "I Have a Thing to Tell You: III," *TNR*, March 24, 1937, pp. 202–07; Thomas Mann, "America and the Refugee," *TNR*, November 7, 1939, (25th anniversary issue), pp. 38–39; Archibald MacLeish, "America of Promises," *TNR*, November 7, 1939 (25th anniversary issue), pp. 46–48.

62. "National Defense: Progressive Policy," *TNR*, March 30, 1938, Part 2.

63. "Get Tough, Mr. President," *TNR*, November 6, 1940, pp. 377–78.

64. Bliven to D. and L. Elmhirst, June 21, 1940; Cowley, *Writer's Trade*, pp. 155–57; Cowley, "A Time of Resignations," *Yale Review*, volume 74 (Autumn 1984). Author's interview conducted with Cowley.

65. "The Race Against Hitler," *TNR*, January 20, 1941, p. 73; and "For a Declaration of War," *TNR*, August 25, 1941, pp. 235–38.

66. Daniel Mebane (publisher), "A Letter to New Republic Subscribers" (advertisement), *TNR*, October 25, 1939, p. iii.

67. Bliven to D. and L. Elmhirst, May 19, 1942; and Cowley to Wilson, (undated, mid to late 1930s).

68. Kazin, *New York Jew*, p. 23.

69. Cowley, "Introduction" In Dorothy Chamberlain and Robert Wilson, eds., *The Otis Ferguson Reader* (Chicago Ill.: December Press, 1982).

70. Cowley to Wilson, (undated, 1935–36).

71. Cowley, *Writer's Trade*, p. 137.

72. Cowley, "Introduction," p. xviiii; interview conducted with author; for L. Elmhirst's trip to the United States, see also Mebane to Cowley, October 8, 1940 (Dorothy Straight Elmhirst Papers, Cornell University Library, Ithaca, New York).

73. Michael Straight, *After a Long Silence* (New York: Norton, 1983), p. 159.

74. Cowley, "Introduction," p. xviiii; Wilson to D. Elmhirst, October 12, 1940 (Cornell); Soule to Bliven, December 31, 1940 (Cornell); Bliven's response (undated, Cornell).

75. Interview with author. If, by radical, Cowley is referring to his view of Stalin and the Soviet Union, he did not differ greatly from Soule and Bliven, as I have tried to demonstrate. For that matter, as Cowley strenuously argues, he was an ardent interventionist by that time, thus squaring with the Elmhirsts.

76. Croly to L. Elmhirst, June 23, 1927.

CONCLUSION

1. For a thorough discussion of the magazine during the war and the Henry Wallace affair, see William L. O'Neil, *A Better World* (New York: Simon & Schuster, 1981), pp. 43–97. Straight's relation to Wallace is detailed in his autobiography, Michael Straight, *After a Long Silence* (New York: Norton, 1983). The previously cited biographical material on Bliven and Soule covers their post-*TNR* years. Cowley recounted his troubles in *Writer's Trade*, p. 157. The Straights' contribution is estimated in W. A. Swanberg, *Whitney Father, Whitney Heiress* (New York: Viking, 1980), p. 543.

2. Bruce Bliven, *Five Million Words Later* (New York: John Day, 1963), p. 168.

3. William L. Chenry, "A Journal of Opinion," *Saturday Review*, November 7, 1936, p. 18.

4. "Check and Double Check," *TNR*, March 14, 1939, p. 152.

5. Walter Lippmann, "Remarks on the Occasion of this Journal's 50th Year," *TNR*, March 21, 1964, p. 14.

Bibliography

MANUSCRIPT SOURCES

Randolph S. Bourne papers, Columbia University Library, New York, New York.

Heywood Broun papers, Library of Congress, Washington, D.C.

Malcolm Cowley papers, Newberry Library, Chicago, Illinois.

Dorothy Straight Elmhirst papers, Cornell University Library, Ithaca, New York.

Felix Frankfurter papers, Library of Congress, Washington, D.C.

The New Republic Historical Files, *The New Republic*, Washington, D.C.

Theodore Roosevelt papers, Library of Congress, Washington, D.C.

Isabel Soule papers, University of Oregon, Eugene, Oregon.

Willard Straight papers, Cornell University Library, Ithaca, New York.

Edmund Wilson papers, Beinecke Library, Yale University, New Haven, Connecticut.

INTERVIEWS

Malcolm Cowley, Interview with author, July 1984.

Alfred Kazin, Interview with author, August 1984.

J. F. Updike, Interview with author, March 1983.

EDITORS' WORKS

Bliven, Bruce. "Introduction" In *New Republic Anthology: 1914–1935*, edited by Groff Conklin. New York: Dodge, 1936.

_____ . *Five Million Words Later.* New York: John Day, 1963.

Cowley, Malcom. *Exile's Return.* New York: Penguin, 1976.

_____ . *And I Worked at the Writer's Trade.* New York: Viking Press, 1978.

_____ . *The Dream of the Golden Mountains.* New York: Penguin, 1980.

_____ . "Introduction." The Otis Ferguson Reader, edited by Dorothy Chamberlin and Robert Wilson. Chicago: December Press, 1982.

_____ . "Echoes from Moscow: 1937–1938." *Southern Review* Volume 20 (Winter 1984): 1–12.

_____ . "A Time of Resignations." *Yale Review* Volume 74 (Autumn 1984).

Croly, Herbert. *Progressive Democracy*. New York: Macmillan, 1914.

_____ . *The Promise of American Life*. New York: Harper & Row, 1962.

Hackett, Francis. *I Chose Denmark*. New York: Doubleday, Doran, 1940.

Johnson, Alvin. *Pioneer's Progress*. Lincoln, Nebraska: University of Nebraska, 1960.

Lippmann, Walter. *Drift and Mastery*. New York: Mitchell Kennerly, 1914.

_____ . *Preface to Politics*. New York: Mitchell Kennerly, 1914.

Lovett, Robert M. *All Our Years*. New York: Viking Press, 1948.

Soule, George. *A Planned Society*. New York: Macmillan, 1932.

_____ . *The Coming American Revolution*. New York: Macmillan, 1934.

The New Republic. 1914–1940 (inclusive).

_____ . "Herbert Croly Memorial Issue," July 16, 1930.

_____ . "Fortieth Anniversary Issue," November 1954.

_____ . "Remarks On the Occasion of This Journal's 50th Year," March, 21, 1964.

Weyl, Walter. *New Democracy*. New York: Harper & Row, 1911.

_____ . *Tired Radicals and Other Essays*. New York: Heubsch, 1922.

Walter Weyl: An Appreciation. New York: Harper & Row, 1965.

Wilson, Edmund. *To the Finland Station*. Garden City, New York: Doubleday, 1953.

The Thirties, edited by Leon Edel. New York: Farrar, Straus, and Giroux, 1980.

Edmund Wilson: Letters on Literature and Politics, edited by Elena Wilson. New York: Farrar, Straus, & Giroux, 1977.

⁝ SECONDARY WORKS

Aaron, Daniel. *Writers on the Left*. New York: Harcourt, Brace & World, 1961.

_____ . *The Strenuous Decade*. Garden City, New York: Anchor Books, 1970.

Aldridge, John W. *After the Lost Generation*. New York: McGraw-Hill, 1951.

Bernstein, Barton J. *Towards a New Past*. New York: Vintage, 1969.

Bernstein, Barton J., and Matusow, Allen, J., eds. *Twentieth Century America: Recent Interpretations*. New York: Harcourt, Brace, Jovanovich, 1977.

Bernstein, Irving. *Turbulent Years: A History of American Workers 1930–1941*. Boston: Houghton, Mifflin, 1970.

Blum, John Morton. *The Republican Roosevelt*. New York: Atheneum, 1963.

Bourne, Randolph. *War and the Intellectuals*. New York: Harper & Row, 1964.

Brooks, Van Wyck. *From the Shadow of the Mountains*. New York: E. P. Dutton, 1961.

Burns, James MacGregor. *Roosevelt: The Lion and the Fox*. New York: Harcourt, Brace & World, 1956.

Conkin, Paul K. *The New Deal*. New York: Thomas Crowell, 1967.

Coute, David. *The Fellow Travelers*. New York: Macmillan, 1970.

De Wolfe, Mark, ed. *Holmes–Laski Letters*. Cambridge, Massachusetts: Harvard University Press, 1953.

Deglar, Carl N. *Out of Our Past*. New York: Harper & Row, 1959.

Diggins, John P. *The American Left in the Twentieth Century*. New York: Harcourt, Brace, Jovanovich, 1973.

_____ . *Up from Communism*. New York: Harper & Row, 1975.

Dilling, Elizabeth. *The Red Network*. Kenilworth, Illinois: Published by author, 1934.

Draper, Theodore. *The Roots of American Communism*. New York: Viking Press, 1957.

Ekirch, Arthur A. *Ideologies and Utopias*. Chicago: Quadrangle Books, 1969.

Forcey, Charles. *The Crossroads of Liberalism*. New York: Oxford University Press, 1961.

Freidel, Frank. *Franklin D. Roosevelt: The Triumph*. Boston: Little, Brown, 1956.

_____ . *Franklin D. Roosevelt: Launching the New Deal*. Boston: Little, Brown 1973.

Gilbert, James Burkhart. *Writers and Partisans*. New York: John Wiley and Sons, 1968.

Goldman, Eric. *Rendezvous With Destiny*. New York: Vintage, 1954.

Graham, Otis. *Toward a Planned Society*. New York: Oxford University Press, 1976.

Hamby, Alonzo L. *The New Deal: Analysis and Interpretation*. New York: Longman, 1981.

Hicks, Granville. *John Reed: The Making of a Revolutionary*. New York: E. P. Dutton, 1934.

Hicks, John D. *Republican Ascendancy*. New York: Harper & Row, 1960.

Hofstadter, Richard. *The American Political Tradition*. New York: Vintage, 1948.

_____ . *The Age of Reform*. New York: Vintage, 1955.

_____ . *Anti-Intellectualism in American Life*. New York: Vintage, 1963.

Hollingsworth, Harold, and Holmes, William F. *Essays on the New Deal*. Austin: University of Texas Press, 1969.

Howe, Irving. *The American Communist Party*. Boston: Beacon Press, 1957.

_____ . *A Margin of Hope*. New York: Harcourt, Brace, Jovanovich, 1982.

Ickes, Harold L. *The Secret Diary of Harold L. Ickes: 1936–1939*, Vol. 2. New York: Simon & Schuster, 1954.

Johnson, Walter. *William Allen White's America*. New York: Henry Holt, 1947.

Josephson, Matthew and Hannah. *Al Smith: Hero of the Cities*. Boston: Houghton, Mifflin, 1969.

Karson, Marc. *Organized Labor in the Progressive Era*. Minneapolis: University of Minnesota Press, 1960.

Kazin, Alfred. *Starting Out in the Thirties*. Boston: Little, Brown, 1982.

_____ . *New York Jew*. New York: Knopf, 1978.

Kempton, Murray. *Part of Our Time*. New York: Simon & Schuster, 1955.

Kennedy, David. *Over Here*. New York: Oxford University Press, 1980.

Kirkendall, Richard S., ed. *The New Deal: The Historical Debate*. New York: John Wiley & Sons, 1973.

Klehr, Harvey. *The Heyday of American Communism*. New York: Basic Books, 1984.

Lasch, Christopher. *The New Radicalism in America, 1889–1963*. New York: Knopf, 1965.

Lawson, R. Alan. *The Failure of Independent Liberalism: 1930–1941*. New York: G. P. Putnam's Sons, 1971.

Leuchtenburg, William E. *Franklin D. Roosevelt and the New Deal*. New York: Harper & Row, 1963.

_____ . *The Perils of Prosperity*. Chicago: University of Chicago Press, 1967.

Levy, David. *Herbert Croly of The New Republic.* Princeton, New Jersey: Princeton Unversity Press, 1985.

Liggett, Walter W. *The Rise of Herbert Hoover.* New York: H. K. Fly, 1932.

Link, Arthur. *Woodrow Wilson and the Progressive Era.* New York: Harper Torchbooks, 1954.

_____ . *American Epoch.* New York: Alfred A. Knopf, 1963.

_____ . *The Papers of Woodrow Wilson.* Princeton: Princeton University Press, 1972.

Ludington, Townsend, ed. *The Fourteenth Chronicle: Letters and Diaries of John Dos Passos.* Boston: Gambit, 1973.

MacKay, Kenneth. *The Progressive Movement of 1924.* New York: Octagon Books, 1966.

Madison, Charles. *Leaders and Liberals in the Twentieth Century.* New York: F. Ungar, 1961.

May, Henry F. *The End of American Innocence.* New York: Oxford University Press, 1959.

McWilliams, Carey. *The Education of Carey McWilliams.* New York: Simon & Schuster, 1978.

Mitchell, Broadus. *Depression Decade.* New York: Harper & Row, 1947.

Mott, Frank L. *A History of American Magazines.* Vol. 3. Cambridge, Massachusetts: Harvard University Press, 1960.

Mowry, George. *Theodore Roosevelt and the Progressive Movement.* New York: Hill & Wang, 1963.

Murphy, Bruce Allen. *The Brandeis and Frankfurter Connection.* New York: Doubleday, 1983.

O'Neil, William L. *A Better World.* New York: Simon & Schuster, 1981.

Pells, Richard H. *Radical Visions and American Dreams.* New York: Harper & Row, 1973.

Rozwenz, Edwin L., ed. *The New Deal: Revolution or Evolution?* Boston: D. C. Heath, 1949.

Schlesinger, Arthur, Jr. *The Crisis of the Old Order.* Boston: Houghton, Mifflin, 1957.

_____ . *The Coming of the New Deal.* Boston: Houghton, Mifflin, 1960.

_____ . *The Politics of Upheaval.* Boston: Houghton, Mifflin, 1960.

_____ . *Early Writings of Walter Lippmann.* New York; Liveright, 1970.

Shannon. David. *The Socialist Party of America.* New York: Macmillan, 1955.

Steel, Ronald. *Walter Lippmann and the American Century.* Boston: Little, Brown, 1980.

Straight, Michael. *After a Long Silence.* New York: Norton, 1983.

Swanberg, W. A. *Whitney Father, Whitney Heiress.* New York: Viking, 1980.

_____. *Norman Thomas: The Last Idealist,* New York: Scribners, 1976.

Taft, Philip. *Organized Labor in American History.* New York: Harper & Row, 1964.

Tugwell, Rexford G. *To the Lesser Heights of Morningside: A Memoir.* Philadelphia: University of Pennsylvania Press, 1982.

Warren, Frank A. *Liberals and Communism: The Red Decade Revisited.* Bloomington, Indiana: Indiana University Press, 1966.

Weinstein, James. *The Corporate Ideal in the Liberal State: 1900–1918.* Boston: Beacon Press, 1968.

Weyl, Walter. An Appreciation. New York, privately published 1922.

MISCELLANEOUS MATERIALS

Aridon, Beulah. "The Nation and New Republic." *Survey Graphic* Volume 29 (January 1940): 21–26.

Chenry, William L. "A Journal of Opinion." *Saturday Review* Volume 13 (November 7, 1936): 4–5.

"George H. Soule Jr. Dies at 82: Ex-Editor of The New Republic." *New York Times,* April 15, 1970.

Kaplan, Sydney, "Effects of World War I on Some Liberals." *Journal of Ideas* Volume 17 (June 1950): 307–69.

"NR Protests to Dies." *New York Times,* October 27, 1938, p. 18 and November 12, 1939, p. 17.

N. W. Ayer & Son's Annual Directory of Newspapers and Periodicals. Philadelphia: Ayer, 1917–40.

"Public Opinion." *Time,* November 13, 1939, pp. 21–22.

"The New Republic Idea" (advertising booklet), 1941.

Whitman, Alden. "Edmund Wilson Dies." *New York Times,* June 13, 1972.

_____. "New Republic Editor Dies." *New York Times,* May 29, 1977.

Index

About the Author

David Seideman was born in 1961 in New York City. He was educated at Georgetown University (B.A. in History and English minor) where he received the 1983 Morris Gold Medal for History and was a member of Phi Alpha Theta, the International Honors Society of history.

From 1979 to 1986 he has worked in various capacities at *The New Republic*. His work has also appeared in *National Wildlife*, *The New York Times Book Review*, and *The Times Literary Supplement*. He edited *The New Republic*'s special seventieth anniversary book in 1984.